Jewish History
The **BIG** Picture

by Gila Gevirtz

Adapted from
The History of the Jewish People
by Jonathan D. Sarna & Jonathan B. Krasner

Behrman House Publishers
www.behrmanhouse.com/historyleadersguide

Designer: Terry Taylor/Terry Taylor Studio
Page Layout and Print Production: Cathy Pawlowski-Ehrhardt
Cartographer: Jim McMahon
Cartographic Consultants: Dr. Itzik Eshel and Prof. Robert M. Seltzer

The author and publisher gratefully acknowledge the many contributions of Abigail Winograd whose extraordinary skill as a copyeditor has greatly enriched this volume.

The author and publisher gratefully acknowledge the cooperation of the following sources of photographs and graphic images: **American Jewish Archives, Cincinnati Campus, HUC-JIR:** 151; **American Jewish Historical Society:** 95, 147, 162, 163, 190, 253; **American Jewish Joint Distribution Committee:** 211, 213, 220; **Beth Hatefusoth Museum of the Jewish Diaspora:** 18; **Bildarchiv Preussischer Kulturbesitz/Art Resources, NY:** 124; **Bridgeman-Giraudon/Art Resources, NY:** 71, 87; **Creative Image Photography:** 272; **Frank J. Darmstaedter:** 19; **Gustov Doré:** 10, 23; **Foto Marburg/Art Resources, NY:** 76; **FreeStockPhotos.com:** 48; **Gila Gevirtz:** 13 (bottom), 35, 50, 58, 62, 90, 91, 126, 258, 259, 262, 266, 267; **The Granger Collection, NY:** 33, 44, 82, 99, 139; **Brian Haviland Studio, Brian Haviland/ Richard Lerner:** 270 (drawing by Ruchy Seligman); **Israel Consulate General Library:** 235; **Israel Ministry of Tourism:** 53, 110; **The Jewish Museum/Art Resources, NY:** 93, 107, 170; **Jerry Lampen/Reuters/Corbis:** 263; **Leo Baeck Institute, NY:** 129; **Erich Lessing/Art Resources, NY:** 11 (top), 28, 29, 40, 45, 113; **Library of Congress** 164; **Richard Lobell:** 2 (bottom); **Eric Pollitzer:** 219; **Arnold Pronto/The Helen Suzman Foundation:** 252; **Réunion des Musées Nationaux/Art Resources, NY:** 8; **Robert F. Wagner Labor Archives:** 189; **Edward Serotta:** 257; **State of Israel Government Press Office:** 177; **World Wide Photos:** 201; **YIVO Institute of Jewish Research Archives, NY:** 225, 238, 239; **Zionist Archives and Library:** 178, 198.

ISBN: 0–87441–838–0
ISBN: 978–0–87441–838–5

Library of Congress Cataloging-in-Publication Data
Gevirtz, Gila.
   Jewish history : the big picture   /   by Gila Gevirtz, adapted from The history of the Jewish people by Jonathan D. Sarna and Jonathan B. Krasner. — 1st ed.
      p. cm.
   Includes index.
   ISBN 978-0-87441-838-5
   1. Jews--History. I. Krasner, Jonathan B. History of the Jewish people.   II. Title.
   DS118.G43 2008
   909'.04924—dc22

                                                                                                2007049282

Manufactured in the United States of America

For Michael, son of Yeḥezkel and Ester

—G.G.

CONTENTS

Part Four: Antisemitism and Zionism

Part Five: Devastation and Rebirth

Foreword

By Deborah E. Lipstadt

An oft-quoted response to the question "Why study history?" is George Santayana's aphorism, "Those who cannot remember the past are condemned to repeat it." But rather than there being a consensus, some argue that, to the contrary, forgetfulness is a blessing, not a curse, a prerequisite for anchoring oneself in the present and planning for the future.

Both arguments are wrong.

If remembering the past ensured that we would not repeat it, then the Cambodian killing fields, the gassing of the Kurds, and the Srebrenica massacres would have been impossible. Yet not only did those genocides occur, but they took place at a time when the Holocaust was being broadly studied, analyzed, and commemorated. Indeed, in each case, a well-tutored world silently stood by, permitting evil to freely run its course.

But if memory does not serve as an insurance policy, neither does forgetfulness. For rather than being the most content people in the world, those who are deprived of their personal or national history often feel unmoored; without a sense of how they came to be or who they are or what they aspired to become, they are set adrift.

Ultimately, it is not the answer but the question itself—"Why study history?"—that is misguided.

Jewish tradition teaches that everything in the world is neutral. Nothing is inherently good or evil. Rather, it is our use of an object or opportunity that determines whether it becomes a curse or a blessing. A knife in the hands of a criminal may lead to murder. Alternatively, in the hands of a surgeon that same tool can help sustain life. Furthermore, some aspects of life whose face value might appear to be bad in fact hold great potential for goodness. Rashi, the great medieval Bible commentator, argued that everything in the world, even our evil inclinations, is necessary for survival. While our unselfish inclinations prompt us to give charity, help those in need, and welcome strangers, our so-called evil or selfish inclinations, Rashi asserted, also serve constructive purposes: They prompt us to build homes for shelter, support our families, and take care of ourselves.

Without these inclinations we not only would leave ourselves unprotected and vulnerable but also might be less able to act responsibly.

We can apply this insight to the study of history. History and the remembrance of things past—even terrible things—are neither inherently good nor inherently bad. They neither cause tragedies nor prevent them. Rather, it is what we choose to *do* with what we learn that creates a constructive or destructive outcome.

We can remember past wrongs and mortgage not just our energies but also those of our children, to avenge those wrongs. Conversely, we can look at the past and determine that never again will we let such evil attach itself to our identity. With historical perspective and knowledge, the choice becomes ours. We can use the history of genocide to justify retaliation or to remind ourselves that unless we name and excise evil as soon as it arises, it may morph into a thing of nightmarish proportions.

The question is not "Why study history?" but rather "What will we do with the history we study?" And, if that is a question we pose regarding world history, how much more so should we ask it about Jewish history. For the existence of the Jewish people is an anomaly. By all rights Jews should be consigned to the pages of history rather than play a vital role in contemporary events. There are so many junctures at which it would have made historical sense for the saga of the Jewish people to have ended: the Babylonian exile, the Roman destruction of Jerusalem, and, of course, the Holocaust.

The study of Jewish history can offer us insight into how the Jewish people have managed to survive. In the opening pages of *Jewish History—The Big Picture*, the author points out that different groups answer that question in different ways. Some look back and see the hand of a loyal God while others see the hand of a determined individual. Some attribute the Jews' survival to the power of a belief system while others attribute it to a cultural heritage.

But there is a danger in using history to justify a particular position. There will be those who selectively read events—relying on intellectual blinders—so that they see only those events that validate their bias. For example, some will stitch together a version of history that focuses on the negative, resulting in what the great historian Salo Baron called a lachrymose theory of Jewish history.

This was the history to which the protagonist, Yudke, in Hayim Hazaz's short story, "Had'rashah" ("The Sermon") subscribed. At a meeting of his kibbutz, Yudke rises and proclaims, "I object to Jewish history. . . . I don't accept it . . . all the edicts, vilifications, persecutions, and martyrdoms, and yet again, edicts, vilifications . . . we have been a people with no history." Yudke, with his uniquely Zionist perspective, took a very particular—and quite distorted—view of Jewish history, which he used to justify his political worldview.

Yudke's rendition of Jewish history was as skewed as those who would ignore those edicts and vilifications in order to produce a more celebratory version of history. Each student of Jewish history may draw a different lesson from it. For that lesson to be valid, however, it must be based on a complete—*not* a selective—reading of Jewish history. That is why *Jewish History—The Big Picture* is so important. It offers readers an unvarnished, comprehensive, and deeply nuanced rendition of Jewish history. It is a rendition that is of value to all readers, including those who simply want to know how it is that the Jews continue to make history.

Without an accurate knowledge of history, it is impossible to know from whence one has come. And those who do not know from whence they have come often have a hard time knowing where they are or should be going.

Thus it is that the award-winning Czech writer Milan Kundera observed in *The Book of Laughter and Forgetting* that "The first step in liquidating a people is to erase its memory. Destroy its books, its culture, its history. Then have somebody write new books, manufacture a new culture, invent a new history. Before long the nation will begin to forget what it is and what it was. The world around it will forget even faster." In the same vein and long before Kundera, the founder of Hasidism, the Ba'al Shem Tov, proclaimed: "Forgetfulness prolongs the exile; remembrance is the secret of redemption."

The pages that follow offer the raw material that will help you to deduce how the Jewish people has survived. It is up to each reader to decide what to *do*—if anything at all—with that information.

How Do They Do It?

"I don't know who discovered water, but I'm sure it wasn't a fish." Curled up inside this clever insight, attributed to the media critic Marshall McLuhan, is a curious conundrum. If fish are oblivious of the water in which they live, what might we humans fail to see, immersed as we are in our daily lives? What challenges and opportunities might we be blind to? And how can we develop a greater awareness and understanding of the things closest to us, the things most essential to our existence?

Not surprisingly, our understanding of the present—the times we live in and the lives we lead—often depends on our knowledge of the past. It is history that can help us as a parent or sage would. Offering the wisdom of experience, it helps us respond to current challenges and opportunities using insights gleaned from the past. Inviting us to stand on its shoulders, history broadens our view of what *is* and what *might be*, as well as the *why* of each perspective.

Perhaps now more than ever we need the benefit of history's wisdom and parenting. We need the breadth of its perspective and the richness of its experience. We need it to shed light on the many personal, communal, and global challenges before us and to help us develop responses that are both thoughtful and practical.

So where do we begin, and whose history do we study?

Jewish history presents a remarkable story of courage, resilience, and adaptation. It spans the globe and the millennia—from the Fertile Crescent to urban North America, from ancient times to the modern age—revealing a civilization that has influenced and been influenced by the many other civilizations it has encountered. Great religions and great cultures have been borne of Judaism, as have great bodies of literature, law, and ethics. At the same time, Judaism has been enriched and renewed through cultural cross-fertilization. Finally, the history of the Jews—a virtual how-to handbook for thriving under adverse conditions—offers diverse models of human persistence and creativity.

How do they do it?

Some think the Jews survive and thrive because of their belief in God and the teachings of the Bible. This view holds that throughout their history religious faith and tradition have provided the Jews with the wisdom and the strength to embrace hope and overcome adversity.

The biblical verse on this Union flag may have comforted many a Jewish soldier during the American Civil War: "Be strong and have courage; do not be terrified or anxious, for Adonai, your God, is with you wherever you go" (Joshua 1:9).

Some think this ancient people's persistence and endurance is fueled by a sense of purpose. Judaism teaches the religious imperative to add justice and goodness to the world. Perhaps it is the nobility of this vision that inspires each generation to cultivate its Jewish identity and values.

Some think it is the Jews' questioning, even skeptical nature. The Israelite prophets preached on the need to examine one's actions—are they righteous or self-serving, truthful or dishonest, just or unjust? Perhaps such probing questions help the Jews identify and assess opportunities and strengths as well as flaws and weaknesses.

The Four Questions are a highlight of the Passover seder. They remind Jews to reflect on the meaning of their rituals.

Jewish History—The Big Picture will provide you with a broad overview of the Jewish experience. As you read this book, you will discover how the Jews succeeded in the larger world while cultivating their distinctive identities. In every century they have adapted to changing times with creativity and purposefulness while holding fast to an enduring set of core beliefs. Their courage and determination have been rewarded as each new generation has contributed to world culture *and* Jewish tradition.

So, read on and see how this determined people has flourished by learning from its past, addressing the needs of the present, and investing in the future. You will encounter many forces at work, many influences, each of which may enrich and inspire you, each of which may inform your own life choices.

Part One
Origins and Exile

Introduction
The Birth of the Jewish People and Monotheism

As Numerous as the Stars

Where does the story of the Jewish people begin? The Bible teaches that it starts with the patriarch Abraham. The Book of Genesis teaches that God commanded Abraham: "Go forth from your land," to the Land of Canaan, which is what Israel was called in ancient times. It also teaches that God made a covenant with Abraham. According to the Covenant, Abraham's descendants, the Israelites, would become as numerous as the stars and would inherit the Land of Canaan.

The Israelites gradually settled in Canaan between 1200 and 1050 BCE. Most of them were farmers, sheepherders, and cattle herders. The Bible describes Canaan as "a land of wheat and barley, of grape vines and figs and pomegranates, a land of olive trees and honey, a land where you can eat food without limit" (Deuteronomy 8:8).

Each autumn, farmers plowed and sowed before the rains. Their labors were rewarded in the spring, first with the barley harvest and, a few weeks afterward, with the wheat harvest. In late summer they gathered the grapes and by late September and early October the

History or Religious Teachings?

The Bible, or Tanach, is a sacred text that serves as both a spiritual guide and an intellectual history of the Jewish people. Much of its language and meaning are not only poetic but also mythic and metaphoric. In contrast, historical scholarship seeks to uncover and articulate the facts of Jewish history. Therefore, if you notice differences between biblical and historical accounts, remember that each presents a different type of knowledge and provides its own unique insight into the Jewish experience.

olives had reached their peak. Men tended the crops and animals. In addition to helping with that work, women spun wool and wove cloth.

The Gift of Monotheism

The religions of the Israelites' neighbors were based on polytheism. Many of the Canaanite gods were associated with different forces in nature. Yam was the sea god; Shapash, the sun goddess; and Yareaḥ, the moon god. The Canaanites believed that their gods competed against one another for power and for the loyalty of human beings.

The Israelites rejected the idea of many gods with humanlike needs and desires. Instead, they based their religion on monotheism, the idea that there is only one God. The Torah, also known as the Five Books of Moses and as the Pentateuch, provides us with insight into the values and beliefs of the Israelites. Its teachings go beyond legal concerns for property and the protection of consumers. The Torah

The early Israelites were divided into twelve tribes, each with its own portion of land.

commanded the Israelites to treat others with fairness and justice—to care for the widow and the orphan, act kindly toward strangers, and feed, clothe, and shelter the poor. These shared values and beliefs not only helped distinguish the Israelites from their neighbors but also helped unite the Israelites.

Monotheism took hold gradually, for few people change their beliefs and habits overnight. Remember that the Israelites lived in a world abounding with polytheistic religions. So at first many of them worshipped Canaanite gods alongside the one Israelite God. Only after centuries of diversity and experimentation did they fully accept monotheism.

This statue of the Canaanite god Ba'al is from 1300 BCE. Many Israelites worshipped both Ba'al and the one Israelite God.

Chapter 1

The Early Israelites
Adapting to a Changing World

The Big Picture

In a classic Peanuts comic strip, Lucy is ensconced in her psychiatrist's booth assuring Charlie Brown that adversity is good. Why? Because it prepares us for yet more adversity. If Lucy had it right, then the lives of the early Israelites abounded in goodness.

Led at first by local chieftains, the Israelites united under a king when the chieftains' leadership proved inadequate. Over time the Israelite kingdom was built, split in two, and destroyed. Many Israelites were forced out of their homeland; those who remained became impoverished. While some exiles eventually returned, others chose to establish themselves more firmly in foreign lands.

Despite numerous challenges at home and abroad, the Israelites continued to adapt while maintaining their core religious beliefs and identity. While other ancient peoples were conquered and absorbed into the dominant culture, the Israelites continued to survive and thrive. How the Jewish people continue to adapt and flourish is what this book is all about.

Time to Unite?

Early Israelite society was tribal. A single clan might constitute a village, and a group of clans formed a tribe. Local judges, or chieftains, ruled over the tribes. Often one judge had authority over a single tribe. Judges were responsible for settling disputes between people and led their tribes in times of war.

TIMELINE

c. 1200–1050 BCE	Canaan is settled by the Israelites, according to the Bible
c. 950 BCE	First Temple is completed
928 BCE	Kingdom of Israel is divided into two mini-states, Israel and Judah
World History	
776 BCE	*First Olympic Games are held, in Greece*
722 BCE	Northern kingdom of Israel is destroyed by the Assyrians
586 BCE	Judah is defeated by the Babylonians; Jerusalem and the Temple are burned to the ground
539 BCE	Babylonian Empire falls to the Persians
c. 516 BCE	Second Temple is dedicated in Jerusalem
445 BCE	Nehemiah travels to Jerusalem, helps rebuild Judah

But eventually the tribal structure could no longer meet the needs of the people. The neighboring Philistines developed superior military technology, such as iron-spoked chariots, and began pushing into Israelite territory. The Israelites needed a more centralized leadership than the local judges could provide. They needed one leader who could unite them in their fight for survival.

In the biblical telling, Saul, at God's command, was anointed the first king of Israel. But Saul was more a tribal chief than a king. The territory he controlled was not especially large and had no palace or capital city. Although he was a great warrior, Saul was unable to unite the Israelites.

Upon her victory in battle, Deborah the prophetess sang "Hear, O kings, . . . I will sing to Adonai, . . . the God of Israel" (Judges 5:3).

A Kingdom Is Built but Cracks

It was Israel's second king, David, who succeeded in uniting the people. David fought back the Philistines and captured the city of Jerusalem, establishing it as the kingdom's political and religious capital. During a reign of more than thirty years, David unified a bitterly divided people and developed Israel into one of the strongest powers in the region. His defeat of the Philistines ensured that they would never again pose a threat to Israel's survival.

The kingdom grew stronger yet under the reign of David's son Solomon. King Solomon centralized Israel's government in Jerusalem and increased its wealth and status by developing Israel into a center of international trade. According to the Book of Kings, Solomon fortified many cities and built a wall around Jerusalem. He is probably best remembered, however, for his massive construction projects. The most famous was the Holy Temple in Jerusalem, which was completed circa 950 BCE.

Despite Solomon's accomplishments, his reign created religious conflicts and economic problems that weakened the kingdom. When Solomon died, the united kingdom of Israel cracked into two mini-states: Israel in the north and Judah in the south. Without a central government and a strong military, each struggled to survive in a dangerous region. The struggle intensified as a new power arose to the northeast: the kingdom of Assyria (modern-day Iraq).

Although Israel and Judah banded together with other small states in the region to try to prevent the Assyrians from taking control, they could not withstand the might of the Assyrian army. In 722 BCE the northern kingdom of Israel was destroyed. According to the Book of Kings, more than twenty-seven thousand Israelites were deported to the

This stone sculpture shows an Assyrian military officer bringing two Judeans from the town of Lachish to the Assyrian king.

northeast. The southern kingdom of Judah was spared when its king agreed to pay the conquering Assyrians a ransom in silver and gold.

The Destruction of Judah

The Assyrian kingdom was eventually brought down by rebellious states outside Judah in the east. But Judah was still at the mercy of greater powers, especially now, as it was sandwiched between two competing powers that filled the vacuum left by Assyria's decline: Egypt to the south and the Babylonian kingdom to the northeast. In 597 BCE the Babylonian king, Nebuchadnezzar, swept into Judah. He forced King Johoiachin and the kingdom's spiritual leaders and leading citizens into exile. On the remaining population, he levied heavy taxes. A few years later, when Judah rebelled, the Babylonian

FAMOUS FIGURES

The Prophet Elijah

In the difficult years between Solomon's death and the Temple's destruction, "prophets" arose among the Israelites. The prophets saw themselves as called upon by God to speak God's word. They preached on God's ethical teachings—such as the values of justice, mercy, and honesty. Sometimes they predicted the future and offered political advice. With their candor came the risk of displeasing those in power. One who put himself at risk in this way was the prophet Elijah.

King Ahab of Israel and his wife, Jezebel, enriched themselves at the expense of their subjects. They also encouraged the Israelites to worship idols and the Canaanite god Ba'al alongside God. When Elijah spoke up, criticizing Ahab and Jezebel, Ahab called him a "troubler of Israel" (1 Kings 18:17) and "my enemy (1 Kings 21:20)." Now seen as a foe and a hostile influence, Elijah was forced to flee the kingdom of Israel.

army returned and laid siege to Jerusalem. In the summer of 586 BCE Jerusalem and the Temple were burned to the ground.

Nebuchadnezzar had not just devastated a city and destroyed a holy temple—he had also destroyed a way of life. For the people of Judah, family, work, and religion had all revolved around the land. Judeans had tilled the soil and then paid tribute to God by bringing the fruits of their labor to the Temple in Jerusalem. Now, deprived of their Temple, land, and leaders, they had no place in which to worship God, no place to farm, and no one to lead them. The impoverished inhabitants of Judah and the devastated exiles were like orphans.

A Message of Hope

Before the exile, prophets such as Amos and Isaiah had criticized the people for their faithlessness and immorality. Now the prophets comforted the Israelites with a message of hope. The God of Israel has not been defeated by the Babylonian gods, Jeremiah taught. Instead, God has used Nebuchadnezzar as a tool to punish the Israelites for their sinful ways. The prophet Ezekiel held out hope that the exiles would return to Israel, saying: "Thus said Adonai God: . . . O my people, . . . [I shall] bring you . . . [back] to the Land of Israel. . . . I shall put My breath in you, and you will live again" (Ezekiel 37:12–14).

There was another great prophet of the exile, whose name has been lost to history. His prophecies make up the final chapters of the Book of Isaiah. This prophet assured the people that God would hear their prayers in exile. Expanding Israel's idea of monotheism, he taught that God rules the entire world: "Your redeemer is the Holy One of Israel, who is called 'God of all the Earth'" (Isaiah 54:5). God, he also taught, is the God of all people, regardless of their religion or their land.

The words of the prophets continue to hearten and inspire the Jewish people. This sign in Israel's Ben-Gurion Airport includes Jeremiah's words of hope, "Your children shall return to their country" (Jeremiah 31:17). The reference alludes to Israel's yearning for the return of its soldiers who are missing in action.

In the time of the exile, the idea that people could worship God from anywhere was an extraordinarily creative and intellectual leap of the imagination. It was an idea that would help the Jewish people survive and even prosper in a new land.

Life in Exile

Since the Babylonian exile more than twenty-five hundred years ago, many Jews have lived in the Diaspora, the countries outside Israel. In fact, living in the Diaspora feels normal to Jews today. But for the Jews in Babylonia, the adjustment was profound.

The prophets recognized the importance of helping the exiles return to the routines of life. Jeremiah sent a letter from Jerusalem to the Jews in Babylon. In God's name he encouraged them to "build houses and live in them. Plant gardens and eat their fruits. Take wives and bear sons and daughters. . . . Multiply there, do not decrease in numbers. And seek peace for the city to which I [God] have exiled you, and pray to Adonai for the city; for in its peace you will have peace" (Jeremiah 29:5–7).

The exiles took Jeremiah's words to heart. They set up communities within the larger non-Jewish population, taking part in business and even politics.

Abandonment Versus Adaptation

The fact that the Babylonians did not discriminate against the Jews on the basis of their religion or nationality helped the Jews achieve economic success and encouraged them to adopt the culture of their new land.

Some Jews not only adapted to their surroundings but also abandoned Judaism. Still, many remained faithful. Religious rituals such as observing the Sabbath, keeping kosher, and performing circumcision (*brit milah*) took on new importance. In addition, Jewish communities came together for communal prayer at city gates, on lakeshores, or near riverbanks. These practices eventually gained widespread acceptance. They further unified the Jews and strengthened their religious and cultural identities.

To Stay or Not to Stay

In 539 BCE, the Babylonian Empire fell to the Persians. Fortunately for the Jews, the Persian ruler, Cyrus, went out of his way to show respect for his new subjects' gods. To gain support and favor with the Jews, Cyrus permitted the exiles to return to Judah and rebuild the Temple.

Despite their joy in hearing this news, most Jews chose not to uproot themselves and resettle in Judah. (Indeed, more than two thousand years later, when the modern State of Israel was declared, most Diaspora Jews made the same choice.) The journey was dangerous, and life would be difficult now that Judah had become an isolated province in a large empire. In contrast, Babylon was a thriving cosmopolitan city.

Returning and Rebuilding

The first Jews to return to Judah began rebuilding the Temple. They completed the Second Temple in about 516 BCE, seventy years after the destruction of the First Temple (the Temple that Solomon had built). The dedication was celebrated with great joy. It was also touched with sadness, for the modest building that now stood in its place paled in comparison to the splendor of the original Temple.

The next fifty years were difficult for the people of Judah. The Persians were willing to let them live in the land, but they would never permit an independent Jewish government. Judah remained sparsely populated and miserably poor.

In 458 BCE, Judah was invigorated when a scribe and religious leader named Ezra led nearly fifteen hundred Jews back from Babylonia. Ezra was determined to revitalize the religious life of Judah. Empowered by the Persian government, he appointed judges and other officials to teach the laws of the Torah and to make rulings based on them.

Ezra sent word to the Jewish community in Babylonia about the difficult conditions in Judah. Nehemiah, who was the highest-ranking Jewish official in the Persian court, was disturbed by what he heard. He persuaded the Persian king to make him governor of Judah. Shortly after Nehemiah arrived in Jerusalem, he set the city's entire population of able-bodied men to work as an emergency force to rebuild Jerusalem's destroyed walls. No longer would the city be raided or threatened by neighboring enemies.

Nehemiah also rebuilt Judah's economy. He ordered a onetime cancellation of all debts and restored the annual Temple taxes. Nehemiah understood that economic revival

A Tradition of Innovation

Reading Torah aloud from a platform (*bimah*) in synagogue on Monday, Thursday, and Shabbat—the Jewish Sabbath—is a time-honored tradition today. But at one time the public reading of the Torah was an innovation. It began with a public Torah reading by Ezra in 444 BCE. Imagine the scene: Massive groups of people descend on Jerusalem and congregate around a wooden platform. Everyone is eager to hear the words of Torah.

Slowly, Ezra makes his way up the platform. As he opens the scroll, men, women, and children rise as one. The crowd hangs on every word Ezra reads from the Torah—these are the beliefs that unite the children of Israel. And they are alive and well! "Amen, amen," the people cry.

Because the Judeans spoke Aramaic, they needed translators to help them understand the Hebrew text of the Torah. Similarly, today, most North American synagogues provide their congregants with English translations of the Torah.

depended on making Jerusalem into an urban center. The city's population was too small to support the changes Nehemiah had in mind. So he resettled 10 percent of Judah's rural population in the city.

New Challenges

Judah made a strong comeback under the leadership of Ezra and Nehemiah. The population of Jerusalem increased, and the city was revitalized. Not only had the Jews figured out how to survive in the Diaspora, but they had also demonstrated an unbreakable tie to the Land of Israel.

But then as now, empires rise and fall, and Jewish communities are often deeply affected by shifts in power. The rise of an extraordinary leader in the Diaspora was about to bring Jews under the control of the Greek Empire, an event that would require yet more changes and adaptations.

Chapter 2

The Age of Hellenism
Strategies for Survival

The Big Picture

In 331 BCE, fewer than two hundred years after the rebuilding of the Temple, Jerusalem was conquered by Alexander the Great. Alexander was king of Macedonia and one of the world's greatest military geniuses. By the time Alexander died, his empire stretched from Greece to India. A lover of Greek culture, Alexander aimed to unite his empire by integrating Greek culture with local customs, religions, and traditions.

Like other peoples who were conquered by Alexander, the Jews viewed the Greeks with ambivalence. On the one hand, Hellenistic culture was exciting and advanced. On the other hand, it threatened the traditional ways of life that many Jews valued.

Changing Times

The Jews living in the Land of Israel around 225 BCE—about a century after the death of Alexander—experienced numerous changes in the world around them. One was that Judah became known by its Greek (and later, Roman) name, Judea. Other changes included the sale of handsomely decorated Greek vases on market day in the larger villages and the increasing popularity of Greek clothing, perfumes, and jewelry, brought back as gifts by Jewish soldiers who served in Alexander's army.

TIMELINE

331 BCE	Alexander the Great conquers Jerusalem
323 BCE	Alexander dies; Egypt and Judea are placed under the control of Ptolemy
200 BCE	Jerusalem becomes part of the Seleucid Empire
c. 169 BCE	Judea rebels against the high priest and the Seleucid king
164 BCE	Maccabees capture Jerusalem; the Temple is purified and rededicated
141 BCE	Seleucids are defeated by the Hasmoneans; Judea is again independent

World History

c. 100 BCE	*Anasazi culture first develops in parts of present-day Arizona, New Mexico, Colorado, and Utah*

But Greek culture did not conquer the ancient Near East as quickly as Alexander's army had. Hellenism, or the integration of Greek culture into the local culture, spread gradually and unevenly. It is natural that the more frequently people come in contact with an idea, language, or culture, the more quickly they adopt it. Thus Hellenism was strongest in urban areas where the population came in contact with Greek soldiers and merchants and where Greek was adopted as the lingua franca, the language in which business was conducted.

Greek colonists brought their literature, theater, sporting competitions, and religious festivals to many of the conquered cities. Greek temples, amphitheaters, and schools began to dot the cityscape. The cultural offerings in newly established "Greek" cities, such as Alexandria in Egypt, attracted Jews and non-Jews alike.

Hellenism came far more slowly to rural areas of Judea, where farmers had less contact with the Greek colonists and their institutions. Even so, all Jews in Judea felt the impact of Hellenism's reach.

Remaining Connected

After Alexander's death, in 323 BCE, his empire was divided among three of his generals— Ptolemy, Lysimachus, and Seleucus. Egypt and Judea were placed under the control of Ptolemy. He and his successors, known as the Ptolemies, were tolerant rulers. The Ptolemies wanted to modernize the agriculturally rich Nile valley. Many immigrants, including Jews, flocked to Egypt where the kings settled them and employed them in the state-run economy. Like other immigrants, the Jews were protected and favored because they worked in the king's service. They were employed as agricultural laborers, metalworkers, weavers, and merchants. Many Jews also served as soldiers in the Ptolemaic army.

Just as Jewish women wove cloth for centuries in the Land of Israel, so, too, did many of them weave cloth in Hellenic Alexandria.

The Septuagint made it possible for Jews who did not know Hebrew to read and understand the Torah. But not everyone supported the idea of translating the Torah. Many Jews argued that the Torah could not be translated without losing much of its meaning because each Hebrew word was chosen by God.

The Jews living in Egypt and other Diaspora communities along the Mediterranean were, in a number of ways, like North American Jews today. They lived near one another so that they could participate in Jewish communal and religious life. They also gathered together in "prayer houses." Although archaeologists and historians don't know exactly what went on in those prayer houses, some think they were the forerunners of synagogues.

Like most Jews of today's Diaspora, Hellenic Jews adapted to their surroundings. Their accommodations included adopting the Greek language and style of dress, and giving their children Greek names and sending them to Greek-style schools.

Despite their adaptation to Greek culture, many Diaspora Jews maintained their ties to Judaism and the Jews of Judea. Their relationship may be compared with that between today's North American Jews and Israeli Jews. On the one hand, both communities share many values and traditions, such as the value of studying Torah and the tradition of celebrating the Jewish holidays. On the other hand, each community has its distinct practices. In the modern State of Israel, for example, the Torah is taught in secular schools as well as in religious schools, and influence over Jewish life is strongly controlled by the government. The experience in the Diaspora is quite different, of course.

Conflict in Judea

The Seleucid Kingdom, named for Alexander's general Seleucus, and formed from the eastern portion of Alexander's empire, was based in Syria. Judea lay on the edge of the Ptolemaic and Seleucid kingdoms. The two kingdoms continually battled over where the boundary line between them should be drawn. In 200 BCE, the Seleucids gained control over Judea.

Eventually a conflict broke out between the high priest, Onias III (Ḥanan), and his younger brother, Jason (Joshua). Onias wanted to limit the influence of Hellenism in Jerusalem, while Jason wanted to turn Jerusalem into a Greek-style city to bring it wealth and culture.

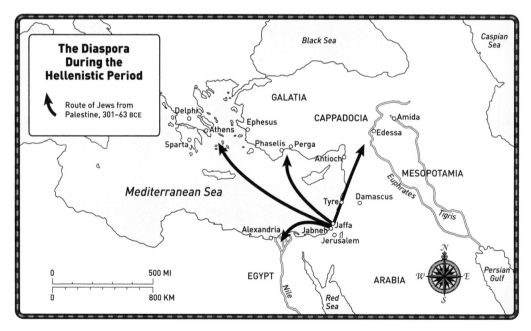

Encouraged by new opportunities available under Hellenic rule, Jews established communities in what is now Egypt, Greece, and Turkey.

Then, in 175 BCE, a new ruler, Antiochus Epiphanes, rose to the Seleucid throne. He quickly earned the hatred of the Judeans by doubling their taxes. Realizing that Antiochus was starved for cash, Jason bribed the king to make him high priest instead of his brother. Jason's move caused a stir in Judea, for the position of high priest traditionally was passed from father to eldest son. With Antiochus's blessing, Jason further divided the population by transforming Jerusalem into a Greek-style city, building, for example, a sports arena next to the Temple. Some of the younger priests neglected their Temple duties because they preferred to take part in the discus and wrestling competitions next door. Traditional Jews were horrified and vowed to resist Hellenism.

The Revolt Against Antiochus

Despite Jason's attraction to Greek culture, his Hellenism had limits. He continued to respect the holiness of the Temple and did not interfere with sacrifices and other rituals. Soon after Jason's appointment, however, a more extreme Hellenist, named Menelaus, offered Antiochus an even larger bribe than Jason had presented. The result: Jason was out as high priest, and Menelaus was in.

Whereas Jason had favored adaptation, Menelaus believed in assimilation. Thus tensions were already high when Menelaus stole money from the Temple treasury to pay his bribe to Antiochus. This was more than traditional Jews could bear. In about 169 BCE, Judea erupted in rebellion against Menelaus and Antiochus.

Antiochus's response was swift and deadly. With his troops he marched into Jerusalem, slaughtered many of the protesters, and sold others into slavery. He looted the Temple and entered the Holy of Holies—a place forbidden to all but the High Priest on Yom Kippur, the holiest day of the Jewish year. Jerusalem became an occupied city, with a new military fortress overlooking the Temple.

"The Hammer"

Antiochus was still not satisfied. Considering the Jews a disruptive force in his empire, he forbade the observance of Shabbat, Jewish holidays, and other Jewish rituals. He outlawed the study of Torah and converted the Holy Temple into a Greek temple. He placed a statue of Zeus near the altar and ordered the sacrifice of pigs in the Temple.

For the next two years a country priest known as Mattathias the Hasmonean, along with fellow collaborators, fought a guerrilla war against the Seleucids. Although they were outnumbered and had only primitive weapons, the rebels had the advantage of knowing Judea. They knew the best routes to take and where to hide. Another advantage they had was the covert assistance of a sympathetic Jewish population.

After Mattathias died, his son Judah took command of the rebels. Judah's men nicknamed their bold leader Maccabee, which means "the Hammer." The rebels thus became known as Maccabees. They lived up to their name, dealing hammer blow after hammer blow to the Seleucids. Although Judah's victories were modest, they were marked by heroic glory because of the courage and daring of the rebels.

Ḥanukkah

In the Jewish month of Kislev in 164 BCE, the Maccabees captured Jerusalem from the Seleucids and purified the Temple. The Temple was rededicated on the twenty-fifth day of Kislev, the third anniversary of the day on which it had been defiled.

Judah and his men styled their dedication according to the eight-day autumn harvest festival of Sukkot, which they had not been able to celebrate a few months earlier. The new

Judah Maccabee

Judah Maccabee was a brilliant military leader who conducted an early form of guerrilla warfare. Because the Seleucid forces were superior in both numbers and arms, Judah avoided open battle. He and his band of rebels executed a successful series of daring night attacks that made use of their superior knowledge of the land.

Judah died on the battlefield in 161 BCE. His brothers succeeded him, eventually securing the independence of Judea. The story of Judah Maccabee is told in the Book of Maccabees.

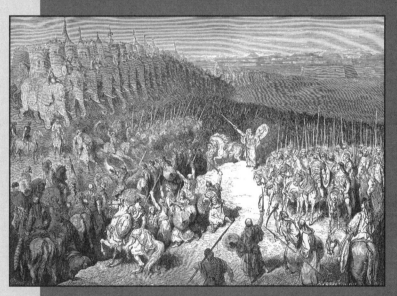

Judah Maccabee and his followers armed themselves with captured weapons.

festival eventually became known as Ḥanukkah, which means "dedication." It is also called the Festival of Lights. To this day, Ḥanukkah begins on the twenty-fifth day of Kislev, which usually falls in December, and is celebrated for eight days.

Independence and Division

The Hasmoneans' struggle to win independence from the Seleucids continued for another twenty-three years. In 141 BCE, the hated Seleucid fortress overlooking the Temple was finally destroyed. The Jews were free once again.

The Oil Story

A legend recorded in the Talmud, the authoritative collection of Jewish law, suggests another reason why the Hasmoneans—the family that led the revolt against the Greeks—created an eight-day festival. When the Maccabees purified the Holy Temple, this story says, they found enough oil to light the Temple's candelabrum for only one day, yet the oil miraculously lasted for eight days.

Mattathias's only surviving son, Simon, was proclaimed high priest and "Prince of the People." This proclamation signaled a change from the past—Simon was not a member of the traditional high priestly family. In the minds of some Jews, he was no more a legitimate high priest than Menelaus had been. Simon's grandson would go one step farther and proclaim himself king of the Jews, a position many Jews believed could be held only by a descendant of King David.

Although Judea was independent, it was still in a region dominated by Hellenism. So the question Jews continued to confront was: Do you support resistance, adaptation, or assimilation? Ironically, the descendants of the Maccabees were in favor of adaptation. For example, they minted coins that used both Hebrew and Greek.

Today, Jews also to face the issue of resisting, assimilating, or adapting to the Diaspora culture. Although the concern remains critical, it hasn't been as divisive as it was in Judea. Under the Hasmoneans the bitter divisions would have tragic consequences. 🐦

Chapter 3

Roman Domination of Judea
Divisions Inside and Out

The Big Picture

Thanks to Hasmonean conquests, the Jewish state grew to include almost all of the biblical Land of Israel as well as the southern Golan and territory east of the Jordan River. The Hasmoneans controlled profitable trade routes, and merchants and large landowners thrived. But it was the less prosperous Judeans who carried the heavy tax burden required to maintain Judea's large army. In addition, resentment of the Hasmoneans grew among their subjects when they forced the non-Jews in the kingdom to convert to Judaism.

While this was a time of great political, economic, and religious diversity—it was also a time of intolerance. One group of Jews went so far as to distance itself physically from other Jews by moving to the desert. Another used guerrilla tactics to intimidate those who opposed them. The deep divisions in Judean society would have been disastrous in the best of times and these were hardly the best of times. In fact, the Jews were about to battle the most powerful empire the world had ever seen.

Judea Divided

Early Hasmonean leaders had helped Judea withstand the strong influence of Hellenism and the rule of the Seleucids. In contrast, the later Hasmoneans adapted

TIMELINE

63 BCE	Roman general Pompey makes Judea a Roman province
37 BCE	Romans name Herod "King of the Jews"
10 BCE	Hillel and Shammai teach in Jerusalem
6 CE	Zadok and Judah the Galilean lead a tax revolt against the Romans

World History

c. 43 CE	*City of London is founded*
66 CE	Roman procurator Florus robs the Temple treasury, sparks a Jewish revolt
70 CE	Roman army conquers Jerusalem; the city and the Temple are destroyed
73 CE	Romans capture Masada; Jewish rebellion is completely crushed

Hellenic influences and weakened Judea by creating deep divisions with those who resisted adaptation. These divisions were exacerbated by the economic gap between the wealthy and the less financially successful, who carried the tax burden.

The situation reached a low point around 90 BCE. While the Hasmonean king, Alexander Yannai, was performing a Sukkot ceremony in the Temple the people began to pelt him with *etrogim* (citrons). Why would the Jews attack their king? The cause of the conflict lay in the Hasmonean kings' decision to declare themselves both high priests and kings; previously, there had been a separation of religious and political leadership. Many also resented the high taxes the king required to support his numerous military campaigns.

The first group to voice its opposition to the concentration of power in the hands of the Hasmoneans was the Essenes. The Essenes led a simple life, emphasizing religious ideals and the study of Torah in minute detail. Wanting nothing to do with the Hasmonean leader, or "wicked priest," as they called him, they moved to the Judean desert, founding the settlement of Qumran by the edge of the Dead Sea.

Rather than head for the desert, other groups stayed in Judea and struggled for power. Two major rivals—actually, religious and political parties—developed. They were the Sadducees and the Pharisees. The two differed largely in their social and economic makeup and in their approach to understanding Torah.

The Sadducees were mostly wealthy priests and aristocrats. They traditionally filled the religious and political leadership roles in Jerusalem. The Pharisees included priests and non-priests, rich and poor alike. Most Jews, however, were not members of either party. Most Judean men were poor farmers, craftsmen, and fishermen who did not have the leisure of thinking about the political schemes of rival groups.

The Pharisees wanted to replace the leadership because they believed that the powers of the king and those of the high priest should be separated. Understandably, kings do not look favorably on people who talk about replacing them. So the Hasmonean rulers allied themselves with the Sadducees. The Pharisees therefore increased their opposition. From here, matters quickly turned ugly.

The End of Independence

This brings us back to the unfortunate *etrog* incident in the Temple—it was the Pharisees who led the revolt against Alexander Yannai. Yannai struck back in the harshest manner. He resorted to a slow and painful Roman execution technique—crucifixion. Yannai tortured many of his political opponents to death by means of crucifixion.

After Yannai's death, the Pharisees regained political influence. Soon after, they attacked the Sadducees. Unfortunately, the Jews were so busy fighting a civil war that they ignored a much more serious threat: the expanding Roman Empire. In 63 BCE, the Roman general Pompey marched into Jerusalem and ended the civil war by making Judea a Roman province.

Pharisees and Sadducees

Of course, in first-century Judea, there was no clear separation between politics and religion in the way there is in the United States and Canada today. The Pharisees and the Sadducees were competing political groups with profoundly different religious beliefs.

The Pharisees believed that the written Torah could be understood only in combination with an oral tradition. As scholars who were knowledgeable about the written and oral traditions of the Torah, the Pharisees considered themselves to be the natural leaders of the people and kept their distance from those who did not agree with their religious interpretations.

The Sadducees, many of whom were members of the high priest's family, rejected the Pharisees' oral tradition. They argued that the Temple priests, whom the Torah designated the religious leaders of the Jewish community, were the only ones qualified to interpret the Torah.

Digging Up the Past

One morning in 1947, a Bedouin shepherd made one of the most important archaeological discoveries of the twentieth century. In a cave near the Dead Sea, he found a group of ceramic jars. Inside were leathery scrolls, many of which turned out to be ancient copies of biblical books, such as the Book of Isaiah. Known as the Dead Sea Scrolls, these are the oldest copies of biblical texts ever discovered.

Scholars believe it was the Essenes who left the scrolls in these caves around Qumran. Some of the scrolls describe the Essenes. Their community was organized as a commune. Life centered on community meals and prayer. The scrolls also tell us why the Essenes left Jerusalem (they disapproved of the Hasmoneans) and what they thought of the Pharisees and Sadducees (their interpretation of Judaism was wrongheaded).

This scroll of the Book of Isaiah was found in Qumran; like the Hebrew of a Torah scroll, its Hebrew contains no vowels.

Herod the Great?

Now Judea was under the authority of Rome. At first, Roman rule was not very different from the rule of the Hasmoneans. Roman leaders were mainly concerned with collecting taxes and keeping the peace. They were content to let a Jewish leader rule the Land of Israel as long as he remained loyal to Rome. In 37 BCE, the Romans named Herod—a general whose family had been forcibly converted to Judaism generations earlier by the Hasmoneans—"King of the Jews."

Herod—known as Herod the Great—was a strong leader who brought over thirty years of calm to the Land of Israel. He was a master builder of cities and fortresses. He rebuilt Jerusalem and expanded the Temple, making it into one of the most beautiful and impressive temples in the Roman Empire. Even the Pharisees, who questioned Herod's Jewishness and argued that his family background disqualified him from leadership, were forced to admit that, "anyone who has not seen Herod's building has never seen a building that is truly grand."

The archaeological remains of King Herod's palace include remnants of a tower, a courtyard with columns, and a synagogue.

Hillel and Shammai

Two of the most famous Pharisees were Hillel and Shammai, who lived during the time of Herod the Great. Both were revered teachers, but they often differed in their interpretations of the Torah. The following Talmudic story highlights differences in the temperaments of these two famous teachers:

One day a non-Jew came before Shammai and said, "I will convert to Judaism if you teach me the whole Torah while standing on one foot." Shammai responded by chasing the man away with a stick. The man then went before Hillel and repeated his challenge. Hillel responded, "What is hateful to you, do not do to others. That is the entire Torah. The rest is commentary. Now go and study [Torah]."

But Herod often seemed indifferent to the Jews. His loyalty was to the Romans. In fact, he placed a large Roman eagle—the symbol of Rome's might—on the Temple gate. When two Pharisees tore down the eagle, Herod had them burned alive. He also deepened the rifts in Jewish society. His ambitious building programs were costly, and the heavy tax burden brought many farmers to the edge of ruin.

Perhaps most destructive were Herod's fits of irrational violence. He went so far as to murder most of his family, suspecting they were plotting against him. He executed many popular figures of the day—including his wife, the Hasmonean princess Miriamne. Fearing attempts on his throne and his life, Herod built massive fortresses to which he could escape in case of rebellion; the most famous of these was Masada. Herod's insensitivities and irrational behavior sparked fear and resentment.

Challenging the Romans

Herod succeeded in stifling opposition because the people feared him. But soon after he died, in 4 BCE, farmers rose up in protest. Many had been forced off their land because they couldn't pay their taxes and their debts. Now some became Robin Hood-style bandits, stealing weapons, looting royal palaces, robbing travelers, and even attacking Roman soldiers.

The Romans soon took direct control of Judea and clamped down on the bandits. (The Galilee and the Golan remained under the control of Herod's sons.) The Roman Senate appointed special commissioners, called procurators, to tend to military, judicial, and civil matters. The high priest controlled religious affairs and other local matters. The Romans auctioned off the office of high priest to the highest bidder, who was usually a Sadducee. Many poorer people resented the close relationship between the Sadducees and the Romans, and they turned to the Pharisees for religious and political leadership.

But even the Pharisees were not fully united on the issue of Roman control of Judea. Some were violently opposed to it. In 6 CE, a Pharisee named Zadok and a popular community leader named Judah the Galilean led a tax revolt against the Romans. Others did not openly oppose the Romans; instead, they prayed for the coming of the Messiah.

Praying for the Messiah

Many Jews turned to God for relief from the troubled times in which they lived. Some believed God would send a messiah to destroy their enemies and rule them as in the days of old. They looked forward to the coming of the Messiah at the "End of Days"—when their suffering would end and a more perfect world begin. So they prayed that the Messiah would come soon.

The Hebrew word for messiah, *mashiah*, means "anointed one." In biblical times, kings were anointed with oil. Thus many people expected the Messiah to be a flesh-and-blood king.

On the Brink of Rebellion

As long as the procurators respected Jewish traditions and didn't tax the people too heavily, things remained relatively calm. But the people's anger toward Rome was building.

The procurators who ruled in the late 40s and the 50s CE were especially insensitive and corrupt. Anti-Roman followers of Zadok and Judah the Galilean responded by launching a campaign of deadly tactics. Their group became known as the Sicarii, or "dagger men," because of the small curved dagger, or *sica*, that they used to assassinate their enemies. Many of the Sicarii's targets were Sadducees, who were hated as traitors for cooperating with Rome.

Meanwhile, tensions between the rich and the poor also increased. The poor despised the rich; the rich feared the poor. Desperate Jewish bandits began raiding the farms of wealthy landowners. The Land of Israel was ready to explode.

The Revolt Begins

The procurator Florus lit the fuse in 66 CE.

Concerned with gaining ever greater amounts of gold and silver, Florus robbed the Temple treasury. When outraged Jews protested, he ordered his soldiers to attack the protesters and loot Jerusalem. The soldiers broke into homes and robbed them, destroyed the marketplace, and slaughtered hundreds, including women and children.

Did Florus want a war? Oddly, yes. A war would give him a reason to pronounce Jerusalem a conquered city and seize the Temple treasury. Florus got what he wanted, for by now even the Sadducees and more moderate Pharisees were swept up in the wave of anti-Roman fury. The Temple priests declared that they no longer would make a daily sacrifice in honor of Nero, the Roman emperor, nor would they ask God to protect the Roman Empire. That was as good as a declaration of war.

War

This would have been the perfect time for Jews of Judea to unite against their common enemy. Instead, the conflicts between the various Jewish parties ripped them apart.

At first the priests and aristocrats controlled the war. But the Sicarii soon besieged Jerusalem, declaring their leader, Menaḥem, to be the Messiah. They tried to gain control of the revolt by murdering aristocrats and looting their homes. When the Sadducees killed the Sicarii's leader, the Sicarii fled to Masada, the mountaintop fortress that Herod had built in the Judean desert. There they stayed until the end of the war, praying for God to destroy their enemies, Roman *and* Jewish alike.

Meanwhile, on the battlefield, Jewish fighters won an early victory over Roman troops sent from Syria to restore order. Ultimately, though, the Jewish war effort was doomed. When the Roman legions under the command of Vespasian attacked in the spring of 67 CE, Jewish resistance quickly collapsed on account of infighting. Joseph ben Matityahu, the general in charge, was captured, and Rome took control of the Galilee. After his capture, Joseph became known by his Roman name, Josephus Flavius, and he turned against the war.

As a general, Joseph ben Matityahu was sent to the Galilee to unite and lead the population. The people were divided. On one side were the residents of wealthy cities such as Sepphoris, who believed that a war would bring ruin. On the other side were bandit groups made up of the poor. They had no trust in Joseph ben Matityahu or in the military leaders in Jerusalem, who mostly came from wealthy families.

Jew Against Jew

In 68 CE, the Roman emperor Nero was overthrown and died. The war came to a temporary halt as Rome was overwhelmed by an internal struggle for control of the empire.

Unfortunately, the Jews of Judea did not use this opportunity to organize their troops, fortify Jerusalem, and store supplies. Instead, poor farmers, laborers, and bandits who had been driven out of the Galilee now gathered in Jerusalem and formed a group called the Zealots. The Zealots attacked the chief priests and aristocrats—other Jews— who were running the war. Soon others who despised the rich and the powerful of Jerusalem joined the Zealots.

As if that were not enough, the Zealots and the other groups next turned on one another. Jerusalem became a battlefield as Jew slaughtered Jew. Leaders of the Pharisees and the Sadducees urged the people to end the civil war. No one listened.

The Fall of Jerusalem

The Romans must have watched in amazement as civil war brought their enemies to the verge of self-destruction. In 69 CE, Vespasian was made emperor. He sent his son Titus to complete the military action he had begun.

By the spring of 70 CE, Titus and his army had Jerusalem under siege. Famine quickly overwhelmed the city. The surviving factions tried to fight off the Roman invaders, but Roman battering rams cracked the city's walls.

The Jewish War

Josephus hated the rebellious Jewish factions, such as the Sicarii and the Zealots, whom he believed had brought the country down. *A History of the Jewish War*, the first book by Josephus, provides an eyewitness account of the war with Rome. Vespasian financed the book, so Josephus avoided accusing him and Titus of wrongdoing, blaming the revolt on Jewish hotheads instead. In the following passage, Josephus describes the state of civil war among the Jews:

All [Jews] who were not fighting with the Romans turned their hands against one another. There was also a bitter contest between those who wanted war and those who wanted peace. At first, this quarrelsome attitude took hold of families who disagreed among themselves; eventually those people who were the dearest to one another lost all control with regard to each other.

This is a model of Jerusalem as it appeared in 70 CE, just before the destruction of the Second Temple. The part of the Temple known as the Holy of Holies is in the foreground.

For the next three weeks the priests fought courageously to keep the Romans out of the Holy Temple. As the fighting raged on the ninth day of the Jewish month of Av, a Roman soldier threw a blazing piece of wood into the Temple sanctuary. Flames shot into the air. The Temple burned into the next day, until there was nothing left but cinder and ashes.

Jerusalem and the Temple were destroyed. The surviving leaders of the Jewish factions were led to Rome in chains. Taken with them were the sacred Temple vessels, captured as spoils of war. Jewish tradition teaches that the underlying cause of Jerusalem's destruction was not the Roman rulers but rather the disunity among the Jews and their baseless hatred, *sinat hinam*, for one another. Had the Jews been unified, they might have saved the Temple.

Last Stand at Masada

Now only isolated pockets of rebels held out against the Romans. The most serious of these was the Sicarii stronghold of Masada. Located high atop an isolated rock surrounded on all sides by steep slopes, at the edge of the Judean Desert, Masada was the perfect place for a fortress, as it provided attackers with no natural shelter.

Mourning Jerusalem: Tisha B'Av

Today, centuries after the fall of Jerusalem and the destruction of the Temple, Jews continue to mourn their losses on holy days that commemorate historical events.

Tisha B'Av, the ninth day of the Jewish month of Av, which falls in the summer, is a day of mourning on the Jewish calendar. For a full twenty-five hours, from sundown to nightfall, it is a tradition to fast. It is not a fast of atonement. Rather, it is a fast of grieving. The Book of Lamentations, which was written after the destruction of the First Temple, is chanted mournfully in the synagogue, like an ancient ballad telling a tale of love and loss. For the twenty-five hours of this holy day, Jews are prohibited from wearing leather, listening to music, and bathing. Those prohibitions, too, are signs of mourning.

Masada held large stockpiles of food and water. What the Sicarii lacked, though, was a defense against Roman technology. The Romans built a ramp up the western side of the rock, pushed a siege tower up to the fortress, and battered down the walls. Rather than risk being taken to Rome as prisoners, the Sicarii committed suicide en masse.

Earlier generations than ours often imagined the Jews on Masada as brave fighters and heroes because they refused to give in to the Romans. But perhaps they are better seen simply as an example of why the revolt failed. The Sicarii were not brave warriors but extremists who refused to fight alongside other Jews because they despised them as much as they hated the Romans. Almost until the end the Sicarii were convinced that they were right and everyone else was wrong, that they would usher in the End of Days, while all their enemies would be destroyed.

Instead of triumphing, the Jewish rebellion was completely crushed. The Jews lost their country and their capital city. They watched their beloved Temple burn to the ground. But all was not lost. How the Jews saved themselves and their religion is the focus of the next chapter.

Part Two
Diaspora and Diversity

מה אהבתי תורתך כל הום

היא שיחתי

זהוא ספר

ספר שני

הלכות קש

Chapter 4

Rabbinic Judaism
Reinventing a Religion and an Identity

Imagine the heartache the people of Judea felt after the destruction of Jerusalem and the Temple. For over a thousand years, with only one short interruption, the Temple had been at the core of Jewish spiritual, political, and commercial life. Temple sacrifice was an essential way the Jews thanked God for their good fortune, pleaded for their needs, and repented for their sins. The Temple priests provided leadership, and business was conducted in the Temple courtyards.

Now God's home among the people had been de-stroyed. Everything that had been essential to their belief system and way of life had been ripped from them. Or had it?

Too Difficult to Bear

After the Jewish Revolt was crushed, many Jews found the bloodshed and loss of the Temple almost too difficult to bear. A poet named Baruch expressed the misery that many felt. He looked at the rich harvests around him and was angered and dismayed that nature went undisturbed while his life lay shattered: "Woe unto us, for we have witnessed the suffering of Zion and see what has happened to Jerusalem. . . . Earth, how can you give forth the fruit of your harvest? Hold back your life-giving crops!" (2 Baruch 10:7–9).

TIMELINE

c. 68 CE	Yohanan ben Zakkai and other rabbis set up a religious court in Yavneh
c. 85 CE	Religious leadership passes to Gamaliel II
c. 100 CE	Rabbis at Yavneh create new prayer services for Jewish holidays

World History

c. 100 CE	*Teachings of Siddhãrtha Gautama, known as the Buddah (c. 563–483 BCE), are introduced in China*
117 CE	Hadrian becomes emperor of Rome
132 CE	Bar Kochba leads a massive Jewish revolt
135 CE	Romans defeat the Jewish revolt; Bar Kochba dies

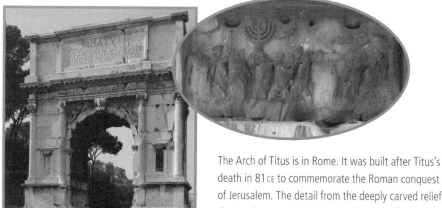

The Arch of Titus is in Rome. It was built after Titus's death in 81 CE to commemorate the Roman conquest of Jerusalem. The detail from the deeply carved relief depicts the Romans carrying spoils of war from Jerusalem, including the Temple's branched candelabrum.

Coping with Tragedy

Tisha B'Av (the holiday that commemorates the day on which the Temple was destroyed) and Yom Hashoah (Holocaust Remembrance Day) are the two saddest days of the Jewish calendar. Separated by almost two thousand years, the tragic events they commemorate are the worst tragedies that have befallen the Jewish people. Both the destruction of the Temple and the Holocaust, during which six million Jews were murdered, threatened the survival of the Jewish people. Both tested the faith and identity of those who survived.

Some Judean Jews responded to their overwhelming grief by becoming ascetics—living a simple life, giving up pleasures, such as tasty foods, beautiful clothing, and comfortable beds. The ascetics of Baruch's time devoted themselves completely to prayer and religious study. Some chose this path as a form of *t'shuvah*, or repentance.

Why did Jews feel the need to repent? Many saw the destruction of the Temple as God's punishment. They reasoned that God was all-powerful and could not be defeated by Israel's enemies. Therefore, the only explanation for Rome's victory was that Israel must have sinned.

Baruch agreed. He admonished the Jews for being disloyal to God by disregarding the laws of Torah. Had they followed God's teachings, he said, they would have lived in peace forever.

The Rabbis Respond

Most of the great scholars of the time were Pharisees or descendants of Pharisees. They called one another *rabbi*, meaning "my teacher." These rabbis agreed with Baruch that the Jews must accept some responsibility for the Temple's destruction; instead of uniting, they had allowed *sinat hinam* to tear them apart. However, the rabbis discouraged the Jews from falling into deep despair.

Rabbi Yohanan ben Zakkai offered Jews a hopeful vision of the future, one that provided new ways to fulfill ancient traditions. One day he and Rabbi Joshua were walking past the ruins of the Temple. "Woe unto us," Rabbi Joshua cried, "that this, the place where the sins of Israel were atoned for, is in ruins!"

"My son," Rabbi Yohanan said to him, "do not be distressed. We can atone for our sins in another way that is equally as effective as [Temple] sacrifice. What is it? It is acts of loving-kindness. As the Bible says, 'God desires mercy, not sacrifice'" (*Avot de Rabbi Natan* 6).

Escape from Jerusalem

During the Roman siege of Jerusalem, Yohanan ben Zakkai realized that the city was doomed. Thousands of Jews were being killed, and thousands more were starving. Rabbi Yohanan wanted desperately to leave Jerusalem so that he could save his people. But the Zealots, who controlled the city gates, permitted no one to leave, for leaving was tantamount to surrendering to the Romans. According to legend, Rabbi Yohanan had his students smuggle him out of the city in a coffin. The Zealots had no choice but to let them out of the gates, for it was forbidden to bury the dead within the city walls.

While many of his friends remained in Jerusalem to fight to the bitter end, Rabbi Yohanan made practical plans for a future without the Temple.

Rabbi Yoḥanan's response was almost shocking. Remember that many Jews believed their ability to be close to God was destroyed with the Temple; it was only in the Temple that they were permitted to make sacrifices to God. But Rabbi Yoḥanan taught that Judaism was not tied to a particular building or to sacrifices. Instead, it was tied to the Torah, which the Jews still had and could take with them wherever they went.

Rabbi Yoḥanan and other rabbis gathered in a town called Yavneh, where they set up a religious court, or *beit din*. They also established an academy, or *beit midrash*, where scholars and the best students could study, debate, and pass on Jewish teachings from one generation to the next.

The rabbis of Yavneh never gave up their hope that the Holy Temple would be rebuilt and the rituals of sacrifice reestablished, but they continued to develop Jewish law, or halachah, to meet the needs of the community. In fact, the ancient rabbis spent most of their time studying Torah, debating, and making Jewish law.

Yavneh quickly became known as the city of learned teachers and rabbis. After Rabbi Yoḥanan died, leadership passed to Hillel's great-grandson, Gamaliel II. Gamaliel was often addressed by the title *Rabban*, meaning "our teacher." Rabban Gamaliel and other rabbis created new prayer services for Jewish holidays, including parts of the Passover haggadah. The religious court officially decided which books would be included in the Bible. It also established official times for prayer. Rabban Gamaliel recognized that eventually prayer would become the main form of Jewish worship. Such wisdom helped Judaism not only survive but also evolve into a modern religion that has continued to attract adherents.

Synagogues as Houses of Worship

Even before the Temple was destroyed, synagogues were established in some Jewish communities. After the destruction of the Temple, the number of synagogues grew and their use as prayer houses became more important. This made it possible for Jews everywhere to join their community in worship.

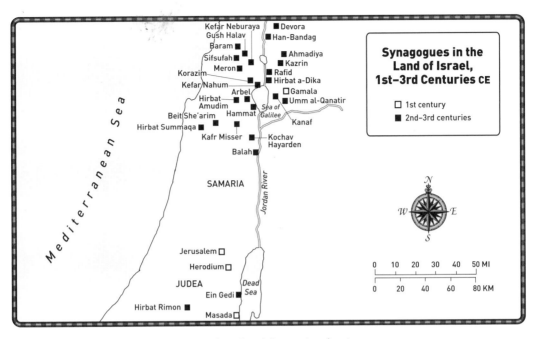

This map shows where archaeologists have found the remains of ancient synagogues.

Both in the Diaspora and in the Land of Israel, the role of the synagogue grew in importance. *Synagogue* is a Greek word meaning "congregation." Early synagogues were a combination of prayer house, Jewish community center, and guesthouse: Synagogues held communal prayers and Torah readings. They also housed social activities, held classes for adults, and offered overnight accommodations for travelers.

Unlike today, rabbis in those days had no official role in a synagogue. Each synagogue was under the control of a local leader, a group of elders, and a group of prayer leaders. Some synagogues adopted practices that the rabbis would have opposed—for example, permitting women to serve as the head of the congregation, praying in Greek and Aramaic rather than Hebrew, and decorating the floors with images of human beings. Scholars suggest that the Judaism practiced in these synagogues may have been quite different from the Judaism that comprised the rabbis' religious teachings and rulings.

A Second Revolt

The Jewish people had shown remarkable determination and creativity. In less than fifty years, Jewish leaders—both rabbis and synagogue leaders—had succeeded in adapting

Judaism to meet the needs of their changing circumstances. Yet many Jews refused to give up hope that the Temple would be rebuilt. And they still dreamed of independence from Roman authority.

But like many other Roman leaders before him, the emperor Hadrian could not understand why the Jews insisted on preserving a separate identity. Determined to undermine those efforts, he announced plans to rebuild Jerusalem as a Greek-style city, and he banned circumcision.

With that, Judea once again exploded in rebellion. Beginning in 132 CE, a leader named Simon ben Kozeva led a massive Jewish revolt. Some people, including the revered sage Rabbi Akiva, believed Ben Kozeva was the long-awaited Messiah. According to tradition, the coming of the Messiah would be announced by a bright star or comet, and so Ben Kozeva's supporters nicknamed him Bar Kochba, meaning "son of a star." (Most people continued to call him Ben Kozeva—as he called himself. Yet today, he is generally known as Bar Kochba.)

But not everyone saw Bar Kochba as a savior, nor were all Jews ready to serve in his army. Bar Kochba responded harshly to his opponents, especially those who sought refuge in other towns. In a letter to the leaders of Ein Gedi, he said, "Concerning all the men of Tekoa who are found in your place—the houses in which they live shall be burned and you, too, shall be punished."

The Bar Kochba Revolt caught the Romans by surprise. Bar Kochba and his army now enjoyed the same advantage that had enabled the Maccabees to prevail—a detailed knowledge of Judea. They hid in underground caves, slipped out to perform daring raids on enemy positions, and then vanished back into the countryside. Although the rebels never captured any cities, they established an independent Jewish government in the Judean hills.

Hadrian probably did not realize that his policies would create so much hostility. He had built many Greek cities throughout his empire, and his law against circumcision was not directed solely at the Jews. In keeping with Greek tradition, Hadrian simply believed that the human body is perfect and should not be altered.

FAMOUS FIGURES

Babata

A Jewish woman named Babata lived at the time of the Bar Kochba Revolt. In 1961, the Israeli archaeologist Yigal Yadin discovered a collection of her personal and legal documents, written on papyrus, in one of the Bar Kochba caves in the Judean Desert.

Babata's documents—thirty-five in all—form the largest collection of ancient documents ever found in Israel. They are important because they shed light on the customs and way of life of the time. They show that Babata had been married and widowed twice, had participated in the business and legal affairs of her stepdaughter, Shalomzion, and had been involved in several lawsuits. Like the lawsuits of today, Babata's court cases dragged on for years.

Also among Babata's documents are deeds to her property and her *k'tubot*—her marriage contracts. Similar to many *k'tubot* today, Babata's marriage contracts protected her by clearly defining the responsibilities of her husband. "If I [Babata's husband] die before you, you will live in my house and receive maintenance from it and from my possessions," states Babata's marriage contract.

This silver coin with a Hebrew inscription and the image of a lyre was issued by Simon Bar Kochba in about 134 CE.

Disastrous Results

Bar Kochba battled for three years. But his army was not strong enough to defeat the Romans, who had the most powerful military in the world. Hadrian sent his most experienced general to Judea. He and his army dealt mercilessly with the Jewish people. Countless villages were destroyed and hundreds of thousands of civilians were killed.

Bar Kochba and his men made their last stand in a village called Beitar, southwest of Jerusalem. The Romans successfully laid siege to the town and slaughtered rebels and villagers alike. Bar Kochba was killed. According to tradition, the fall of Beitar occurred on the ninth of Av (Tisha B'Av), the same day as the destruction of the Temple.

Jewish Life Ends in Judea

Hadrian treated the surviving Jews harshly. He rebuilt Jerusalem as a Greek city, banning Jews from entering its gates except on Tisha B'Av. He forbade the Jews of Judea to observe some of their most basic religious laws and customs, including the public reading of the Torah and the observance of Shabbat. Hadrian also tried to erase the Jewish nature of the land by renaming the entire Land of Israel "Palaestina," or Palestine, after the Philistines.

As a result of the war, the Jewish population of Judea was dramatically reduced. Some Jews had been killed, others had been captured, and yet others fled in search of safety. After more than a thousand years, Jewish life in Judea was over. The center of that life, including the religious court at Yavneh, moved north to the Galilee, to towns and villages that had not been ravaged by the war. Here, rabbis began building a new future.

Fortunately, the many adaptations to the new circumstances that had arisen after the destruction of the Temple now helped Jews face the future. Synagogues and schools were being built, and Jews were encouraged to worship God through Torah study, prayer, and acts of loving-kindness. Jews had not only survived dark and uncertain times with courage and creativity; they had also developed new ways of thinking about and practicing their religion.

Chapter 5

Judaism and Christianity
A Parting of the Ways

The Big Picture

Roman rule over Judea was a time of great change and turmoil—Herod's reign, the building of the Second Temple, conflict between the Pharisees and Sadducees, two major Jewish rebellions, and the destruction of the Second Temple. If there had been newspapers in Judea, these stories would surely have made the headlines. But one story that might not even have been reported was the story of a Jew named Jesus.

Now, more than two thousand years later, you cannot hope to understand Jewish history without knowing the story of Jesus. That is because his life and teachings led to the birth of a new religion—Christianity—which changed the course of not only Jewish history but also world history.

A Longing for Change

To begin the story we must go back in time to the early part of the first century CE, before the two Jewish rebellions against Rome and the destruction of the Temple. Disheartened by foreign rule, Jews in the Land of Israel longed for political freedom and dreamed of a return to the golden age of King David. Many believed that Roman rule would be swept away and replaced by a messianic age, a time of peace and plenty. In these tense times, people who claimed to be a messiah, prophet, or revolutionary often attracted a large following.

TIMELINE

c. 4 BCE	Jesus is born
c. 26 CE	John the Baptist preaches and baptizes his followers
c. 33 CE	Jesus is arrested and crucified by the Roman governor of Judea
c. 50 CE	Paul begins to teach his interpretation of Christian beliefs
60–90 CE	The Gospels are written
c. 73 CE	Some Christians develop the belief that Christianity is meant to replace Judaism

World History

79 CE	*Mount Vesuvius erupts; first detailed eyewitness account of a volcanic eruption is recorded*
300s CE	Christianity becomes the official religion of the Roman Empire

One Jew who attracted attention was a man named Yoḥanan, known to history as John the Baptist. Like an ancient Hebrew prophet, John reprimanded the Jews for disregarding God's teachings. He warned that the End of Days, when all people would be judged by God, was near and that sinners would not be permitted to enter God's kingdom. "Repent, for the Kingdom of Heaven will soon be here!" he urged (Christian scriptures, Matthew 3:2).

John created a new ritual, which became known as baptism. Baptism was based on the Jewish purification ritual of *mikveh,* which requires that a person dunk his or her entire body in water. John taught that repentance purifies people of their sins and that baptism is an outward sign of that purification. Even today some Jews wash themselves in a *mikveh* on certain occasions, such as after they have touched a dead body. The *mikveh* ritual has also become part of the Jewish conversion process.

Jesus of Nazareth

One of John's followers was a young man named Jesus, who had grown up in Nazareth, a small town in the Galilee. After he was baptized, Jesus became a traveling preacher. Like John, he urged people to repent for their sins. In addition, he spoke out against greed and unjust treatment of the poor.

What little we know about the life of Jesus comes from stories that were written after his death. Jesus began traveling and preaching when he was about thirty. Just as the stories about many religious leaders of his time describe the miracles they performed, so do the stories about Jesus—in this case, healing the sick, turning water into wine, and walking on water. Soon Jesus had a following. Some accepted him as a prophet in the tradition of Elijah. Others thought he was the long-awaited Messiah.

This mosaic comes from the city of Sepphoris, which was less than four miles from where Jesus grew up.

According to Christian tradition, Jesus made a bold decision in about 33 CE. He took his message outside the rural parts of the Galilee, straight to the center of Jewish life: Jerusalem. Jesus and his followers arrived in Jerusalem in the weeks before the festival of Passover, along with thousands of holiday pilgrims.

Arrest and Execution

Jesus spoke to large crowds at the Temple. Like the great Jewish prophets, he was critical of rich and powerful figures, accusing them of engaging in corruption and making large donations to the Temple while ignoring the poor. He also spoke out against the corruption of the priests, whom he blamed for cooperating with the Romans. One day as Jesus neared the outer area of the Temple, he began overturning the stalls and tables of the merchants who sold birds for Temple sacrifice and the money changers who sold Roman coins.

The high priest, Caiaphas, and other Jewish leaders were angered by Jesus's criticism and hostile actions. They also knew that with the city streets packed with people preparing for Passover—a festival celebrating freedom from oppression—Jesus might easily arouse the Jews to rebel against the Romans, whom many saw as modern-day oppressors.

The Roman procurator of Judea was Pontius Pilate, a man who used brutal tactics to crush even the hint of rebellion. Thus Caiaphas and the other priests worried that if Jesus should stir up the people, Pilate might respond by setting his troops loose on Jerusalem's pilgrims, creating a bloodbath. Indeed, the historian Josephus reported that thousands of Jewish rebels and bandits were crucified by the Romans.

According to tradition, Jesus was arrested and handed over to Pilate, who condemned him to death and executed him by crucifixion.

From Jesus to Christ

This was the end of Jesus's life—but the beginning of his importance in history. His execution surely devastated his supporters. They may have sought comfort in the Jewish belief that God can restore people to life. Indeed, shortly after his death some followers reported seeing Jesus resurrected—raised from the dead. His supporters came to believe that Jesus was not only an earthly king but also a spiritual king and that the End of Days would soon arrive.

Over time, Jesus's followers began to identify themselves as a separate community within the Jewish tradition. The main difference between this new community and other Jews

The Church of the Holy Sepulchre in Jerusalem is an especially holy place for Christians. According to Christian tradition, it is built on the site where Jesus was crucified. Many Christians also believe that the church houses the tomb where Jesus was buried.

was its members' belief in Jesus as the Messiah. The community became known as Christians, from the Greek word *christos*, which means "messiah" and is the source of the name Christ. Early Christians continued to follow Jewish laws and to make sacrifices at the Temple. At first it was possible to be both Christian and Jewish but two factors eventually led to a complete break between Judaism and Christianity.

Seeking New Followers

In the first century, Jews often tried to persuade people to convert to Judaism, usually without success. Although the concept of monotheism and the close-knit nature of Jewish communities appealed to many non-Jews, few were interested in following Judaism's restrictive laws. For example, they were resistant to following the laws of kashrut, which limit the foods that one can eat.

Around 50 CE, a Jew named Paul began to teach that gentiles need not convert to Judaism or follow Jewish law in order to become Christians. Belief that Jesus had died for one's sins and the performance of Christian rituals, such as baptism, were enough. Paul's teaching attracted many people. The Christian leaders in Jerusalem, however, including Peter and Jesus's brother James, opposed some of Paul's more extreme teachings. In opposition to them, Peter and James instructed Paul's converts to obey the Torah, including the laws of kashrut and male circumcision.

Paul pressed forward, seeking new followers in the Diaspora. He founded and supported Christian communities in cities along the eastern coast of the Mediterranean. Aside from making visits to those communities, Paul's main means of communication was through letters, or epistles. He used epistles to educate the new Christians and to build their morale. Years later Paul's epistles became the earliest books to be included in the Christian sacred writings, known by Christians as the New Testament. Christians believe that those writings reflect a new covenant with God. The Christian scriptures are composed of the books of the New Testament and the books of the Hebrew Bible, which Christians know as the Old Testament.

As Christianity spread, it encompassed a patchwork of communities with differing membership requirements and differing views of whether or not its members had to observe the laws of the Torah. Communities even differed on such basic questions as the significance of Jesus, the meaning of his death, and reports of his rising from the dead. Under the influence of some pagan religions, which had traditions relating to the death and rebirth of their gods, many Christians of non-Jewish origin came to believe that Jesus was divine. They believed that he literally was the son of God.

Breaking Away

The Jewish Revolt (66–73 CE) confronted Jewish Christians—Jews who had accepted Christian teachings—with the same question it confronted all other Jews: Why had God permitted the destruction of the Temple, God's dwelling place? Jewish Christians came to believe that God was punishing the Jews for rejecting Jesus as the promised Messiah. Christian beliefs and practices, they asserted, were meant to replace Judaism.

The Bar Kochba Revolt further distanced Jewish Christians from the Jewish community. Christians already had a messiah, so they were not interested in joining Bar Kochba. In addition, after the revolts, Christians may have seen few advantages to maintaining their Jewish identity. Roman-Jewish relations had hit a low point. Jews throughout the empire were forced to pay a special tax, and the Roman government no longer recognized the authority of Judea's Jewish leaders.

As we saw in chapter 4, the Jewish community was in crisis. Jews throughout the empire, weakened spiritually by the loss of the Temple in Jerusalem and politically by the lack of effective leadership in Judea, had no means by which to protest the Roman persecutions. Early Christians, also persecuted by the Romans, sought to minimize their suffering by identifying themselves as Christians, not as Jews. Any association with the despised Jewish community also interfered with their missionary efforts among pagans. Over time, many Christians began to think of themselves as members of a separate religion. Others, however, continued to identify themselves with Jews and Judaism until as late as the fourth or fifth centuries.

Shifting Blame

Members of some Christian communities began to gather and edit Jesus's sayings and stories about his life creating books that came to be called the Gospels, *gospel* meaning "good news." Christians considered the stories about Jesus to be good news, because they told about the coming of the Messiah.

The authors of the Gospels lived in a world dominated by Roman power. Not wanting to offend Roman leaders, they shifted the blame for Jesus's crucifixion from the Romans. Thus the Gospels were interpreted as teaching that Jews not only had denied that Jesus was the Messiah but also had been guilty of his murder. As Christianity and Judaism became separate religions, sections of the Gospels became the basis of misunderstanding and hatred.

A Scene from the Gospels

Pontius Pilate was known to be a cruel Roman governor. Yet in the Gospels a story is told in which he agrees to set one Jew free from prison as a goodwill gesture to the Jews at the time of their holiday. The crowd chooses to release a bandit rather than Jesus.

Pilate asks the crowd, "What should I do with Jesus who is called the Christ?" The crowd responds, "Let him be crucified!" The Gospel then describes Pilate symbolically washing his hands before the crowd, declaring, "I am innocent of his blood." The crowd responds, "Let his blood be on us and let it be on our children!" (Christian scriptures, Matthew 27:22, 24–25).

FAMOUS FIGURES

Jesus of Nazareth

The exact day and month of Jesus's birth are not known, nor is there certainty about the year in which he was born. Historians believe that Jesus was probably born sometime around 4 BCE. His Hebrew name was Yehoshua, which in the Galilee may have been pronounced "Yeshua."

The Gospels do not provide much information about Jesus's youth. They do say, however, that he was circumcised and that he was interested in Jewish religious teachings. After he was baptized, Jesus traveled throughout the Land of Israel, particularly in the Galilee, preaching to large crowds that often included laborers, fishermen, and other people of simple means. He emphasized the importance of compassion and offered hope of a better world, a coming "Kingdom of God" on earth to those who suffered.

Christian tradition teaches that Jesus miraculously fed thousands of his followers with only five loaves of bread and two fish. The Church of the Multiplication of the Loaves and the Fishes in the Galilee was built on the site where this miracle is said to have happened. This mosaic from the church shows the fish and a basket of bread.

It is important to remember, however, that the Gospels were written *before* Christianity had split from Judaism and that most of the authors were Jewish. Those authors debated as brothers and sisters with the Pharisees and other survivors of the Jewish Revolt. Together they questioned the meaning of the life and death of Jesus and the destruction of the Temple. True, some of those arguments were vicious, but family arguments, too, can be emotionally charged, as are some arguments among today's Jews. The tragedy is not that insults were hurled but that after Christianity split from Judaism, the understanding of the times in which this family feud took place was forgotten.

Christianity's Influence

The Christians were not the only ones who were critical of their rivals. Rabbis hurled insults at Christians and sought to limit their growth and influence. But rabbis had little power under the Romans. In contrast, Christianity was spreading quickly and gaining influence. Three hundred years after the death of Jesus—by the fourth century—Christianity had become the official religion of the Roman Empire.

Christians and Jews Living in Peace

Just as today's political advertisements may distort the degree to which a community or a country is divided, so, too, would our understanding of ancient history be distorted if our knowledge were limited to information on the religious leadership. In fact, although Jewish and Christian leaders were often in conflict, many Jews and Christians interacted peacefully.

Before the Christianization of the Roman Empire, Jews, Christians, and pagans interacted freely in the Galilee and in many Diaspora communities. Even in the fourth and fifth centuries, churches, synagogues, and pagan temples existed side by side in urban centers, including Rome. Some Christians even worshipped with Jews in their synagogues.

THE RISE OF CHRISTIANITY AND ITS SPLIT WITH JUDAISM

- The Romans oppress the Jews; dejected, many Jews yearn for liberation through a messiah.

- John the Baptist criticizes the Jews for their sins and offers forgiveness through baptism.

- Jesus is baptized, begins to preach, and develops a following.

- Jewish leaders are concerned that, in reaction to Jesus and his followers, Pontius Pilate will unleash troops in Jerusalem.

- Jesus is crucified; reports of his resurrection inspire faith in him as the Messiah.

- Jesus's followers identify themselves as a separate community within the Jewish tradition; the main difference is their belief in Jesus as the Messiah.

- Around 50 CE, Paul teaches that gentiles can become Christians without converting to Judaism; he establishes Christian communities along the eastern coast of the Mediterranean.

- By 90 CE, some Christian communities have developed the belief that Christianity is meant to replace Judaism.

- By the fourth century Christianity has become the official religion of the Roman Empire.

- Judaism and Christianity each become more centralized.

The Christianization of the Roman Empire greatly deepened the rift that had grown between Christianity and Judaism. Now Christian leaders were able to use the power of Rome to enforce their prejudices. By the fifth century Jews were officially denied many of their traditional rights and privileges, including the right to build new synagogues, hold state office, and serve in the army.

The rift grew even greater as both religions became more centralized. Christian leaders, called bishops, were recognized as religious authorities and determined the proper practices and religious guidelines for their dioceses, or regions. The chief bishop, who headed the diocese in Rome, became known as the pope.

Judaism, too, became more centralized. Banned from participating in many of the public activities of the Christianized Roman Empire, Jews were forced to turn inward. Local synagogues and Jewish communities increasingly became the centers of Jewish life. As a result, community elders, synagogue leaders, and rabbis grew in influence and power.

Thus Judaism and Christianity eventually became two separate religions, and centuries of hostility between Christians and Jews followed. Once the seeds of hatred and misunderstanding had been planted, they grew and blossomed into repeated acts of violence. The consequences were tragic and became a central theme in Jewish history.

Chapter 6

Babylonia
The New Center of Jewish Life

The Big Picture

After the disastrous Bar Kochba Revolt, as Christianity spread throughout the Roman Empire, many Jews left Judea in hopes of a better life. Many moved north, to the Galilee or to Syria and other parts of the Hellenic world. But others traveled east, to Babylonia, where Jews had lived for generations after the destruction of the First Temple.

Jewish life in the Galilee eventually weakened because of the intolerance of the Roman Empire's Christian rulers. As the Galilee declined in population and influence, Babylonia grew more powerful. For more than five hundred years, Babylonia served as the center of Jewish learning and growth. During this period, Jews found new ways to enrich Jewish traditions and values as they adapted to and prospered in their new country.

Collecting the Law

After the Bar Kochba Revolt, small Jewish communities survived in Judea, now renamed Palestine by the Romans. Rabbi Judah the Prince was one of the many rabbis who remained in Palestine. He dedicated his life to developing a standardized record of Jewish law. Much of it was based on "oral law"—legal rulings that had been passed on by word of mouth from one generation to the next. In about 200 CE, Rabbi Judah and his students completed this collection,

TIMELINE

c. 200	Mishnah is completed
c. 400	Palestinian Talmud is completed
c. 500	Babylonian Talmud is completed
c. 570	Muhammad, prophet of Islam, is born in Mecca

World History

596	*Pope Gregory I sends the monk Augustine to convert the English to Christianity*
638	Jerusalem comes under Muslim control
642	Babylonia, a center of Jewish life, comes under Muslim control
711	Spain, a center of Jewish life, comes under Muslim control
882	Saadiah ben Joseph (Saadiah Gaon), a great scholar, is born in Egypt

which became known as the Mishnah. The Mishnah was a revolutionary work. Its legal rulings allowed Judaism to adapt to the reality of life without the Temple.

Next Step: The Talmud

The Jewish population of Babylonia had declined after the rebuilding of the Temple when Jewish leaders returned to Israel. After the destruction of the Second Temple, the Babylonian Jewish community began to grow. Jews lived, worked, and worshipped in peace. Scholars traveled from Palestine—where they had learned the rabbinic tradition—to Babylonia, bringing their teachings with them. In 219 CE, the Babylonian sage Rav, who had spent years studying in Palestine with Rabbi Judah the Prince, returned to Babylon. Upon Rav's return it was said, "we became like the Land of Israel." The rabbis of Babylonia and their students discussed the Mishnah with great excitement.

Many of these discussions are recorded in the Babylonian Gemara, a compilation of discussions of Jewish law, interpretations of the Bible, parables, stories, traditions, and folklore. (Gemara comes from the Aramaic word *gamar*, meaning "study.") Much of the Gemara is written in Aramaic, the language of Babylonia. Unlike the Mishnah, which makes little direct reference to the Torah, the Gemara often refers to the Torah to support its opinions.

Meanwhile similar conversations were going on in Tiberias and other rabbinic centers in the Galilee. These discussions were also compiled; they were known as the Palestinian Talmud. (Talmud comes from the Hebrew word *lamad*, meaning "study" or "learning.") The Palestinian Talmud was completed circa 400 CE, whereas the Babylonian Gemara continued to be expanded and edited into the sixth century.

These are the remains of a Talmudic village in the Golan Heights, north of the Sea of Galilee.

The Palestinian Talmud was compiled in haste because of the chaos in the Roman Empire and the growing intolerance for Jews in the Galilee. Interestingly, the Gemara, which was produced in the Diaspora of Babylonia, became far more influential in Jewish life. Where the two works disagree on a matter of Jewish law, the Babylonian Gemara is generally given precedence.

Today, both the Palestinian Talmud and the Babylonian Gemara are popularly known as the Talmud. Indeed, because the Mishnah is printed in every edition of the Talmud, the term *Talmud* is often used to refer to the Mishnah as well, even though it is a separate work.

The Talmud and its commentaries fill thousands of pages. The largest volumes deal with the issues of day-to-day living. For example, there are laws concerning property rights, the obligations of employers and employees, and which foods to eat and which to avoid. There are also laws that discuss how to observe special occasions, such as Shabbat and holidays. In addition to such practical laws, the rabbis discussed and recorded laws that were no longer practical, such as the laws of sacrifice. In fact, they discussed these laws with the same fervor that they discussed practical laws. They did so to preserve them for the time when the Holy Temple would be rebuilt.

Operating as a guide to Jewish living, the Talmud helps adapt Jewish law to life in the Diaspora. For example, it calls for Jews to follow the laws of the countries in which they live. In matters of civil law, so long as "the king" acts fairly, the Talmud declares, "the law of the land is the law."

Before the Talmud, biblical Judaism had been the foundation of Jewish life. Among the most influential leaders of biblical Judaism were the Temple high priests. Many of them were Sadducees. In contrast, the Pharisees were in a good position to lead the community after the Temple's destruction, for they emphasized the importance of studying and interpreting Jewish law over performing Temple rituals. Although many Jews at first resisted rabbinic law, rabbinic Judaism, based on the Talmud, slowly became the foundation of Jewish life. It continues to be the basis of Judaism to this day.

A Land of Opportunity

When Jews first arrived in Babylonia, back in 586 BCE, they were impressed by its agricultural wealth. It was a fertile land and many Jews became successful farmers. Others worked in

Each page of the Talmud has a clear structure. The Talmud text is in the middle, surrounded by the commentaries of later generations.

manufacturing or trade. Some Jewish traders eventually traveled as far as China to buy or barter for raw silk. Other Jews processed the raw silk then sold it. There were also Jewish bankers, Jewish tax collectors, Jewish soldiers, and even Jewish elephant riders.

While living under the rule of the Babylonians, the Jews separated political and religious authority within their communities, just as they had in the days of the kings, the prophets, and the Temple priests. Their political leader was the exilarch, a word meaning "head of the Jewish community of the exile." The exilarch's primary duty was to settle conflicts between the Jewish community and the Babylonian government. The exilarch was also responsible for collecting taxes and appointing judges in the Jewish community.

The heads of the great Jewish academies in Babylonia provided religious leadership. These rabbis were known as *geonim* (singular: *gaon*), meaning "geniuses" and "learned." The *geonim* were great scholars of the Talmud. We know little about the daily life of Babylonia's Jewish community and the extent to which Jews accepted rabbinic Judaism and the leadership of the *geonim*.

The Challenge of Islam

In the first half of the seventh century, Arab armies swept out of Arabia and conquered most lands in which Jews were living. The armies brought with them a new religion, called Islam, meaning "submission (to the will of God)." The founder and central prophet of this new faith was Muhammad. Muhammad had been raised in the Arabian city of Mecca, where he had lived among both Jews and Christians. There he came to believe in one God. He warned of a coming day of judgment and declared himself the last and greatest of the prophets. Muhammad introduced a new sacred text, which became known as the Koran, the holy book of Islam.

Muhammad and his successors waged war against their neighbors. They achieved spectacular success, capturing Jerusalem in 638, Babylonia in 642, and much of Spain in 711. All the great centers of Jewish life were now under Islamic rule. This meant that Islam was the state-sponsored religion in those places. Other religions could be practiced only to the extent permitted by the Muslims.

The Roots of Islam

In the eyes of Muslims, acceptance of Muhammad's teachings includes acceptance of Allah as the one God and the source of the sacred texts (including the Bible), and recognition of the importance of the prophets (including Moses and Jesus). Because Muhammad recognized the influence of other monotheistic religions on his teachings, at first he did not consider what he preached to be a new religion. Instead, he expected Jews and Christians to voluntarily accept his ideas as additions to their traditions. But they did not, so Muhammad chose to emphasize the differences.

Muhammad instructed his followers to turn away from Jerusalem when they prayed and to turn instead toward Mecca. He made Friday the day of holy assembly and, in contrast to Judaism and Christianity, permitted work on that day. Most of Judaism's dietary laws were rejected, although a few continued to be observed, such as the ban on eating pork.

Yet to this day, there continue to be commonalities and shared traditions. Many stories in the Koran originated in the Bible, including stories about Abraham. Numerous Jewish teachings and ethical sayings are included in the Muslim oral tradition, known as Hadith. And among the holy places of Islam are the tomb of Abraham, in Hebron, and what is considered the burial site of John the Baptist's head, in the Great Mosque of Damascus.

In Babylonia and elsewhere, Muslims usually granted Jews the right to practice their religion without interference. In fact, Islam recognized both Jews and Christians as "people of the book" (the Bible), or monotheists, and granted them protected status. But as protected non-Muslims, Jews had secondary status. For example, they had to stand aside when passed by a Muslim in the street. Synagogues had to be smaller than neighboring mosques. Jews were encouraged to convert to Islam (which some did), but Muslims were forbidden to convert to Judaism. Still, for centuries, Jews enjoyed greater freedom under Islam than under Christianity.

The rise of Islam created additional challenges for the Jews of the Middle East, including the Jews of Babylonia. First, Islam made Arabic the primary language of their world. Less educated Jews, who knew Arabic but not Hebrew and Aramaic, found themselves cut off from Judaism's most important texts. In addition, the Arabs developed new forms of scholarship, including grammar, commentaries on texts, philosophy, science, and medicine. The traditional Jewish focus on law suddenly seemed insufficient in a world that valued more diverse knowledge and skills.

The Dome of the Rock in Jerusalem is the oldest Islamic building to survive in its original form. It is one of Islam's holiest sites. Muslims believe that it is the place from which Muhammad rose to heaven. It was built on the site of the Second Temple.

Determined to meet these challenges, the Jews of Babylonia produced Jewish books in Arabic and Judeo-Arabic, which used Hebrew letters to write Arabic words. Under the influence of their neighbors, they also explored new fields of study, creating commentaries, grammars, and philosophic works of their own. Many of those works blended traditional Jewish teachings with Arabic teachings, making it possible for Jews who might otherwise have completely assimilated, or abandoned their Judaism in favor of the Babylonian culture, to live in both worlds. Furthermore, they enriched not only Jewish culture but also the larger, general culture.

CHALLENGE	ADAPTATION
• Dispersal of the Jews had made communication of the oral tradition difficult.	• The oral tradition was recorded in the Mishnah.
• Jews spoke Arabic, the primary language in Babylonia after the Islamic conquest, and many of them forgot Hebrew	• The Bible and a prayer book were translated into Arabic; the Judeo-Arabic language was developed.
• The general principles of the Mishnah did not present practical laws to guide real-life situations.	• The Gemara and additional commentaries were written.
• The temptation to assimilate was great.	• Jewish leaders focused on Judaism's strengths.
• Some Jews saw a conflict between the law of the land and Judaism.	• The geonim declared that as long as the civil laws were just, Jews must honor them.
• Secular society valued diverse knowledge and skills.	• Jewish studies were broadened to include such subjects as philosophy, Hebrew grammar, and commentary on texts.

Life in Babylonia presented the Jews with challenges that became opportunities through the process of adaptation.

FAMOUS FIGURES

Saadiah Gaon

Saadiah ben Joseph was the greatest of the *geonim*. Born in Egypt in 882, he studied in Israel and Babylonia before becoming the *gaon* of the Babylonian academy of Sura.

Saadiah, also known as Saadiah Gaon, translated most of the Bible into Arabic and produced a prayer book with Arabic instructions and explanations. He wrote the first Hebrew grammar book, a Hebrew dictionary, and Hebrew poetry. Because Greek philosophy was valued by many educated and assimilated Jews in the Arab world, Saadiah wrote (in Arabic) *The Book of Beliefs and Opinions,* in which he showed how one could believe in both the Torah and the Greek philosophers.

Most earlier *geonim* had focused on the Talmud and Jewish law. Saadiah demonstrated that Jews could take what they learned from the surrounding culture, including language, philosophy, literature, and values, and adapt it in ways that strengthened Judaism. He proved that Judaism could not only survive, but also thrive in the Diaspora. Saadiah died in 942.

The Karaite Challenge

Diaspora Jews were challenged not only by Islam. They were also challenged by Jews who, influenced by Islam, followed only the explicit teachings of the Torah rather than the interpretations and directives of the rabbis. Those Jews denied the authority of the Talmud, the exilarch, and the *geonim*. Although resistance to rabbinic authority dated back to the time of the Temple, the new challengers were particularly noteworthy because there were so many of them, their views were in tune with Islamic culture, and the man they considered their founder enjoyed a distinguished reputation.

Anan ben David, born sometime in the eighth century, was learned and pious; he was even said to be a descendant of King David. According to some, he was in line to be appointed exilarch but was passed over because of his strict, uncompromising ways. Respected as a scholar and righteous man, Anan soon became the guiding light of the Ananite sect. Following his death, he also became the guiding light of the Karaites, Jews who insisted that the Bible alone is the source of God's law.

Following a statement in Psalms, the Karaites declared that "the Torah of Adonai is perfect" and need not be interpreted to be understood. Their views brought them into conflict with the rabbis. For example, the rabbis permitted Jews to keep a fire burning throughout Shabbat as long as it was lit beforehand. In contrast, Karaite leaders, taking literally the biblical commandment to kindle no fire on the Sabbath day, ruled that their followers must spend Shabbat without fire for light and heat.

Karaites also refused to follow the traditional Jewish calendar set by the rabbis. Applying the literal words of the Torah, they declared that the holiday of Shavuot must always fall on the first day of the week. In addition, based on the teachings of the prophets, the Karaites favored elaborate mourning rites for the destruction of the Temple and the exile of the Jewish people from the Promised Land. Some of their synagogues resembled mosques, and like Muslims they removed their shoes before entering their place of worship.

The *geonim* considered the Karaites heretics and sought to undermine the basis of Karaite beliefs. For centuries, however, mainstream Jews and Karaites not only interacted but also intermarried, for each considered the other a part of the Jewish people. But over time the two communities grew further apart, much as Jews and early Christians had, until the differences in belief and practice proved too great to bridge. By the sixteenth century the rabbis had decreed that Jews may not marry Karaites. Yet the Karaite community lived on; today most of its thirty-five thousand adherents reside in Israel.

Beyond Babylonia

The influence of the *geonim* and the Talmud grew in the Muslim countries of North Africa, such as Egypt. It especially grew in Spain, where the economy was strong. Jewish communities were also developing in parts of Christian-controlled Europe, including France and Germany. Those new centers of Jewish life drew scholars and rabbis from Babylonia. The Talmud that had been written in Babylonia was soon being studied in Jewish communities in Europe, Asia, and Africa. It enabled Jews in diverse Diaspora communities to discuss and observe the same collection of laws.

The Babylonian model of Diaspora life remained highly influential. Living as a minority in a non-Jewish environment, Jews had learned to adapt their lives to new surroundings, borrow selectively from neighbors, and renew Jewish life.

Chapter 7

Sepharad and Ashkenaz
Judaism's Increasing Diversity

Just as many Jews had left Judea in search of a better life, so, centuries later, did many leave Babylonia. In time two new centers of Jewish life developed in the areas that are known today as Spain and Germany.

Thanks to modern modes of transportation, we can now travel from Spain to Germany in about the time it takes to play a baseball game. But a thousand years ago people didn't often make the more than nine-hundred-mile trip. Also, without the benefit of such technologies as telephones, televisions, and computers, they lived more isolated lives than we do.

As a result, the Jews of Spain and of Germany developed in different ways. Each community was influenced by its surrounding culture—the non-Jewish population—and especially by that culture's attitudes toward Jews. As always, the Jews adapted to the world around them, and in the process, Judaism became richer and more diverse.

The Golden Age of Spain

In the year 711, Muslim armies, originating in Arabia and North Africa, crossed the Strait of Gibraltar into Spain. Within four years most of the Iberian Peninsula (modern-day Spain and Portugal) lay under Muslim rule. As a result, Spain became religiously and culturally diverse: Muslims ruled;

TIMELINE

711	Muslim armies cross the Strait of Gibraltar into Spain and soon conquer most of Spain

World History

800	*Charlemagne is crowned the first Holy Roman emperor*
950	Golden age of Spain begins
993	Shmuel Hanagid, a scholar, rabbi, and military commander, is born in Spain
1040	Rabbi Solomon ben Isaac (Rashi), a biblical and Talmudic scholar, is born in France
1135	Moses Maimonides (Rambam), a great scholar and author of the *Mishneh Torah*, is born in Spain
1286	Moses de Leon writes the the *Zohar*, the basic textbook of the Kabbalah

Sephard adla · 67

Christians were tolerated; Jews, being neither Christian nor Muslim, served as valuable intermediaries. People of different ethnic and cultural backgrounds, Middle Easterners and Europeans alike, came to know one another and work together.

Under Islam, cities grew, and Spain became a land of opportunity, a crossroads for international trade. Jewish immigration swelled, and Spain—or Sepharad, as the Jews called it—developed into a leading center of Jewish learning and culture. The milieu was so rich in Judaism that this period in Jewish history is known as the golden age of Spain.

The golden age began in the mid-tenth century and lasted about two hundred years. Inspired by Muslim poets, Jews began writing beautiful poetry in Hebrew and Arabic. Jews also made contributions to the study of philosophy, medicine, science, Bible commentary, Jewish law, music, dance, and the visual arts.

Shmuel Hanagid (*nagid* being the title of the head of the Jewish community) was born Samuel ibn Nagrela in 993. Considered one of the most influential Jews of his time, Shmuel was a great secular and Jewish scholar and a brilliant statesman, poet, rabbi, and military

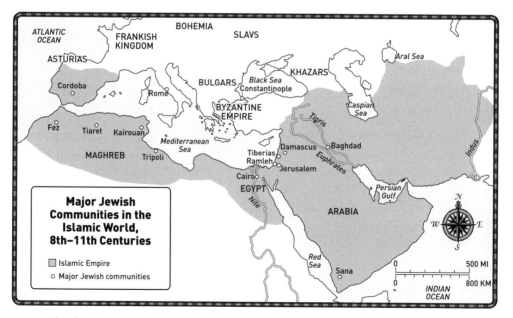

As the Islamic Empire grew, thousands of Jews migrated to the west, especially from what are now Iraq and Iran. Strong ties developed between the Jews of Sepharad and those who remained in the east.

commander. In fact, he became the vizier, or commander, of the city of Granada and spent eighteen years in command of a largely Muslim army. He wrote three books of poetry, commentaries on the Bible, and a major work dealing with Jewish law.

Judah Halevi, who lived from circa 1075 to 1141, was also a shining star during the golden age of Spain. In addition to being the greatest of Spain's Jewish poets—some eight hundred of his poems are studied to this day—he was also a leading philosopher, physician, and merchant. As a young man, he wrote secular poetry and lived a carefree life. But when he was about fifty years old, he turned his back on his easygoing life and dedicated himself to his faith in God. He often wrote of his desire to settle in the Land of Israel. Eventually he did travel east, first to Egypt and then to Palestine, where he died two months after his arrival.

Judah Halevi believed that the Jewish people were distinguished by their closeness to God, sacred language, tradition, and worship. This view had a strong influence on Jewish mystics, who rejected the idea that God was unknowable.

The teachings of the mystics eventually became known as the Kabbalah. In addition to study, mystics used fasts, chants, and meditation in an attempt to glimpse the secrets of God's world. They thought that human beings could interact with angels and work to counter the forces of evil.

major key

In Spain in 1286, Moses de León wrote most of the *Zohar* (*Book of Splendor*). The *Zohar*, composed in Hebrew and Aramaic, became the basic textbook of the Kabbalah. It offers "hidden" mystical explanations of selected biblical words and verses. For example, the letters of a word might be scrambled to uncover a new meaning in a passage. Kabbalists, or followers of Kabbalah, believed that by discovering such hidden meanings, one can learn much about God, the creation of the world, God's relationship to human beings, and good and evil.

Students of Kabbalah still read the *Zohar* today. But just as many Jews in our time are not mystics, so, too, during the golden age of Spain not all Spanish Jews were mystics. Some Jews considered efforts to uncover the secrets of God's world to be dangerous. In fact, there is a tradition that mysticism should be seriously explored only by scholars who are at least forty years old.

A Poet and a Scholar

Although education was rare among women of this time, there were exceptions. Qasmunah, a poet from a leading Spanish Jewish family, was one of them. Unfortunately only three of her short poems, written in Arabic, were preserved. This one describes her feelings of loneliness:

> *Oh deer, you who continually graze in the fields,*
> *I am much like you in the wildness and blackness of the eye.*
> *We are both alone, friendless; and*
> *We always mound blame on fate's decree.*

Another highly educated woman of this time was the daughter of a community leader in Baghdad who gave lessons in Torah and Talmud. A scholar who taught men, she went to great lengths to conduct herself with modesty. According to Rabbi Petachia of Ratisbon (the modern-day Regensburg, Germany), who visited the Jewish community of Baghdad, her modesty led her to teach male students through a window: "She herself is inside the building, while her students are below, outside, and do not see her."

The most learned and famous Spanish-born Jew was Moses Maimonides, also known as the Rambam (an acronym for Rabbi Moses ben Maimon). Maimonides criticized the mystics for insisting that Judaism was full of secrets. Instead, he taught that Judaism is essentially a religion of reason. He believed that, like philosophy and science, Judaism makes sense when it is studied and reflected on. Maimonides wrote the first complete code, or detailed summary, of Jewish law, a fourteen-volume work known as the *Mishneh Torah*.

This fourteenth-century illuminated manuscript is from the second section of Maimonides's *Mishneh Torah*. It includes the laws of the Sh'ma and Amidah. At the top of the page is a quote from the Book of Psalms 119:97. It begins: "How I love Your Torah."

A Jewish Frontier

While Sephardic Jewry was flourishing, important centers of Jewish life were developing in northern France and western Germany. Jews called these areas Ashkenaz, based on the Hebrew word for Germany. Small Jewish communities had existed in this part of Europe since the time of the Roman Empire, when Jews emigrated to work as sailors, traders, and artisans. As time went on, Jews also became shopkeepers, tailors, peddlers, butchers, poets, and doctors. In addition, some Jews became moneylenders. (Christians needed non-Christians to serve as their moneylenders because their religious law forbade them to charge interest on loans made to other Christians.)

The Jewish population of Ashkenaz was modest in comparison to that of Spain and the Middle East. According to the twelfth-century Jewish traveler Benjamin of Tudela, only

FAMOUS FIGURES

Maimonides

Maimonides was born in Córdoba, Spain. Just about the time of his bar mitzvah, a fanatical Muslim sect known as the Almohads conquered Córdoba. They persecuted Jews and sought to convert them by force. In 1135 the family of Maimonides was forced to flee and after many years of wandering it settled in Fostat, the old city of Cairo, Egypt.

Maimonides eventually became the court physician to the vizier of Egypt, but medicine was only one of several interests. He was also a great rabbi, author, philosopher, and community leader.

As Saadiah Gaon had done in Babylonia, through his work Maimonides helped the Jews of Spain understand how they could adapt to the surrounding culture in ways that strengthened Judaism. He wrote *The Guide of the Perplexed* in which he sought to teach the "science of [Jewish] Law," and asserted that Judaism was compatible with the study of science. He taught, for example, that the laws of kashrut have both physical and spiritual purposes. He said that the foods forbidden

by the Torah are all unhealthy in some way. In addition to his books on Judaism, Maimonides wrote comprehensive medical guides, describing such essential knowledge as how to survive snake bites and how to maintain a healthy lifestyle.

So respected was Maimonides as a leader and teacher that some Jews compared him to the biblical Moses, declaring that "from Moses to Moses there has been no one like Moses."

six thousand Jews lived in the six largest French communities. Germany's Jewish population was no more than twenty thousand. But the population grew steadily until the fourteenth century, especially in France, which by 1300 may have had as many as one hundred thousand Jews.

Reynette of Koblenz: Moneylender

By the thirteenth century married and widowed Jewish women had become successful moneylenders in England, France, Germany, and Spain. Reynette of Koblenz was a moneylender who lived in Germany in the fourteenth century. At first she worked with her husband, Leo. Later, after she was widowed and had remarried, her success grew. Eventually the size of her financial dealings exceeded those of both her husbands.

In many communities the rights, privileges, and obligations of Jews were spelled out in detailed legal charters. Under the terms of those charters, Ashkenazic Jews largely governed themselves. The Church, which had a strong influence in secular matters, discouraged the kind of social and cultural relationships that Jews and Muslims had in Spain.

As a result, Ashkenazic Jews generally did not write religious works in the local language, nor did they pursue scientific and secular studies, as they did in Spain. The leading communities—such as Mainz and Worms in Germany and Troyes and Sens in France—became centers of commerce where Jews and Christians traded with one another. However, creative Jewish scholarship was restricted to the Hebrew language and was mostly limited to the study of traditional Jewish texts.

Ashkenaz was a Jewish frontier land in the eleventh century, far from other centers of Jewish life. Communication with those distant Jewish communities was infrequent and difficult. Jewish traders and merchants were the main sources of news from far away. As a result of their isolation, Ashkenazic Jews formed tight-knit communities that were less open to outside influences than those of Sepharad. Ashkenazic Jews living in larger towns often settled in the same neighborhood. Families were thus within walking distance of one another, the synagogue, and other Jewish amenities, such as a kosher butcher.

Passover Traditions

Because of their physical separation and limited communication, the Jews of Ashkenaz and the Jews of Sepharad developed some different customs. For example, although both communities observed the traditional celebration of Passover, in contrast to the Sepharadim, the Ashkenazim developed a tradition not to eat legumes, such as peas and beans, on Passover. To this day, many Ashkenazic Jews observe this custom, whereas Sephardic Jews do not.

Jewish community leaders, called *parnasim*, sought to develop a system of communal government, including a court system and rules concerning fair business practices. The *parnasim* were usually the elders of their community. Most often they came from wealthy and leading families. Some had close ties to the secular authorities and could speak with them on behalf of the community when a problem arose. Others were respected as Torah scholars.

In each community *parnasim* organized an independent board, called a *kahal*, which managed day-to-day affairs. The *kahal* collected taxes from the community to provide such services as schools and tzedakah, or charity. The *kahal* strictly regulated community behavior. Those who did not follow its standards could be excommunicated—excluded from the community and shunned by its members.

The work of Gershom ben Judah, known as Rabbenu Gershom Me'or Hagolah ("light of the Diaspora"), helped to set Ashkenazic Judaism on its own course. Gershom, who lived in Ashkenaz from circa 960 to 1028, established an academy in Mainz that served as a training ground for Ashkenazic rabbis. He also issued a series of rulings that adapted Jewish law to the circumstances the Jews found in Ashkenaz. His most famous ruling banned polygamy, a practice that the Jews' Christian neighbors considered immoral. This ruling was a break from Jewish tradition in Muslim lands.

Rabbi Solomon ben Isaac, who lived from 1040 to 1105 and became known as Rashi, extended the work of Rabbenu Gershom. His academy in Troyes drew students from across Ashkenaz. Most important, Rashi produced a series of writings that offered short, clear, simple explanations of difficult words and concepts in the Bible and the Talmud. He also translated difficult words into French, the language spoken by French Jews. (His commentaries contain about ten thousand French words.)

Eleventh-century Worms was a center of Jewish learning. Rashi was among the great scholars who studied there. The first synagogue of Worms was founded in 1034.

In this way, Rashi made Judaism's greatest texts accessible to the Jews of his day and thereby increased their ability to honor and pass on Jewish tradition. In addition, because his works are replete with rulings based on Jewish laws, he helped the Jews of his time live as Jews in their European homelands. Rashi's work is still studied today.

After Rashi's death, his students continued his work. Many of them were known as *tosafists*, meaning "those who add." The *tosafists* contributed new commentaries on the Bible and the Talmud.

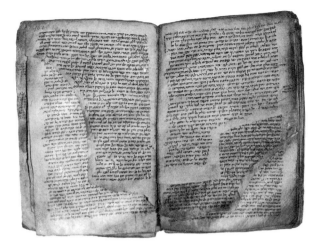

This edition of a Rashi commentary on the Later Prophets was produced circa 1250.

As in Spain, some Jews in Ashkenaz studied mysticism. These mystics had much in common with the ascetics who gave up life's pleasures after the destruction of the Second Temple. The mystics, too, devoted themselves to religious study and prayer as a form of repentance. Their religious observance went far beyond what Jewish law demanded and they added special prayers to the liturgy that, they thought, would draw them closer to God.

The mystics of Ashkenaz were known as Ḥasidei Ashkenaz, "the pious Jews of Germany." Many of the prominent leaders were members of one extended German Jewish family, the Kalonymus family. The teachings of Ḥasidei Ashkenaz spread throughout Germany, France, and Italy.

Like Father, Like Daughter

Among Rashi's accomplishments was that he raised three learned daughters: Yocheved, Miriam, and Rachel. All three were Torah and Talmud scholars and experts on kashrut. It is said that when her father was ill, Rachel ably wrote a response to a question of Talmudic law posed by Rabbi Abraham Cohen of Mainz.

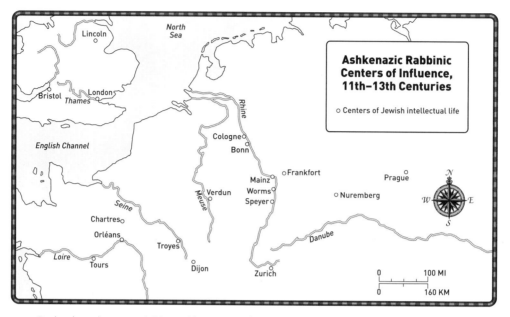

By the eleventh century, thriving Ashkenazic Jewish communities, such as those in Troyes, Mainz, and Worms, had become centers of Jewish learning and trade.

A Tradition of Diversity

Both Sephardic and Ashkenazic Jews remained committed to the values and traditions of Judaism. They believed in the same Torah, studied the same Talmud, celebrated the same holidays, and founded their communities upon the same rabbinic heritage. Yet their understanding and practice of Judaism differed in significant ways. The Jews of Sepharad developed a tradition that was strongly influenced by the Muslim world with which they interacted. In contrast, the Jews of Ashkenaz were more isolated. They did not integrate as much of their surrounding culture into their observance of Judaism. Unfortunately, one common experience that both the Sephardic and the Ashkenazic Jewish communities were about to face was a sharp rise in intolerance and violence.

Chapter 8

Medieval Europe
The Rise of Religious Persecution

By the eleventh century the Jewish communities in Ashkenaz were strong and well established. Christians and Jews lived side by side in relative peace. But the world of medieval Ashkenaz was complex. Periods of calm often were shattered by outbreaks of anti-Jewish violence and persecution. The first major outbreak began in 1096, after Pope Urban II called for the liberation of the Holy Land from the Muslims.

Response to the appeal was swift and enthusiastic. The pope promised forgiveness of sins and eternal reward for those who joined in the effort. Many Christians saw this call to action not only as a holy war but also as a great adventure and an opportunity to gain wealth.

So began the series of wars known as the Crusades, which started with anti-Muslim feelings among the Christians but grew to include anti-Jewish feelings. The events that followed robbed the Ashkenazic communities of their sense of security and strained Jewish-Christian relationships for centuries.

Warning Signs

Pope Urban II publicly challenged Christians to form armies, march to Palestine, and capture the Holy Land from the Muslims who controlled it. He referred to Muslims as infidels.

TIMELINE

1095	Pope Urban II issues a call to liberate the Holy Land from the Muslims
1099	Christian armies conquer Jerusalem; crusaders slaughter Muslims and Jews
c. 1148	First known charge of blood libel is made, in Norwich, England

World History
1211	*Genghis Khan ("universal ruler") invades China*
1215	Pope Innocent III requires Jews to dress differently from Christians
1290	Jews are expelled from England
1306	Jews are expelled from France
1348	Plague sweeps across Europe

Jews feared the Christian armies, which were heavily armed and aroused by religious fervor. In their passion the Christian soldiers could easily turn on the "infidels" next door—the Jews—rather than the Muslims far away.

Sensing the threat, French Jews held a day of fasting and prayer for the entire Ashkenazic community. "May God save us and save you from all distress and suffering," the German Jewish leaders wrote to the Jews in France. "We deeply fear for you. However, we have less reason to fear [for ourselves] for we have not heard so much as a rumor of the Crusade."

Ironically, French Jewry escaped relatively unharmed. The German Jews were not as lucky. As the French Crusaders swept through the Rhineland, they stirred up the local population against infidels. Disorganized violent bands of the poor and the ignorant attacked Jews, who were closer at hand than Muslims. Often they were joined by middle-class townspeople who resented the Jews as business competitors. Violence first broke out in Speyer, where Jews were slain in the streets by an angry mob. The rest of the Jewish community was saved only by the town's bishop, who gave them refuge in his castle.

As news spread up the Rhine to the Jewish community in Worms, panic also spread. Some Jews fled to the local bishop, offering him gold and jewels in return for protection; others hid in their homes. When the violent mob reached Worms, the townspeople joined in the murderous rioting. Jews were dragged from their homes and slaughtered. The fortunate ones were given a choice: convert to Christianity or die.

A Martyr: Minna of Worms

Minna was well-known and respected in both the Jewish and the Christian communities of eleventh-century Worms. Records of the Crusades tell how she hid in the cellar of a house outside Worms. The Christian people of the city gathered around her, pleading with her to convert so they would not be forced to slay her. But Minna preferred martyrdom to the sacrifice of her ideals. And so in the same spirit as the many Jewish martyrs before and after her, she responded, "Far be it from me to deny God in Heaven. For God's sake and for God's holy Torah slay me. Do not delay."

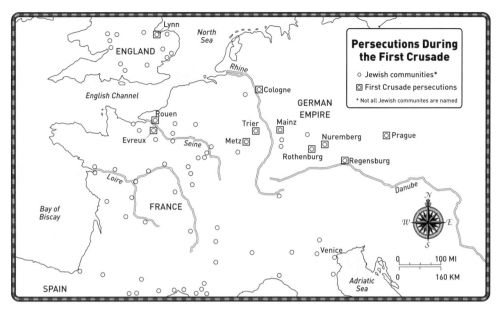

Jewish communities in Europe were sometimes attacked and destroyed by bands of crusaders. Despite the devastation, in most cases the communities quickly rebuilt what they had lost.

Similar horrors shook the towns of Mainz and Cologne. The Jews did all they could to resist the attackers, but in the end they were overwhelmed. Thousands of Jews were murdered, and some of the most important Jewish communities in Germany were destroyed.

As terrible as the massacres of the First Crusade were, they were still isolated events. Yet even when it appeared that life was changing for the better, seeds of conflict continued to be sown.

Sleepy Towns No More

Europe was changing. Forested land was being cleared, roads were being built, and new technologies, such as iron plows and water mills, were increasing farmers' productivity. More efficient agriculture enabled people to produce more food than they needed and trade the surplus. Trade in everyday goods—timber, grain, wine, metal utensils, and wool—expanded. The broad effect was that sleepy towns were transformed into lively market centers.

At first the Jewish communities of Ashkenaz viewed these changes favorably. The bustling economy created opportunities for Jewish merchants. Moneylenders became more important as they helped establish new businesses. Christians were guided by the religious teaching that profit-making is ungodly and that "love of money is the root of all evil" (Christian scriptures, 1 Timothy 6:10). As a result, both trade and moneylending were dominated by Jews.

From the eleventh to the thirteenth centuries, four major Crusades and numerous other expeditions sought to capture the Holy Land from the Muslims and to defend the land that had been captured.

The Crusades Reach Palestine

The First Crusade also affected the Jews in Palestine. When the Christian armies conquered Jerusalem in 1099, Crusaders slaughtered both Muslims and Jews. Under Christian control the city was forbidden to Jews. However, large Jewish populations were still permitted to live in coastal cities such as Acre and Ashkelon, as well as in Tiberias, on the Sea of Galilee.

Ironically, while the Crusades were the cause of great suffering, they also resulted in closer ties between Jews in Europe and Jews in the Holy Land. With the European Christians in charge of Palestine, travel between Europe and Palestine became easier. In 1267, Moses ben Naḥman, a Spanish rabbi, Jewish legal scholar, Bible commentator, kabbalist, and community leader known as Naḥmanides, or Ramban, settled in Palestine. A small migration of rabbis and scholars continued even after the Muslims recaptured the land.

CHANGES IN TECHNOLOGY	ADAPTATIONS IN CHRISTIAN SOCIETY	ADAPTATIONS IN JEWISH SOCIETY
New technologies enabled fewer farmers to produce more food and trade the surplus. Small towns grew as trade increased.	Fewer people needed to live on small farms and in villages. Large cities developed. Money was needed to expand businesses.	Jewish communities were urbanized. A middle class of Jewish traders developed. Jews became bankers to provide loans to Christian businesses.

Competition and Conflict

Soon, however, Christians gave precedence to the financial rewards of trade over the teachings of the Roman Catholic Church. Increasingly, Christians became merchants, and Jewish merchants became their competitors. Christian merchants used their religion, which was the official religion, to great advantage. They won the right to govern their towns without interference from kings and nobles. They set up their own guilds, which allowed them to control the quality, quantity, and price of goods. Jews were forbidden to join the guilds or enjoy their benefits. The result: Jews were forced out of trade.

Laws were passed that made the lives of Jews not only more difficult but also more insecure. In Germany, for example, Jews were forbidden to bear arms and thus were denied the right to display what was in effect a sign of honor in the Middle Ages. Many rulers stripped Jews of their freedom, legally defining Jewish people as royal property. Rulers then demanded large sums of money from the Jewish community in the form of special taxes. Jews were pushed from both sides: hated as moneylenders by the general population and taken advantage of economically by kings and nobles.

Another threatening trend was the growing power of the Catholic Church. Church leaders used their increasing political influence to attack those whom they considered enemies, both at home and abroad. They also used their influence to persecute the Jews. In most cases the Church did not encourage physical violence against the Jews, but it did not want the Jews to prosper. Its policy was based on the teachings of Saint Augustine of Hippo: Jews were to be segregated from the rest of society; they were to be kept in a lowly position to serve as witnesses to the truth and wisdom of Christianity.

FAMOUS FIGURES

Dolce of Worms

Dolce of Worms lived in twelfth-century Germany. The wife of a well-known rabbi, she earned money to help support her husband's study of Torah. Dolce lent money, spun wool, made ritual objects such as wicks for the synagogue candles, and cared for the daily needs of her husband's students who boarded with the family. She also taught the women in her community how to chant prayers and sometimes led special prayer services for women in a separate room connected to the synagogue.

Dolce's ability to provide both financial support for her family and spiritual leadership for the Jewish community inspired her husband to write these words about her after her death:

> Her husband trusts her completely. She fed and clothed him in dignity so that he could take his place among the elders of the land, and offer Torah study and God's command-ments. . . . She sings hymns and prayers. . . . In all the towns she instructed women . . . [so they can] chant songs; she knows the sequence of the morning and evening prayers, and she arrives early to the synagogue and stays late.

Moneylending: A Dangerous Profession

One profession that Jews continued to dominate was moneylending. The reason was simple: In many places, it was the only profession legally open to them. At best this was a mixed blessing: Some Jewish lenders became wealthy, but social tensions increased. Christians of all classes needed loans but resented the people to whom they ended up owing money. The Jews, who were restricted in their professional options by the guilds and the government, had no choice but to charge interest in order to make a profit and earn a living.

The resentment that developed toward the Jews often led to prejudice and violence. It is believed that Dolce of Worms (see page 84) was killed by thugs who were unable to negotiate what they considered agreeable terms for a loan. Seeing the valuables in her home, they robbed and savagely murdered Dolce and her two daughters.

Church leaders preached fiery sermons against the Jews, stirring uneducated peasants with accusations that the Jews had killed Jesus. They repeatedly spoke of the Jewish connection to moneylending and taught that the Jews were in league with the devil.

The Jews Are Accused

In this poisonous environment, Jews soon found themselves accused of horrendous crimes. One common charge was that Jews had murdered young children and used their blood for religious rituals. The first known charge of blood libel, or ritual murder, in the Middle Ages was made by a clergyman in Norwich, England, in about 1148. He made up a story, claiming that in 1144 the Jews of Norwich had taken a young boy and reenacted Jesus's last hours by torturing and crucifying him. Recognizing the charge as a lie, the local sheriff protected the Jews. But the story spread from England to France and Germany, where accusations of ritual murder often set off violent anti-Jewish riots.

The Catholic Church, meanwhile, issued new orders designed to separate Christians and Jews. In 1215, Pope Innocent III required Jews to dress differently from Christians. In some communities, Jews were already distinguishable by their beards and clothing, so the pope's edict had little effect. But in the larger cities, such as Paris, Jews and Christians were almost indistinguishable. In such cities, Jews were required to wear special badges on their clothing.

In 1233 the Church set up a court known as the papal Inquisition to investigate and remove heretics—people who disagreed with Church teachings and rulings. Although inquisitors mainly concerned themselves with Christian heretics, Jews were sometimes targeted. Some of the most zealous inquisitors were Jews who had converted to Catholicism. Unlike other Church leaders, they had a deep and personal knowledge of Judaism. In order to prove the truth of Christianity to the general population, the former Jews challenged the rabbis to public disputations, or debates.

The inquisitors who had converted from Judaism were able to embarrass the Jews by pointing to passages in the Talmud that spoke ill of Christians and insulted Jesus and Mary. They also tried to use their knowledge of the Hebrew Bible to point to passages that could be interpreted as demonstrating the truth of Christianity.

Cultural Borrowing Continues

Despite the competition and conflict between the Christians and Jews of Ashkenaz, the two groups lived and worked side by side in relative peace throughout most of the twelfth and thirteenth centuries. As a result of mixing on social and business occasions, the Jews were influenced by Christian practices. For example, many customs associated with the Jewish holiday of Purim originated in Christian Germany. Traditions such as dressing up in costumes and drinking alcohol on Purim were inspired by carnival, a celebration that occurs at about the same time of year and involves drinking, dancing, and masquerades.

Pope Innocent III called a meeting of bishops and other leaders, both religious and secular, to create a program to deal with people who disagreed with Church teachings. This meeting was known as the Fourth Lateran Council. The Council issued decrees designed to separate Christians and Jews.

The Talmud on Trial

Church leaders challenged rabbis to a series of public disputations. Church scholars sought in particular to discredit the Talmud. They believed that if they could discredit that sacred text, more Jews would convert to Christianity.

The Talmud itself was put on trial in a famous disputation in Paris in 1240. More than ten thousand books and scrolls had been seized from synagogues throughout France. Nicholas Donin, who had converted from Judaism to Christianity, led the prosecution. Donin charged that the Talmud was a wicked collection of books that insulted Christians. A rabbi named Yehiel ben Joseph led the defense team. It was hardly a fair trial: Yehiel and his colleagues were locked in separate prison cells when the hearings were not in session. No one was surprised when the Talmud was condemned and all the seized copies were burned.

The situation grew worse. In 1290 the small Jewish community of England was expelled, followed in 1306 by the expulsion of Jews from France. The royal treasuries confiscated all Jewish property and possessions. The order was devastating: More than one hundred thousand Jews were forced from their homes. Some crossed the border into Germany; others sought refuge in other countries on the Mediterranean coast, such as Italy.

In the Grip of Terror

Then, between 1348 and 1350, the Black Death swept across Europe. It was the deadliest epidemic the world had ever seen, killing about one-third of all Europeans. A terrified population, helpless against a disease they did not understand, frantically searched for causes.

Despite the deaths of many Jews from the plague, some Europeans blamed the Jews for the epidemic. In the grip of terror and irrational hatred, they charged Jews with spreading the sickness by poisoning wells and rivers. Rioting mobs killed thousands of Jews. It would be more than five hundred years before scientists would discover that the disease was carried by fleas living in the fur of black rats and that humans contracted it from fleabites (or in the case of some strains of the plague, from contact with infected human beings).

On the Move Again

The Jews of Ashkenaz learned a bitter lesson: They were not safe in that part of the world. Repeating the pattern of their ancestors, many families packed up their belongings and set off in search of a better life. This time Jews moved east, flocking to the underdeveloped regions of Lithuania and Poland, where their skills as merchants were welcomed.

Why were many Sephardic Jews also looking for a new home at this time? That question brings our story back to Spain, where the Golden Age had come crashing to an end.

Chapter 9

The Sephardic Diaspora
Rebuilding Jewish Life

If asked what you think of when the year 1492 is mentioned you might be likely to say it was the year in which Christopher Columbus set out from Spain and sailed to America. But for the Jews of Spain, that year had a profoundly different significance, for in 1492 King Ferdinand and Queen Isabella issued an order expelling "all Jews and Jewesses of whatever age they may be" from Spain. Jews were warned: Never return, even as travelers.

The expulsion was a catastrophe for the Jews of Spain. Yet they not only survived; they thrived. Sephardic families spread out in many directions and built Jewish communities from Asia and Africa to the Americas. Working together and developing new traditions, they enriched Judaism, and their contributions continue to illuminate Jewish life to this day.

Secret Jews Go Underground

Conditions in Spain had been changing for centuries. Beginning in the eleventh century, Christian armies slowly wrested control of Spain from the Muslims. At first, Christian rulers were welcoming to Jews. In fact, many Jews moved from Muslim areas, where tolerance was waning, to regions controlled by Christians.

TIMELINE

1391 Thousands of Jews are murdered in anti-Jewish riots in Spain

World History

c. 1455 Johannes Gutenberg's newly invented movable type is used to print copies of the Bible

1481 Spain's Catholic Church introduces the Inquisition

1492 King Ferdinand and Queen Isabella expel all Jews from Spain

1497 Jews are expelled from Portugal

1569 Isaac Luria, whose ideas revolutionize Jewish mysticism, moves to Safed

1665 Shabbetai Zevi is claimed to be the long-awaited "King Messiah"

1666 Shabbetai Zevi is arrested by the Ottoman government, converts to Islam

The Santa Maria la Blanca, in Toledo, founded in 1180, is the city's oldest synagogue. The structure and design were strongly influenced by Islamic architecture and art. In the fifteenth century, Christians seized the synagogue and converted it into a church.

By the late 1300s, however, as the Catholic Church gained power in Spain, Jews faced increasing persecution. Thousands of Jews were murdered in a series of anti-Jewish riots in 1391. Thousands more saved their lives only by converting to Christianity. Those Jews, known in Spanish as *conversos*, were forbidden by the Catholic Church to return to Judaism.

Many *conversos* became faithful Catholics. Others went back and forth between Judaism and Catholicism. But some *conversos*, women in particular, began to practice Judaism in secret. For such Jews, no law, not even the threat of death, could sever them from their faith and traditions. These *conversos* became crypto-Jews, or secret Jews. For example, they secretly lit Shabbat candles on Friday evening and recited Jewish prayers only in the privacy of their homes. Often they were encouraged and aided in their underground practices by Jews who had not converted. Those suspected of being secret Jews were sometimes known by the insulting term *marrano*, a Spanish word meaning "swine."

The Jews Are Expelled

Determined to expose Jews who practiced their faith in secret, Spain's Catholic Church introduced the Inquisition in 1481. The Spanish Inquisition focused on uncovering and punishing secret Jews.

Church officials accused thousands of people of being secret Jews. The accused were arrested, questioned, and in many cases tortured. Those who repented by agreeing to abandon Judaism were punished, often by having their property confiscated. Those who refused to repent were burned at the stake.

When they saw that even the Inquisition could not stamp out Judaism in Spain, Ferdinand and Isabella issued an order in 1492 expelling all Jews. Only Jews who converted to Christianity were permitted to remain. In early August 1492, just as Jews around the world observed the saddest day of the Jewish calendar, the fast of Tisha B'Av, some twelve hundred years of Jewish life in Spain came to an end.

The Search for a Home

Many Jews who left Spain settled nearby, in Portugal. Then, in 1496 the royal families of Spain and Portugal united in marriage and the following year the king ordered the expulsion of Portugal's Jews. The king changed his mind, however, and instead of sending the Jews away he forced the conversion of as many as possible. Thus in a movement that came to be known as the Sephardic Diaspora, Jews from Spain and Portugal spread out in search of new homes.

El Banys Arabs ("Arab Baths"), built in the old Jewish Quarter of Girona, in the late twelfth century. The baths reflect the diverse cultural influences on the Spanish city, including those of Islamic, Italian, and Greek architecture. The Romanesque columns with Corinthian capitals support a cupola that lets light in.

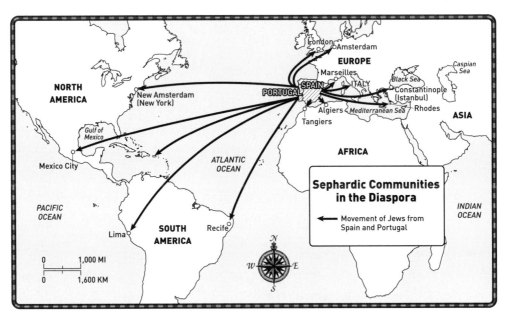

The expulsion of the Jews from Spain and Portugal in the fifteenth and sixteenth centuries created an extended Sephardic Diaspora. It stretched as far east as the Ottoman Empire and as far west as the Americas.

Some traveled across the Mediterranean Sea to North Africa and Italy. Others found a tolerant home in Western European states, such as the Netherlands, that had rejected Catholicism for the new "Reformed Christianity" known as Protestantism. Still others, in the following century, made the trip across the Atlantic to newly established colonies in Central and South America, which lay beyond the reach of the Inquisition.

Like today's victims of war and ethnic conflict, many Jews of the Spanish Diaspora were tortured and jailed, their wealth was taken from them, and they found few countries willing to accept them. Ultimately large numbers of Sephardic Jews settled in the Muslim-ruled Ottoman Empire, which included present-day Turkey, much of the Middle East, and southeastern Europe.

The Ottoman emperor considered Jewish artisans and merchants valuable newcomers. Under Muslim law, Jews were *dhimmi*, members of a protected monotheistic minority faith. As *dhimmi*, they were not the equals of Muslims and had to pay special taxes in return for the safeguarding of their lives and property. But they were permitted to enjoy a great deal of economic freedom and to practice their religion openly.

FAMOUS FIGURES

Doña Gracia Nasi

Doña Gracia Nasi, often known simply as Doña Gracia, was one of the greatest Sephardic Jews of her day. Born to a family of Spanish Jews that had been forced to convert to Christianity, she grew up in Portugal as a secret Jew. In 1542, when she was thirty-two years old, Doña Gracia took control of her family's banking and trading business.

Doña Gracia was constantly on the run from those who eagerly sought to prove that she was a secret Jew and then seize her fortune. Not only did she continue practicing Judaism, but she also boldly used her money to help persecuted *conversos* escape from Portugal.

Doña Gracia finally settled in Turkey where she lived openly as a Jew. She continued to be an active and outspoken defender of Jewish communities and even established a synagogue—perhaps the first Jewish woman to do so.

Portrait medals, such as this one of Doña Gracia, were commissioned by rulers, church officials, and the middle-class. This is the earliest identified medal of a Jewish person that includes a Hebrew inscription. Doña Gracia's name has been inscribed in Hebrew on the left side of the coin.

Repairing the World

Generations of Sephardic Jews struggled to make sense of their expulsion from Spain and Portugal. Some considered it a punishment by God. Others came to believe that the expulsion was part of a series of events that would lead to the coming of the Messiah and the return of all Jews to the Land of Israel.

Could Jews help bring the days of the Messiah closer? Many believed that in the Land of Israel they could. Some ten thousand Jews settled in the city of Safed, in the Galilee. Dedicating themselves to study and prayer, they became especially devoted to the study of Kabbalah. They meditated, engaged in all-night study sessions, and prayed passionately, hoping that their intense spiritual efforts would help bring the Messiah.

The most influential religious leader in Safed was Rabbi Isaac Luria, known to his followers as the Holy Lion, Ha'ari Hakadosh. Although only thirty-eight at his death, his ideas revolutionized Jewish mysticism and even changed the way Jews prayed. Most important, Ha'ari introduced the idea of *tikun* ("repair"), the belief that through prayer, meditation, and the performance of *mitzvot* (God's commandments), an individual can help repair the world, or restore it to a more perfect state. Ha'ari emphasized how much human beings might accomplish if they took action instead of waiting for God to act. In the twentieth century, Jewish thinkers broadened the concept of *tikun* to *tikun olam*, or acts of social justice that make the world a better place.

Rebecca Machado Phillips was born in New York in 1746 to crypto-Jews who had fled Portugal. As an adult, Phillips became a wife, mother, fundraiser, and social activist. She helped raise money for Mikveh Israel, a synagogue in Philadelphia, and was a founder of the Female Association for the Relief of Women and Children in Reduced Circumstances.

The Long Road to New York

Seeking to escape the Inquisition, some *conversos* crossed the ocean in the mid-1500s and settled in such places as Lima, Peru, and the Portuguese colonies in Brazil. Under Portuguese rule, those who practiced Judaism in secret lived dangerously. When the more tolerant Dutch captured parts of Brazil, those Jews once again were able to observe their religion openly. But in 1654, when Portugal recaptured the Dutch colonies of Brazil, the Inquisition returned and Jews as well as Protestants were forced to leave.

In September 1654, twenty-three of those Jewish men, women, and children stepped off a ship in the Dutch colony of New Amsterdam, where they established the first Jewish community in North America. Just ten years later, the British captured New Amsterdam and renamed it New York. Today New York City is home to about one million Jews.

> **Come, My Beloved**
>
> One of the Safed kabbalists, the poet Solomon Halevy Alkabetz, composed the poem "L'cha Dodi" ("Come, My Beloved"), which Jews throughout the world sing on Friday evening as they greet Shabbat. Its next-to-last stanza reveals the poet's deepest hopes:
>
> *Right and left, burst forward,*
> *And honor Adonai.*
> *One from Peretz's line [the Messiah] is coming,*
> *And we will rejoice and find delight.*

The Shulhan Aruch Helps to Unify the Jews

Rabbi Joseph Caro further strengthened the power of Jews to repair the world by observing *mitzvot*. Having fled from Spain to Portugal to the Balkan States, and finally to Safed, he witnessed firsthand the many disagreements among Jews about how laws and customs should be observed. In an attempt to solve the problem and promote Jewish unity, Caro published the *Shulhan Aruch (Prepared Table)* in 1565, a book that clearly describes how Jewish law should be practiced.

The *Shulhan Aruch* was widely circulated and became the best place for individual Jews to find answers to their religious questions. Although differences in customs and traditions persisted, particularly between Sephardic and Ashkenazic Jews, the *Shulhan Aruch* remains to this day the code of Jewish law that traditional Jews turn to first when they have a religious question.

False Messiahs

Sometimes people want to believe something so badly that their judgment becomes clouded. Because many of the refugees of the Sephardic Diaspora yearned for the coming of the Messiah, they were willing to believe in men who were not worthy spiritual leaders. Several such men attracted large followings by claiming to be the Messiah.

One of the most infamous of the false messiahs was Shabbetai Zevi, a Jew from Turkey. Shabbetai Zevi spent his youth studying Kabbalah. He traveled to Israel and gained followers, including a brilliant student from Gaza named Nathan. In 1665, Nathan announced that he was the prophet Elijah and that Shabbetai Zevi was the long-awaited "King Messiah." Nathan declared that the world was finally "repaired" and would soon be redeemed, returned to a more perfect state.

Shabbetai Zevi quickly built a huge following among Sephardic and Ashkenazic Jews throughout the Ottoman Empire and Europe. Meanwhile, Jews who had doubts quietly waited to see what would happen.

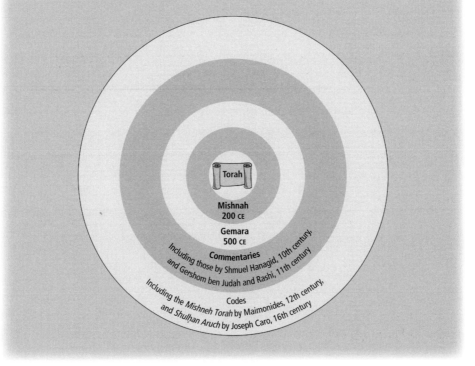

The Development of Jewish Law

The Torah is at the center of Jewish law. Over the centuries the law has evolved based on the rulings, commentaries, and compilations of leading Jewish sages and rabbis. This chart shows the main progression of that evolution through the sixteenth century.

Torah

Mishnah
200 CE

Gemara
500 CE

Commentaries
Including those by Shmuel Hanagid, 10th century, and Gershom ben Judah and Rashi, 11th century

Codes
Including the Mishneh Torah by Maimonides, 12th century, and Shulḥan Aruch by Joseph Caro, 16th century

Shabbetai Zevi's followers believed he was born on the ninth of Av (Tisha B'Av), in keeping with the tradition that the Messiah would be born on the anniversary of the Temple's destruction. He died in 1676 on Yom Kippur.

Alarmed by the growing messianic movement, the Ottoman government arrested Shabbetai Zevi in 1666. The government gave him a choice: convert to Islam or die. Shabbetai Zevi converted. Deeply shaken, most of his supporters quickly abandoned him. Some, however, sought to justify his conversion and continued to believe in him. Not even his death, in 1676, convinced them that he was a false messiah.

Say What You Think

In the Dutch city of Amsterdam, meanwhile, some Sephardic Jews were working on entirely different ideas about how to repair the world. Inspired by a freedom they had never known in Spain or Portugal, Jews explored both religious and secular subjects, such as science and philosophy. Freedom of thought and expression, they came to believe, was the key to improving the world.

One of the leading thinkers of this time was Baruch (Benedict) Spinoza, born in 1632 in Amsterdam to a family of former secret Jews. From a young age, Spinoza was unusually well-read and had a strong curiosity. He studied with the city's leading rabbis, learned Latin, read the latest philosophical works, and spoke with the brightest and best-educated people of his day. The more he studied, the more he questioned basic Jewish beliefs. Was Adam really the first human being? Had Moses really written down the Torah? Was the Torah really the only legitimate source of law?

Such questions threatened the belief system of the mainstream Jewish community. It might have endangered Holland's small Jewish community, whose members worried that it would be blamed for permitting one of its own to spread "heretical" ideas. And so in 1656, Amsterdam's rabbis excommunicated Spinoza, officially cutting him off "from the nation of Israel." Rather than repent, Spinoza insisted on his right to think and write freely. Earning a living as a lens grinder, he continued his philosophical explorations. His writings, which have influenced both modern philosophy and modern biblical scholarship, stress the importance of human reason and freedom of thought. "Every man," Spinoza wrote, "should think what he wants to and say what he thinks."

This Dutch postage stamp, issued in 1977, honored Spinoza on the three hundredth anniversary of his death.

Keep in Touch!

Regardless of *where* they settled—in the Old World or in the New—and regardless of *how* they practiced Judaism—in secret or in public—Jews in the Sephardic Diaspora remained connected to one another. Recalling their common origins in Spain and Portugal, their shared religious and social traditions, and their close family ties, generations of Sephardic Jews married, helped, and traded with one another.

Judaism by now had long been divided into two distinctive branches, one consisting of Sephardic Jews, with roots in Spain and Portugal, and the other consisting of Ashkenazic Jews, with roots in Germany and France. Many Jewish communities had two synagogues, one for Sephardic Jews and another for Ashkenazic Jews. In some communities Sephardic and Ashkenazic Jews rarely interacted and would not even marry each other.

But the experience of the Sephardic Jews left its mark on *all* Jews. First, all Jews learned never to take their security for granted. Even in a country where they had flourished for centuries, conditions could change for the worse and Jews could be persecuted and forced to leave. Second, the Inquisition reminded Jews to value the ties that united all Jewish people no matter what their differences. By risking their lives to help one another, they succeeded in holding on to their religious beliefs and identities for generations, if only in secret. Finally, both Sephardic and Ashkenazic Jews were reminded that they had to be flexible and adaptable, and never give up hope.

Part Three
Enlightenment and Emancipation

Chapter **10**

The Polish Kehillah and German Enlightenment
Isolation Versus Integration

The Big Picture

Our story has been moving back and forth between Sepharad and Ashkenaz. Now we pick up the trail of the Ashkenazic Jews who were driven out of Western Europe and settled in Poland and Lithuania. Beginning in the 1500s, these Eastern European lands became leading centers of Jewish life, in which Jews experienced increasing opportunities for self-rule.

The Jews of Eastern Europe were largely separated from non-Jews. Christians and Jews lived on different streets, spoke different languages among themselves, wore different clothing, observed different holidays, attended different schools, worshipped in different ways, and even had different tax and court systems. But the Jews were not completely isolated. Exciting and challenging new ideas reached them from the larger secular community, as did episodes of sudden anti-Jewish violence.

Living Apart

Community has always been at the center of Jewish life. To this day, Jewish communal organizations, such as synagogues and religious schools, attend to the essential needs of Jewish life. They provide places for worship,

TIMELINE

1500s	Eastern European lands become leading centers of Jewish life
1516	First Jewish ghetto is founded, in Venice
c. 1550	Polish Jews establish the Council of the Four Lands
World History	
1564	*William Shakespeare is born*
1648	Bogdan Chmielnicki leads revolts against Polish nobles
c. 1700	Ba'al Shem Tov, founder of Ḥasidism, is born
1720	Elijah ben Solomon Zalman (Vilna Gaon), a great scholar, is born
1770s	Enlightenment becomes known among Jews as the Haskalah

educational services, social and political networks, and assistance for those in need. Jewish life in Poland and Lithuania also revolved around the *kehillah,* or organized Jewish community. But a major difference between modern Jewish community and a *kehillah* was that the Jews of Eastern Europe were *legally required* by the secular government to belong to the organized Jewish community.

In the United States, where the separation of church and state is a founding value, it is a matter of personal choice to participate in the Jewish community or join a synagogue. In contrast, in sixteenth-century Eastern Europe, where religion and government were closely linked, every Jew was required to belong to the organized Jewish community. It legally represented the Jewish community to the government, it passed laws that all Jews had to follow, and it levied taxes that all Jews had to pay.

Behind Ghetto Walls

Today the word *ghetto* is used to describe poor urban neighborhoods. It originally referred specifically to Jewish neighborhoods. In the early 1500s, a small group of Jews moved from Germany to the Italian city of Venice. They were allowed to stay—but only if they lived in a limited area enclosed by a high wall. This Jewish neighborhood was called Ghetto, named for the nearby *ghetto,* or foundry—a place where metal is melted and molded.

The policy of requiring Jews to live in ghettos spread to a number of other cities in Italy, as well as to Germany and Eastern Europe. Ghetto gates were usually locked at night, to keep Jews inside and protect them from non-Jews, who remained outside. These walled neighborhoods became extremely crowded as Jewish populations grew. Still, Jews managed to thrive by working, studying, and worshipping together and helping one another through hard times.

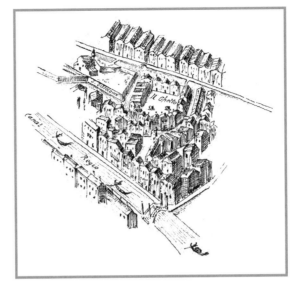

The ghetto of Venice.

The requirement that Jews be members of the *kehillah* led to the strict segregation of Jews from non-Jews. However, Jewish leaders took pride in their community's distinct lifestyle. They believed that segregation strengthened Jewish life, promoted the observance of Jewish law, and prevented intermarriage and assimilation. But it also prevented Jews and their neighbors from learning about and from one another; and it sowed the seeds of misunderstanding and mistrust.

Yiddish was the primary language of the Jews of Eastern Europe. A mixture of Hebrew, Aramaic, and German, it developed in Germany. In the countryside, Jews built their communities in *shtetls*—Yiddish for "little towns." Shtetls were comprised of a few streets of small wooden homes, shops, and a synagogue, which was at the center of shtetl life. In larger cities, Jews tended to live in "Jewish quarters," neighborhoods that were largely separated from non-Jews.

Determined to be self-governing in a land in which Catholicism was the state-sponsored religion, leading Jews from cities and small towns in Poland formed a central Jewish government, called the Council of the Four Lands ("Four Lands" referring to Poland's major provinces). The council maintained its authority from the mid-sixteenth to the mid-eighteenth century.

Jewish Self-Government

Just as the exilarchs of ancient Babylonia and the *parnasim* of medieval Sepharad oversaw Jewish communal concerns, so, too, did the Council of Four Lands. The council issued laws, collected taxes, and settled disputes among Jewish communities. Council members usually met twice a year, gathering at important trading fairs.

This was not exactly the form of democracy we enjoy today—power was in the hands of just a few wealthy council leaders. But the council was a source of pride for Polish Jews. Thanks to it, the Jews largely governed themselves, under the protection of the Polish government.

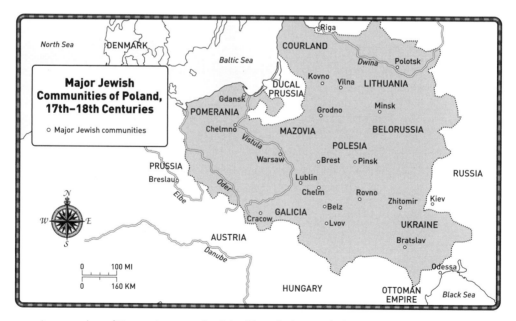

Large numbers of German Jews moved to Poland from the fourteenth through the sixteenth centuries. There they found a more welcoming environment and greater economic opportunities.

From Prosperity to Catastrophe

From about the mid-sixteenth century to the late nineteenth century, the Jews in Poland thrived. They worked as merchants, traders, and artisans. They also managed the estates of Polish nobles, supervised farms, and harvested timber. Some lived well and amassed huge fortunes.

Thanks largely to this prosperity, Poland became a great center of Jewish learning, with a focus on the study of the Talmud and its commentaries. Academies sprang up in many cities. It was said that there was scarcely a Jewish house in the entire kingdom of Poland where there was not at least one member of the family engaged in serious religious study.

Focused as they were on Jewish life and law, the Jews unfortunately failed or chose not to notice the suffering of those around them. Polish peasants, as well as the neighboring Ukrainians, were brutally oppressed by Polish nobles. In 1648 these oppressed peoples revolted under the leadership of Bogdan Chmielnicki.

The Wolpa Synagogue in Wolpa, Poland (modern-day Belarus), was built in 1643. According to an old story, a Polish prince was passing through Wolpa when his son became very ill. The Jewish community prayed for and took care of the boy. It is said that when his son recovered, the prince expressed his gratitude by giving the congregation money to build the synagogue.

In a period known in Poland as the Deluge, bloody battles raged between Chmielnicki's supporters and the Polish nobles. The Jews were caught in the middle of this war. For years some had worked for Polish nobles, managing their estates and collecting taxes. Chmielnicki associated all Jews with the hated nobles and their policies. As many as one out of every four Polish Jews died during the Deluge, many of them brutally massacred by Chmielnicki and his followers.

Jews with Different Views

In the aftermath of the Deluge, some Jews began to move westward into Germany and the countries of Western Europe. But most Polish Jews stayed and attempted to rebuild their lives. This was especially true in Lithuania. Vilna, the capital, developed as a new center of Jewish life and learning. Its reputation was so great that it became known as the Jerusalem of Lithuania.

Glückel of Hamelin

Glückel of Hamelin lived in seventeenth-century Germany. In 1648, when Chmielnicki was pursuing Jews in Poland, Glückel was a little girl in Germany. As was the custom, by age fourteen Glückel was married. She and her husband had thirteen children and built a successful business together.

Glückel wrote a detailed memoir, which was published after her death. It tells much about the daily life of European Jews in the seventeenth century. Glückel wrote about her childhood, her marriage, the lives of her children, and how her in-laws planned to follow the Turkish Jew Shabbetai Zevi to Palestine, believing he was the Messiah. She also wrote about her travels and her business: "I had an excellent business in seed pearls. I purchased [seed pearls] from all the Jews, picked and sorted the pearls, then sold them where I knew they were wanted."

The leading scholar of Vilna was Elijah ben Solomon Zalman, known as the Vilna Gaon, the genius of Vilna, who lived from 1720 to 1797—about the time that George Washington lived. No branch of Jewish learning went unexplored by the Vilna Gaon. In addition to Torah, Talmud, and Jewish mysticism, he studied Hebrew works on astronomy, geometry, algebra, geography, grammar, and medicine. He believed that all those subjects were necessary to fully understand Jewish law. The focus of Judaism, as he taught it, was in study. To him, study was even more important than prayer.

The growing movement of Ḥasidism did not share the Vilna Gaon's priorities. The Hebrew word *ḥasid* means "pious," and to followers of the Ḥasidic movement, simple piety—the joy of worshipping God with all one's might—was more important than study.

The founder of Ḥasidism is believed to have been Israel ben Eliezer, known as the Ba'al Shem Tov ("master of the divine name"), who was born circa 1700 and died in 1760. The Ba'al Shem Tov taught that even those who lacked the education to study Jewish law could embrace God by praying, singing, and dancing with joyful passion and by observing God's commandments, or *mitzvot*. "What is important," he declared, "is not how many commandments we obey, but rather the spirit with which we obey them."

The Ba'al Shem Tov was about twenty years older than the Vilna Gaon and came from modest roots. His teachings were often delivered through stories that uplifted and strengthened the spirit of humble Jews. Many such Jews had suffered at the hands of

Chmielnicki and had felt powerless in the face of the wealthy leaders of the Jewish community. Now, through the Ba'al Shem Tov, they gained a sense of power.

As the Ba'al Shem Tov's followers spread his ideas through Eastern Europe, the Vilna Gaon and his followers sought to stamp out the Ḥasidic movement. Calling themselves Mitnagdim ("opponents"), they attacked Ḥasidim, warning that passionate singing and dancing were no substitute for devotion to the study of Torah. They thought Jews should focus on Jewish learning and the strict fulfillment of each commandment.

Over the years the Ḥasidim and Mitnagdim influenced each other, but their priorities and emphases remained different. The two groups followed different rabbis, used different prayer books, and observed different customs. In the end, however, both contributed to Judaism by developing unique ideas of what it means to be a Jew and by creating new options in Jewish life.

Today, Ḥasidic men usually wear long black, belted robes. Married men often wear fur hats on festive occasions. The style of their dress is quite similar to that worn by Eastern European noblemen over two hundred years ago.

A Ḥasidic Tale

Just as the ancient sages taught through stories based on biblical texts, so, too, did the great Ḥasidic rabbis teach through stories. Thus the story is told of the Ḥasidic rabbi Moses of Kobryn, who, upon looking up at the sky, cried:

> Dear Angel! It is no trick to be an angel in heaven. You don't have to eat and drink, and earn money. Come down to earth and worry about these things, and we shall see if you remain an angel. (Martin Buber, Tales of Hasidism)

T'ḥines: Personal Prayers

An adaptation that enabled larger numbers of Jews, particularly women, to participate more fully in Judaism was the translation of personal prayers from Hebrew into Yiddish. In addition, new prayers, called *t'ḥines* (singular: *t'ḥine*), were written in Yiddish for women.

Many *t'ḥines* were written by women as personal prayers for the welfare of children and husbands. *T'ḥines* generally address "God of our Mothers, Sarah, Rebecca, Leah, and Rachel." For example, a *t'ḥine* written by Serel Rapoport, to be read on the High Holidays, pleads with the Jewish matriarch Sarah: "Mother, have mercy on us, your children, and pray for our children, that they not be separated from us."

Today, following in the tradition of composing *t'ḥines,* some synagogues encourage congregants to write personal prayers in English to celebrate life-cycle events, such as baby namings and bar and bat mitzvah services.

"Dare to Know!"

In the early 1700s modern ideas about freedom of thought and what it means to search for the truth were spreading to Jewish communities in western Poland and Germany. Many were similar to the assertion of the Jewish Dutch philosopher Baruch Spinoza that "every man should think what he wants to and say what he thinks."

Supporters of these new ideas insisted that truth could be discovered through scientific experimentation and reason. Above all, they placed their faith in the creative powers of the human mind. By the 1770s this movement, which secular historians call the Enlightenment, had become known among Jews as the Haskalah (Hebrew for "enlightenment"). Jews who followed this path were known as Maskilim (meaning "enlightened ones").

Instead of focusing on Jewish law, as the Mitnagdim did, or on piety, as the Hasidim did, followers of the Haskalah sought to open Jewish life to the latest scientific and philosophical ideas from the non-Jewish world. They believed that Jews should become broadly educated and seek truth everywhere. In response, increasing numbers of Jews began to attend universities. The German Enlightenment philosopher Immanuel Kant had a particularly great influence on the Maskilim. "Dare to know!" he proclaimed. "Have the courage and strength to use your own intellect."

THREE ADAPTATIONS TO LIFE IN POLAND AND LITHUANIA

HASIDIM	MITNAGDIM	MASKILIM
You need not be highly educated. Pray and perform *mitzvot* with passion and joy.	Study Jewish law and strictly observe *mitzvot*.	Study science, reason, philosophy, and Judaism; then make personal decisions about what to believe and how to live.

Change Is in the Air

For many Jews the Haskalah was no less controversial than Hasidism. Its ideas challenged the authority of traditional rabbis and the basis of Jewish separatism. Most important, it

FAMOUS FIGURES

Moses Mendelssohn

Among the small group of Jews who developed Enlightenment ideas, the best known was Moses Mendelssohn. Mendelssohn lived from 1729 to 1786, during the time of the Vilna Gaon, the Ba'al Shem Tov—and Thomas Jefferson. The child of a poor Hebrew scribe, he was small and suffered from a deformed spine. But Mendelssohn proved to be a brilliant student, and at age fourteen he set out from his hometown of Dessau to Berlin. In Berlin he studied not only the Bible and the Talmud but also Jewish philosophy, general philosophy, Hebrew, Latin, Greek, modern languages, and mathematics.

Mendelssohn remained a faithful Jew even as he befriended and shared ideas with non-Jews. He called upon Jews and non-Jews alike to pursue truth and promote the ideals of freedom and tolerance. As long as someone is honest and law-abiding, he wrote in a book titled *Jerusalem,* that person should "be allowed to speak as he thinks, to speak to God in his own way. . . and to seek eternal salvation wherever he thinks he can find it."

Traditional rabbis worried that people who followed Mendelssohn's path would give in to the social pressure to convert. That is just what happened in Mendelssohn's own family: Some of his children converted to Christianity.

created a new type of Jewish leader—the Maskil. The Maskil was not a rabbi or a traditional student of sacred texts but instead a thinker, a writer, and a scholar, at home in Jewish and secular culture alike.

To its credit, the Haskalah paved the way for Jews to become integrated into modern society. By teaching Jews about the world around them, it helped change their attitudes toward non-Jews and, in time, it helped change non-Jews' attitudes toward Jews. It created the ideal of the Jew who masters both secular and Jewish learning, and it paved the way for Jews to begin working and living with their non-Jewish neighbors. In short, it helped create many of the opportunities *and* challenges of modern Jewish life. 🦌

Chapter 11

Revolution and Emancipation
The Challenge of Freedom

What comes to mind when you hear the word emancipation? You might think of the end of slavery in the United States or the Nineteenth Amendment to the U.S. Constitution, which gave women the right to vote in 1920. But had you been a nineteenth-century European Jew, you probably would have thought of your own struggle for equal rights.

Although not literally enslaved, most Jews lived in countries that denied them the full rights of citizens, such as the right to vote, run for public office, or own land. Emancipation meant the end of those inequities; it meant that Jews could eventually become full-fledged citizens of the countries in which they lived.

Before emancipation, Jews were often forced to live separately from their non-Jewish neighbors. In addition, they were often pressured by their community—family, friends, neighbors—to follow Jewish law and tradition. After emancipation they no longer had to actively maintain their Jewish identity or their ties to the Jewish community. Both decisions became matters of personal choice.

Freedom's Call

As Protestant countries established colonies in the New World, Diaspora Jews made the great journey and joined in

TIMELINE

1654	First Jewish community is founded in North America
1776	Continental Congress issues the Declaration of Independence
1787	U.S. Constitution is drafted
1789	French Revolution begins
1791	French Jews are granted full citizenship and legal equality
World History	
1818	*Frankenstein, by English author Mary Shelley, is published*
1858	Jews gain the right to hold seats in British Parliament
1871	German Jews are given full legal rights

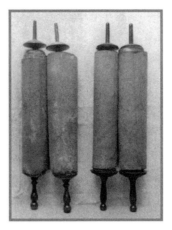

These Torah scrolls were brought to Savannah, Georgia, in 1733 and 1737.

their settlement. Colonies such as Recife and Suriname in South America, Curaçao and Jamaica in the West Indies, and New Amsterdam (later New York) in North America became home to significant Sephardic Jewish communities.

As we saw in chapter 9, the first Jewish community in North America was founded in 1654 by twenty-three Jews who settled in New Amsterdam. Over the next century the Jewish population of the thirteen British colonies that would become the United States grew to about twenty-five hundred. These colonial Jews lived mainly in the East Coast port cities of Savannah; Charleston, South Carolina; Philadelphia; New York; and Newport, Rhode Island. Many were small shopkeepers who sold hardware and dry goods, such as fabric and needles; others were farmers, silversmiths, tailors, bakers, tobacconists, and saddlers. While the rights of the Jews in the thirteen colonies were curtailed, the Jews were safer there and enjoyed more freedom than did Jews in other parts of the world.

By the early 1770s, the Jews were as angered by British taxes and policies as the other colonists, and when the Continental Congress declared independence in 1776, most Jews sided with the new nation. As many as one hundred Jews fought against the British in the American Revolution.

The coming of peace had special significance for the Jews, for Congress announced the end of fighting in the spring of 1782, just before the start of Passover, the Jewish holiday of freedom. In 1783 a peace treaty was signed, ending the Revolutionary War and recognizing the independence of the American colonies. The Jews eagerly watched to see what their legal status would be in the new nation. Would colonial-era restrictions on their rights to vote and run for office be lifted? Would the statement in the Declaration of Independence that "all Men are created equal" apply to them?

Haym Salomon

The best-known Jewish patriot of the revolutionary era, Haym Salomon, was born in Poland circa 1740. Settling in New York City in 1772, Salomon became a successful merchant and a supporter of American independence. He was arrested for anti-British activities when the British occupied New York City.

Salomon was freed when the British learned that he spoke fluent German. They made him an interpreter for the German mercenaries fighting in the British army. Salomon used the opportunity to persuade the mercenaries to desert to the American side. For this the British charged him as a spy (which he was) and sentenced him to hang. But he escaped and made his way to Philadelphia, where he raised money for the revolutionary government and the Continental army.

Celebrating America's Victory in Jewish Prayer

Jews quickly wove the celebration of America's independence into the fabric of Jewish tradition. In New York City a special Hebrew prayer, composed for Congregation Shearith Israel, celebrated America's victory as it echoed Passover's themes of deliverance and freedom and a yearning for the Messiah:

> As You granted to these thirteen states of America everlasting freedom. . . . so, too, may You bring us forth again from slavery into freedom. . . . Hasten our deliverance . . . send us the priest of righteousness to lead us upright to our land . . . may the redeemer come soon to Zion [Jerusalem] in our days.

The answer came in the form of the U.S. Constitution, written in 1787. The Constitution made religious liberty a basic right of all Americans. Religious tests used to qualify candidates for political office were outlawed. And most famously, the federal Constitution's First Amendment (adopted in 1791) established the separation of church and state, declaring, "Congress shall make no law respecting the establishment of religion, or prohibiting the free exercise thereof."

Despite the new government's guarantee of religious freedom, at first not every state in the Union honored that guarantee—even when it was written into a state's constitution. In practice some states gave only Protestants full rights. Although it took a hundred years before Jews were accorded full legal equality in all the states, by the end of the eighteenth century most American Jewish men enjoyed both the right to vote and the right to run for government office.

The United States now treated Jews with the same legal rights as all other citizens. Importantly, Jews received those rights under the U.S. Constitution along with other Americans, not, as in so many European countries, through a separate privilege or, as it was often called, a "Jew bill" that set Jews apart as a group.

France Breaks with the Past

The success and ideals of the American Revolution inspired change in Europe, beginning with the French Revolution in 1789, which swept from power France's eight-hundred-year-old monarchy. "All men are born and remain free, and are equal in rights," declared the new revolutionary National Assembly. "No one will be mistreated for his opinions, even for religious opinions."

Despite the changes in France, Jews were not accorded citizenship nor could they run for public office. Instead, they remained organized in traditional self-governing communities, living in four areas on the country's perimeter. But if the French Declaration of Rights did not immediately affect France's forty thousand Jews, it did offer them hope.

Inspired by the United States' Declaration of Independence and the American Revolution, the French soon sparked a wondrous change in Jewish life. In 1791, after much debate, Jews were granted full citizenship and legal equality. Discriminatory taxes and degrading anti-Jewish laws were abolished.

Freedom Brings Challenges

In the years following the French Revolution, Jews enjoyed the status of full-fledged French citizenship. But freedom brought new challenges. French Jews had always lived in separate, self-governing religious communities, just as the Jews of Babylonia, Spain, and Poland had. In contrast to their non-Jewish neighbors, Jews lived according to the rhythms of the Jewish calendar and under the guidelines set forth by Jewish law.

That quickly changed. French leaders expected Jews to adapt to the larger French culture. "To the Jews as a nation, nothing; to the Jews as individuals, everything," one French supporter of equality for Jews declared. In other words, Jews had to accept the authority of secular judges and courts in place of their own separate legal system. By focusing on individual Jews rather than on Jews as a group, French supporters of equality believed that eventually Jews would become like all other French citizens; they would lose their distinguishing Jewish characteristics.

Emancipation Spreads

Napoleon used his powerful military to spread the French Revolution by force, marching his troops into Belgium, the Netherlands, western Germany, and Italy. In the lands he conquered, Napoleon sought to extend the principles of the revolution, including the emancipation of the Jews. Working side by side, French soldiers and young Jews tore down the ghetto walls that had isolated European Jewish communities for centuries. Jews were freed and granted legal equality on the same basis as the Jews in France.

Unfortunately, in some places the anti-Jewish laws were revived when the French armies retreated. Particularly in Frankfurt, as well as in other places including Bavaria and Baden, promises to Jews were made on paper but never delivered. Yet not all European Jews viewed the backpedaling with chagrin. Some rabbis welcomed the reinstatement of restrictive laws, for they feared that Jews would shed their Jewish values and ties if they were free to live as equals among non-Jews.

Napoleon's Questions

Jews in France were full citizens according to the law—but in reality suspicion of and discrimination against Jews continued in everyday life. The emperor Napoleon Bonaparte, who ruled France after the revolution, was willing to promote the rights of Jews as full French citizens. He called an Assembly of Jewish Notables in 1806 to reconcile traditional Jewish beliefs with "the duties of Frenchmen" and posed twelve questions concerning the relationship between Jewish law and French law.

The Jewish notables told Napoleon what he wanted to hear: that France's Jews were thoroughly patriotic, accepted the duty of military service, and upheld the law of the land over their own law. Playing down the aspects of peoplehood that the French found objectionable, the notables defined Judaism largely in religious terms.

Satisfied, Napoleon called a seventy-one member "Sanhedrin" in 1807 to ratify the Assembly's responses. (In ancient Israel, the Great Sanhedrin was an assembly of Jewish judges who made up the supreme court and legislative body of the land.) Meeting amid great splendor, the rabbis and lay leaders who participated in the Sanhedrin underscored central principles that would make it possible for Jews to live as citizens in the countries that granted them equality.

Three principles proved particularly important: (1) that the central beliefs of Jews were "in keeping with the civil laws under which we live"; (2) that Jews had no reason to separate themselves from society at large; and (3) that it was a religious obligation for Jews to obey the state "in all matters civil and political."

FAMOUS FIGURES

Grace Aguilar

Grace Aguilar, who lived from 1816 to 1847, was an English Jew of Sephardic descent whose ancestors had been crypto-Jews. Aguilar believed that women should be taught to understand Jewish values and observances, not trained to accept them blindly. She also believed that new opportunities for Jewish education and spiritual growth were opening up in emancipated countries, like England and the United States. Aguilar insisted that Jews were now "free to become mentally and spiritually elevated." In her book *The Spirit of Judaism,* Aguilar expressed not only her pride as a Jew but also her faith in an emancipated England. She wrote:

> We shall go forth, no longer striving to conceal our religion through SHAME (for it can only be such a base emotion prompting us to conceal it in a free and happy England);— strengthened and sanctified by its blessed spirit, we shall feel the soul elevated within us.

Aguilar wrote several other books including *The Jewish Faith*, which is composed in the form of letters offering spiritual and moral guidance to a Jewish girl, and *Women of Israel: Characters and Sketches from the Holy Scriptures,* which focuses on the contributions of women of the Bible.

But the majority of European Jews craved the rights and privileges of citizenship. They saw that emancipated Jews enjoyed many more opportunities to choose where they would live and how they would earn a living. Emancipated Jews dressed as they pleased, educated their children in the best schools, and participated in public life. Emancipation, they insisted, did not mean the end of Judaism: Instead, it offered new and exciting ways to live as a Jew.

A Double-Edged Sword

The process of emancipation varied from country to country. Jews gained a great deal of freedom in England but they won the right to hold a seat in Parliament only in 1858 and only after a long political struggle. In some German states, Jews won and lost rights repeatedly as governments changed hands. Complete legal emancipation did not come to Germany until 1871. In Russia and Poland, where the majority of the world's Jews still lived, the legal status of Jews slowly improved in the nineteenth century. Formal emancipation came only in the twentieth century, however, and was not fully enforced even then. As the Jews learned again and again, it takes more than legislation to stamp out prejudice.

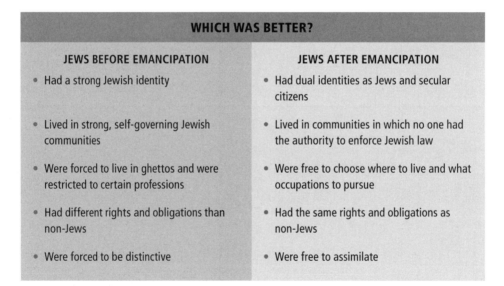

WHICH WAS BETTER?	
JEWS BEFORE EMANCIPATION	**JEWS AFTER EMANCIPATION**
• Had a strong Jewish identity	• Had dual identities as Jews and secular citizens
• Lived in strong, self-governing Jewish communities	• Lived in communities in which no one had the authority to enforce Jewish law
• Were forced to live in ghettos and were restricted to certain professions	• Were free to choose where to live and what occupations to pursue
• Had different rights and obligations than non-Jews	• Had the same rights and obligations as non-Jews
• Were forced to be distinctive	• Were free to assimilate

In both Europe and the United States, emancipation proved to be a double-edged sword. On the one hand, it brought great benefits to Jews—for example, by expanding educational and professional opportunities and providing the chance to serve in government. On the other hand, it carried the risk that Jews would abandon their beliefs and practices. Now not only could one choose to live as a Jew, one could also choose *not* to live as a Jew.

Chapter 12

Judaism and the Modern World
Finding a Balance

The Big Picture

Throughout their history Jews have tried to strike a balance between Jewish tradition and modern ideas. When Judea was part of the Greek Empire, many Jews integrated elements of Greek culture—Greek language, names, styles of dress, and concepts of beauty—into Jewish culture.

Jews have made such choices again and again—in ancient Babylonia, medieval Spain, eighteenth-century Poland, and nineteenth-century Europe. As Jews had done so many times before, newly emancipated European Jews struggled to find their place in a changing world. Some Jews resisted modern culture. Others completely assimilated, shedding their Judaism in order to fit in. But like most of their forebears the vast majority of Jews chose the middle road. Rather than abandon their heritage, they adapted Judaism to the changing times.

Jews Join the Middle Class

Between 1815 and 1880 the Jews of Central and Western Europe witnessed—and experienced—rapid change. The change was most obvious in Germany, home to the largest Jewish community in Western and Central Europe. In the early 1800s, the great majority of German Jewish men were working in occupations that were considered dishonorable—such as peddling, moneylending, and selling used clothes—

TIMELINE

1784	Jewish philanthropist Moses Montefiore is born in Italy
1831	Zechariah Frankel becomes the first rabbi in Bohemia with a secular education
by 1840s	Ideas of the Haskalah spread to the Pale of Settlement
mid-1800s	Samuel Holdheim and Abraham Geiger help create what is now Reform Judaism
1855	Alexander II becomes czar of Russia; grants Jews more freedom

World History

1876	*Alexander Graham Bell patents the telephone*
1881	Czar Alexander II is assassinated in Russia

A Jewish merchant selling used uniforms circa 1850.

and were barely making a living. At that same time, 20 percent of Jewish men were beggars or thieves. But by 1870, 80 percent of German Jewish wage earners had worked their way up to the middle and upper-middle classes. Many were involved in trade and commerce, working, for example, as shopkeepers, merchants, and bankers.

Many Jews abandoned the Yiddish language and their distinctive style of dress. Instead, they adopted the German language and German fashions. They abandoned as well the traditional Jewish school, the *ḥeder,* sending their children to secular schools or to schools that taught both secular and Jewish subjects. This broader education made it possible for more young Jews to pursue higher-status, higher-paying, and more secure jobs outside the Jewish community.

Soon many Jews accepted secular middle-class values. The time-honored ideal Jewish male— the Torah scholar—was replaced by a new ideal—the culturally well-rounded gentleman who knew the ways and values of the secular world. Women, who traditionally had helped their husbands in business, now focused on household duties. They became responsible for their children's religious education, formerly a duty their husbands had attended to. Some women extended their domestic obligations to include volunteer work for charities and educational organizations.

Different Experiences

Emancipation came at different times and in different ways to various European countries. As a result, Jews had very different experiences as they entered the modern world. The cases of England and Germany highlight the differences.

In England, where emancipation was a gradual process, the social and economic integration of Jews came early and with relative ease. Jews felt little pressure to abandon their religious traditions. They took great pride in their synagogues, schools, and social welfare agencies.

The Changing Family

Jewish families in nineteenth-century Europe were beginning to look and live more like their middle-class neighbors—and more like middle-class families in North America today. Men were waiting until they were financially secure to marry and so were marrying later. Couples were having fewer children and in their free time many attended concerts and art exhibitions; and many arranged for their children to take music lessons and gymnastics classes.

English Jews benefited from the tolerant attitude of many of their non-Jewish neighbors. For example, many Christians expected the Jews to remain a separate group and admired them for their ability to survive in the Diaspora.

The situation in Germany was quite different. Jewish emancipation had been imposed on the German states by Napoleon's conquering armies. After Napoleon's defeat, numerous states withdrew the citizenship of Jewish residents. Many Germans considered Jews unfit for citizenship. They believed that Judaism was backward and taught hatred of outsiders. Others worried that if the Jews became integrated into society, they would compete with Christians for jobs. Jews found themselves barred from many professions and excluded from German society.

Frustrated, many Jews worked hard to prove they could live both as Jews *and* as citizens of modern Germany. They pursued a secular education and adopted the middle-class lifestyle of their neighbors while remaining faithful to Judaism. Others gave up their Jewish beliefs and customs. Some went to the extreme of converting to Christianity.

The most famous convert was the brilliant poet Heinrich Heine, who lived from 1797 to 1856. Heine realized that as a Jew he could never advance in the academic world of Germany. So when he was twenty-seven, he converted to Christianity. He referred to his baptism as a "ticket of admission to European culture." But he and others who converted to advance their careers found that even this most radical step did not satisfy their non-Jewish neighbors. After repeated attempts to secure a university position ended in failure, Heine left Germany for Paris. He later spoke regretfully about his conversion, telling a friend: "I make no secret of my Judaism, to which I have not returned, because I never left it."

FAMOUS FIGURES

Moses Montefiore

British Jews were living well, but that did not diminish their sense of responsibility for Jews in other lands. One of the great Jewish philanthropists of this time was Moses Montefiore. He was born in Italy in 1784 to an Anglo-Italian Jewish family that soon returned to England. By the time he was forty, Montefiore had made a fortune as a stockbroker. He dedicated the next sixty-one years of his life to helping Jews around the world.

Montefiore visited Palestine seven times. There he used his money to build homes, farms, and synagogues for the Jewish community. He traveled to Russia, Romania, Morocco, and other countries, urging world leaders to abolish anti-Jewish laws. In 1840, he learned that several Jews in Damascus, Syria, had been accused of killing a Christian

monk to use his blood in preparation for Passover. Montefiore quickly organized a delegation to see the Syrian ruler and eventually won the Jews' release from prison. Montefiore's actions helped create a model for international communal support of Jews who are in need.

Montefiore built this windmill in Jerusalem to provide a source of income for the settlement of Mishkenot She'ananim. Today it houses a museum dedicated to the story of Montefiore's life.

Responding to Changing Times

German Jews tried to modernize themselves by adapting their Judaism to the changing times. In the process they hoped the prejudice of their non-Jewish neighbors would disappear. They also hoped that a modernized Judaism would appeal to more Jews and encourage the many intellectuals who had abandoned Judaism to return. Their hopes inspired a variety of creative solutions.

Reform Judaism

Experimentation began in 1810, when Israel Jacobson, the head of the Jewish community of the short-lived German kingdom of Westphalia, dedicated a grand "temple" that had been built to look like a church. Inside was an organ, and outside a clock tower housed a bell that pealed on the hour. Jacobson, often called the Father of Reform, shortened the prayer service and made it more orderly and dignified. Soon similar "temples" opened in Hamburg and Berlin.

More serious changes were introduced in 1819, when the Hamburg Temple adopted a prayer book that dropped all mention of a messiah and all references to the Jews' return to the Land of Israel. Many early Reform Jews were uncomfortable with the national aspect of Judaism: They were concerned that it might cast doubt on German Jews' patriotism.

In the mid-1800s two German rabbis, Samuel Holdheim and Abraham Geiger, helped create what we now call Reform Judaism. However, Reform leaders could not always agree on how quickly to push for change. Holdheim was willing to abandon all Jewish laws and traditions that separated Jews from non-Jews, including male circumcision and the ban on intermarriage. His Reform congregation in Berlin was the most radical in Germany. Skullcaps and prayer shawls were not worn, and the shofar—ram's horn—was no longer sounded on Rosh Hashanah.

Geiger believed that the Torah was written by human beings. He also insisted that throughout history, Judaism had adapted to the times and the needs of the Jews. However, Geiger did not support controversial innovations that threatened to divide the Jewish community. He believed that the value of Jewish unity, *klal Yisra'el*, required a more gradual approach to change, such as reciting some prayers in German and others in Hebrew.

In his sermons, Geiger emphasized what he called "prophetic Judaism." By that he meant the universal values taught by the ancient Israelite prophets, such as caring for the poor, the orphaned, and the widowed. Like the prophets, Geiger stressed the value of social justice.

Change Over Time Is a Constant

Many supporters of the new "Reform Judaism" were inspired by the work of scholars who were associated with the Society for Jewish Culture and Science. These scholars had found that change over time was a constant feature of Judaism. The reformers argued that they were restoring Judaism's original ethical spirit by shedding rabbinic innovations that had become meaningless in modern times.

Today Reform Judaism continues to emphasize Judaism's ethical *mitzvot,* especially the pursuit of social justice. Yet both the return to earlier traditions and the spirit of innovation also remain hallmarks of Reform Judaism. In the 1930s the Reform movement officially reversed its opposition to Zionism, the commitment to establish and support a modern Jewish state in the Land of Israel. And in recent years many Reform congregations have increased their use of Hebrew, and embraced the tradition of wearing skullcaps and prayer shawls during prayer services. Reform Jews were the first to publicly ordain female rabbis, beginning with Sally Priesand in 1972.

The Responsa Committee of the Central Conference of American Rabbis, an international organization of Reform rabbis, provides guidance on changes in Reform tradition. The committee bases its opinions on a scholarly review of Jewish tradition and modern values. Individual Reform rabbis and congregations decide how to apply the committee's recommendations in their communities.

Conservative Judaism

For many Jews who supported the principle of change over time, the Reform movement was moving too quickly and too radically. The final straw came when some reformers backed the elimination of Hebrew as the language of Jewish prayer. These Jews believed that the association of Hebrew with the Land of Israel defined Judaism as a *national* rather than a *universal* religion, such as Christianity or Islam.

Zechariah Frankel was learned not only in Talmud but also in secular spheres, such as philosophy and science.

Rabbi Zechariah Frankel, a moderate reformer, strongly disagreed. Hebrew, he argued, united world Jewry and was a key to Jewish survival. Like other German Jews, Frankel and his supporters had no interest in reviving the Jewish nation as a political state in the Land of Israel. But they believed that Judaism was a culture as well as a religion. They did not want the cultural part of Judaism to be discarded.

Frankel's followers broke from the Reform movement and became the forerunners of the Conservative movement (which was formalized only in the twentieth century). They retained Hebrew in their synagogue services, along with prayers for the Messiah and the rebuilding of Zion (Jerusalem). Frankel advocated "positive historical Judaism," by which he meant that past Jewish experience served as a positive value. Although Frankel agreed with the Reform Jews that Judaism was an evolving tradition, he believed that changes should be made gradually, be based on historical research, and that they should be respectful of Jewish law and the traditions of the people.

Orthodox Judaism

Not all Jews accepted the idea that Judaism needed modernization. Leading the struggle against the innovators was Moses Sofer, a German Jew who lived in Hungary where he was a highly respected congregational rabbi. Sofer rejected the idea of change. Even cultural adaptation must be opposed, he wrote, because it could lead to religious changes. "Be forewarned not to change your Jewish names, language, and clothing—God forbid. . . .

Never say: 'Times have changed!' We have an old Father—praised be God's name—who has never changed and shall never change."

Other traditional Jews were eager to find ways of adapting to the modern world without abandoning Jewish law, or halachah. Led by Samson Raphael Hirsch, they became known as neo-Orthodox in contrast to Sofer's "ultra-Orthodox" followers. (Neo-Orthodox Judaism was the forerunner of Modern Orthodox Judaism.)

Hirsch supported Jewish emancipation. He encouraged his followers to pursue a secular education and adopt the dress and language of the dominant society. He even allowed Jewish men to shave their beards. But Hirsch rejected the principle that halachah and Jewish rituals had changed over time. He believed that the Torah and its laws were revealed by God on Sinai and could not be altered.

Tradition and Change Conservative-Style

Conservative Judaism has also continued to adapt Judaism to meet the needs of the modern world. Where once there were no female Conservative rabbis, now there are many. And where once men and women sat separately during prayer services and women were not permitted full religious rights and duties with men, now many Conservative congregations offer women full equality with men.

Conservative Judaism tries to innovate within the bounds of traditional Jewish law. The rabbis of the Committee on Jewish Law and Standards rule on issues such as whether it is permissible to drive to a synagogue on Shabbat. If there is a clear majority, the ruling becomes a binding practice for the Conservative movement. If the vote is split, Conservative rabbis may choose to follow either the majority or the minority opinion, basing their choices on the needs and circumstances of their congregations and their own understanding of Jewish law.

By the end of the nineteenth century, there were almost five million Jews in the Pale of Settlement. Labels for the locations use present-day place-names.

Little More Than a Dream

Whereas emancipation was delayed until the mid-nineteenth century in Germany, it was little more than a dream for the millions of Jews in the Russian Empire. In fact, the entire idea of a modern nation-state populated by citizens was foreign to the Russians. Jews had no rights, but neither did the rest of the population. Russian czars ruled without limits on their power.

Historically Russia had been home to few Jews. But in the late 1700s it conquered huge sections of Poland, which had a large Jewish population. Driven by anti-Jewish prejudice, Russian leaders decided they did not want the Jewish population to spread throughout Russia. They drew an imaginary line around part of the land that had once been Poland (comprising much of present-day Lithuania, Poland, Belarus, Ukraine, and Moldova) and declared that all Jews must live there. That area became known as the "Pale of Settlement."

The czars hoped that the Jews would assimilate into Russian society and lose their connection to Judaism. One of the most effective government policies was the drafting of Jewish boys and men into the Russian army. During their long years of service, Jews could not observe their religion and were often pressured to convert to Christianity.

Parents would do almost anything to keep their sons out of the army. *Kehillah* leaders frequently arranged for the children of the rich and influential to avoid serving. They filled the community requirements by sending agents, called *chappers* ("snatchers"), to kidnap poor children, who were then enlisted in lieu of the children of the privileged. As a result, many Jews lost faith in their leaders, and Jewish unity was severely weakened.

New Ideas

By the 1840s the ideas of the German Jewish Enlightenment, the Haskalah, had finally begun to spread to the Pale. The Russian government actively encouraged Jewish modernization. In 1844 it opened schools in which Jewish children were taught the Russian language and culture. Traditional Jews were suspicious, but Russian Jews who favored modernization—Maskilim—supported the schools. They believed that a broad education was the key to social and economic advancement.

Russian Jewish supporters of Enlightenment ideas were given a new cause for optimism when Alexander II became czar of Russia in 1855. Alexander treated the Jews more humanely than previous Russian rulers had. He even allowed some to leave the Pale.

Everyday Life: Parents and Children

As the Enlightenment spread to Russia in the 1840s, arguments between parents and children became a regular part of Jewish family life. "There was tremendous pressure for Enlightenment among young people," remembered Pauline Wengeroff, who lived from 1833 to 1916 and whose memoirs teach us much about Jewish life at the time. "No matter how angry and upset parents became, eventually they had to give in."

One day Pauline heard her older brothers-in-law talking excitedly about the arrival of modern works of science and literature. "We shall find the books," one of them said. "We will just have to be extremely careful and sneak the work into our Talmud time. But don't allow the parents to catch on." Of course the parents did catch on—Pauline's mother walked in on them and caught them studying German poetry. A bitter argument ensued.

More Jews began studying at Russian high schools and universities. In time a Jewish middle class developed in cities such as Warsaw, Cracow, Odessa, and St. Petersburg. The spirit of the period was captured by the Jewish poet Judah Leib Gordon in his 1866 poem "Awake My People!":

> Awake my people! How long will you sleep?
> Night has passed and the sun is shining brightly . . .
> This Land of Eden [Russia] now opens her gates to you,
> Her sons now call you "brother"!

Unlike the Maskilim in Western and Central Europe, the Russian Maskilim were not interested in reforming the Jewish religion. Those who wanted to maintain their Jewish identity created a secular Jewish culture. They devoted themselves to a revival of Yiddish and Hebrew culture, creating new literature and poetry in those languages.

Between Two Worlds

The rapid changes throughout Europe left some Jews feeling as though they were living between two sometimes colliding worlds. Yeshaya Perelstein, a yeshiva student living in a small Polish town in the mid-nineteenth century, became curious about the world around him, and although his father disapproved, he taught himself Russian and began to devour the great books of Western literature. "A change came over me," he wrote. "I discovered. . . a universe that enchanted me with its originality, its beauty, its rich colors. . . . Slowly my heart was filled with doubt, doubt as to whether the Talmudic sages were truly the greatest sources of human wisdom, whether the Talmud was truly the highest level of knowledge and Truth." Yeshaya later changed his name to Harris.

Hannah Rachel Werbemacher

Whereas some Eastern European Jews of this era chose to assimilate, others were more deeply drawn to Judaism. Hannah Rachel Werbemacher, known as the Maid of Ludomir, was born in Poland circa 1805, a time when it was extraordinary—to some, even unacceptable—for a Jewish woman to be a scholar. Yet Werbemacher was determined to become learned, and she succeeded. After her parents died, she used her inheritance to establish her own synagogue. It was called *die Grüne Schule* ("the green synagogue"). There Werbemacher gave sermons on Shabbat to her Ḥasidic followers. She later immigrated to the Land of Israel, where she continued to study mysticism and worked to speed the coming of the Messiah.

Like so many Jews of this time, Perelstein found himself caught between the familiar world of his childhood and the new one outside. Slowly but surely, he said, the "exciting and enchanting new universe" was winning out. "I felt a terrible emptiness inside. I yearned for the happiness I had known before. . . . I wanted to turn back the clock, but I could not."

Most Jews in Western Europe, though, had no interest in turning back the clock. They were more than willing to face the challenges of modern life but they were concerned that the laws of emancipation and Jewish efforts at integration were not solving the problem of anti-Jewish prejudice. In fact, Jewish success seemed to stir up new resentment, providing more fuel for anti-Jewish feelings. Similarly, in Eastern Europe hopes for a brighter future were dimmed. Alexander II was assassinated in March 1881. His death was blamed on the Jews, and anti-Jewish riots broke out throughout the Pale.

Chapter 13

The Rise of Antisemitism
Nationalism and the Search for Scapegoats

The Big Picture

By the mid-nineteenth century the Jews of Western and Central Europe were becoming less and less distinguishable from their non-Jewish neighbors. They spoke the same language, lived next door to one another, enjoyed the same music and literature, and wore the same fashions.

To Europeans who opposed Jewish equality and integration, this was cause for alarm. In the past, hatred of Jews was often based on religious differences, such as the Jews' rejection of Jesus as the Messiah. Now it was expressed in ethnic terms, with attacks on the Jews as a nation rather than as a religious group. It also was expressed in racial terms, with claims that Jews were an intellectually and morally inferior race.

"Us" and "Them"

In 1871 the many German states were brought together to form the unified German Empire. It was a time of growing nationalism. Unification made many Germans more conscious of the ties that bound them together: common language, culture, history, and land. And this nationalism made them less tolerant of those who did not share their ancestry, including Jews, because they were seen as a threat to German unity and "national purity."

TIMELINE

early 1800s	Industrial Revolution spreads from Britain to other Western European nations

World History

1869	*Cincinnati Red Stockings become the first professional baseball team*
1871	Germany is unified
late 1800s	Antisemitism becomes an aspect of everyday life in much of Europe
1894	Alfred Dreyfus, a Jewish officer in the French army, is falsely accused of espionage
1897	Antisemitic politician Karl Lueger is elected mayor of Vienna
1906	Dreyfus is declared innocent of all charges of espionage

Natonalism was on the rise not just in Germany but throughout Europe, encouraging people to think of the world in terms of *us and them*. When nationalism becomes extreme and inspires feelings of superiority, it turns into chauvinism. In Europe, as nationalism turned into chauvinism, people began to question what the Jews were: Were they truly French, Germans, Russians, Dutch? Or were they a nation within a nation?

US AND THEM	
GERMANS ("US")	JEWS ("THEM")
• We speak German.	• They speak German *and* Yiddish.
• We live according to German traditions.	• They have different customs and holidays.
• We have German ancestors.	• They have Semitic ancestors.
• We have allegiance to Germany alone.	• They have allegiance to Germany and the Land of Israel.

Searching for Scapegoats

The Industrial Revolution was another source of tremendous change. As jobs moved from farms to urban factories, people in rural areas uprooted their families in search of work. Families that had lived on farms for generations now crowded into chaotic, polluted cities. Many found it hard to adjust. They felt as if their world and all they valued were being destroyed.

In difficult times, people can be tempted to look for a scapegoat, and in nineteenth-century Europe, Jews were a common scapegoat. Because so many Jews already lived in cities, they were associated with city life. Also, because they were doing well, enjoying middle-class jobs and a middle-class lifestyle, they inspired envy in Europeans who were less successful at adapting to urban life.

A common complaint was that as the Jews were rising into the middle class, they were taking jobs from non-Jews. In reality, Jews made up a small percentage of the population, and in all professions they were far outnumbered by successful non-Jews. But antisemitism distorted the facts. Not only did it make the Jews scapegoats for the failures and problems of others, but it also made the Jews' relative success a cause for feeling great frustration.

By the late 1800s, antisemitism was a common feature of everyday life in much of Europe. Right-wing politicians found they could win elections by running openly antisemitic campaigns. In the Austrian capital of Vienna, for example, a violently antisemitic candidate named Karl Lueger was elected mayor. Throughout Germany, signs appeared barring Jews from the best hotels and restaurants. Antisemitic speech became acceptable in classrooms, shops, and government offices.

The "Science" of Racism

The nineteenth century was dominated by important technological and scientific advances. Sewage systems were installed in many cities; vaccines were widely used to prevent many devastating diseases; and doctors began sterilizing their instruments before operating on patients.

Impressed by the power of science to strengthen society, many people turned to science to justify their prejudices. In Philadelphia a white doctor, Samuel Morton, announced that races could be ranked by the size of the brain. By measuring skulls of whites and blacks, he "proved" that whites were superior. Morton's "science" found many adherents on both sides of the Atlantic Ocean.

Antisemites were obsessed with Jews' bodies, which they claimed were inferior to "Indo-European," or "Aryan," bodies. In books and cartoons they portrayed Jews with flat feet, hawk-shaped noses, thick lips, and dark complexions. Antisemites also charged that Jewish men could not measure up to the masculine ideal. They portrayed them as weak and nervous—the opposite of "real" men. In the nineteenth century many people believed such stereotypes were scientific truths.

Émile Zola's famous letter in defense of Dreyfus was printed on the front page of *L'Aurore*, a literary magazine.

"Death to the Jews"

In the autumn of 1894, Captain Alfred Dreyfus, a Jewish artillery officer in the French army, was placed on trial for selling military secrets to the Germans. Throughout his trial the antisemitic press warned of an "international Jewish conspiracy" and demanded that Dreyfus be convicted. Despite weak evidence, Dreyfus was found guilty. Jews were shocked not only by the lack of evidence but also by the vicious antisemitism of Dreyfus's accusers.

After the trial the military stripped Dreyfus of his rank at a humiliating public ceremony. "Soldiers!" he protested. "An innocent is dishonored." But his pleas were drowned out by the crowd's chants of "Death to Dreyfus! Death to the Jews!"

Some non-Jews spoke out in support of Dreyfus. "J'Accuse!" ("I accuse!") screamed the headline of the passionate defense by France's popular author Émile Zola. Zola's open letter to the president of France was published on January 13, 1898. But antisemites were equally passionate. Antisemitic riots swept through many French cities and towns. As for Zola, he was forced to flee France.

The Dreyfus Affair, as the matter is commonly known, divided France for over a decade. "Because he was a Jew he was arrested," wrote Bernard Lazare, one of Dreyfus's Jewish supporters. "Because he was a Jew he was convicted, because he was a Jew the voices of justice and truth could not be heard in his favor!"

In 1906, Dreyfus was finally cleared of all charges and allowed to resume his army career. But the lasting message of the Dreyfus Affair was not the eventual legal victory. It was that more than a century after the emancipation of French Jews, antisemitism was still a force in French social and political life.

The Plague of Self-Doubt

Although antisemitism was opposed by many non-Jews throughout Europe, the antisemitic atmosphere could not help but affect Jews. Jewish reactions varied. Some more assimilated Jews found their own scapegoats for antisemitism. They blamed newly arrived Eastern European Jews, many of whom were streaming into Central and Western European cities during this period.

The Eastern Europeans seemed to be the living image of the antisemitic stereotype. They dressed differently and had not adopted middle-class values and lifestyles. Many spoke with heavy accents or, worse, spoke only Yiddish. In short, Central and Western European Jews were embarrassed by their Eastern European brothers and sisters.

Many Jews started to doubt themselves. After hearing the anti-Jewish rants for so long, they began to wonder: *Could there be some truth to what they are saying?* Some were so plagued by doubt that they were driven to self-hatred. Among the most notorious self-haters was the Jewish-born philosopher Karl Marx, who claimed, "Money is the jealous God of Israel and that God has become the Lord of the universe."

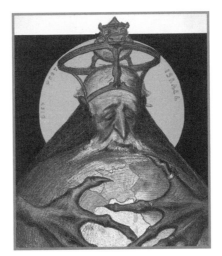

This antisemitic cartoon shows the world in the grasp of the Jews, as symbolized by James (Jacob) Rothschild, a leading member of a wealthy European Jewish banking family.

Jacques Joseph

Jacques Joseph, a son of a rabbi, was born Jakob Lewin Joseph, in 1865. Joseph is considered by some to be the father of modern facial plastic surgery. By the early 1900s, he had become one of the most sought-after surgeons in Berlin. Joseph's life would not be of special interest, but for the fact that the majority of his patients were Jews. Most felt inferior on account of their appearance and requested that Joseph perform a "nose job." He boasted that by operating on his patients' noses, he cured their heads of their emotional problems.

In Germany, many Jews tried to become more German than the Germans. They embraced the German idea of self-improvement through culture and education. Jewish men, in particular, tried to improve their appearance, and thus their self-image, by joining gymnastics associations. They tried to prove their masculinity by learning to duel. A scar on one's face made by a duelist's blade was a mark of honor. When duelists were cut they had their wounds treated such that the scars would be permanent.

Looking Ahead

Despite their experience with antisemitism, at the end of the nineteenth century many Jews were still optimistic. They believed in progress and considered antisemitism to be an ancient prejudice that would eventually die out. After all, many Central and Western European Jews were succeeding professionally and gaining the acceptance of non-Jewish neighbors.

Others were not convinced that Jews would ever be accepted as equals in European countries. Looking across the ocean, they saw hope for a better life in the United States. They wondered if it were worth packing up everything they owned to sail across the Atlantic and start their lives over in a new world. For more and more European Jews, the answer was *yes*.

Chapter 14

U.S. Jewry, 1820–1880
Balancing Freedom with Tradition

The Big Picture

In the mid-1800s the United States experienced one of the greatest economic expansions in world history. Factories were booming in cities and a growing system of canals and railroads was revolutionizing travel and commerce. To keep the economy growing, the United States needed workers—specifically, immigrants. Millions poured in from Ireland, Germany, China, and many other lands.

Among the new arrivals in search of a better life were thousands of European Jews, their journey fueled by Europe's rising wave of antisemitism. In the United States, Jews found the economic opportunities and freedom they had dreamed of. They also found new challenges that threatened the unity of the Jewish community.

Seeking a Fresh Start

Abraham Kohn was one of approximately 150,000 Jewish immigrants who came to the United States from Germany, Lithuania, western Poland, and other parts of Central Europe between 1820 and 1880. He came from a small town in Germany and had little education. Facing a doubtful economic future and legal discrimination, he decided to take a chance and come to the United States. There he traveled the countryside as a peddler until he had earned enough money to open a store in Chicago.

1849 Jewish forty-niners join the California gold rush

1851 Chicago has a synagogue, kosher butcher, and Jewish day school

1854 A forerunner of the first Young Men's Hebrew Association is founded in Baltimore

1860 There are 150,000 Jews in the United States and more than two hundred synagogues

1875 Hebrew Union College is established in Cincinnati by Isaac Mayer Wise

1883 Emma Lazarus writes "The New Colossus," which is later inscribed on the Statue of Liberty

1886 The Jewish Theological Seminary, eventually the heart of Conservative Judaism, is established

World History
1897 *Klondike gold rush begins in the Yukon*

Peddlers like Kohn created new Jewish communities across the United States, from Portland, Maine, to Portland, Oregon. By 1851, for example, Chicago had a synagogue, a kosher butcher, and a Jewish day school. Some Jews remained traditionally observant. Others intermarried and shed their Judaism. Still others experimented with liberalizing Jewish laws and Americanizing Jewish worship. Jews of all stripes were creating a uniquely American Jewish culture.

Jewish Forty-Niners

In 1849 everyone—including the Jews—was talking about the discovery of gold in California. Many Jewish "forty-niners" rushed west, hoping to scoop golden nuggets from the streams of California. Others saw a different opportunity; the chance to earn a living by supplying goods to the settlers, including the miners.

The High Cost of Earning a Living

Peddlers filled their packs with anything and everything they could carry and sell—dishes, sewing supplies, tools, and secondhand clothing. The peddler's life was not an easy one and often the observance of Jewish ritual and laws was difficult. Abraham Kohn tried to spend the week's end in towns that had other Jews with whom he could observe Shabbat. He was often disappointed. As he reveals in his diary entry for July 29, 1842, life in America challenged Jewish observance and unity:

> Thousands of peddlers roam about America—young, strong men wasting their strength by carrying heavy burdens in the heat of summer and losing their health in the freezing cold of winter. And so they entirely forget their Creator. They cease to put on their tefillin [phylacteries]; they do not pray on workdays or on Shabbat. Indeed, they have given up their religion for the packs on their backs. Is such a life not enslavement rather than freedom?

On March 23, 1787, Solomon Raphael received this license to work as a peddler in Pennsylvania.

From Peddler to Merchant

Many peddlers eventually succeeded in opening their own stores. The "Jew's Store" became a regular fixture on the main streets of small southern and western towns. Some peddlers succeeded in building their businesses into department stores that are household names today. These stores include Macy's, Bloomingdale's, and Neiman Marcus. In New York, by 1880 Jews owned about 80 percent of all retail and 90 percent of all wholesale clothing firms. Outside New York about 75 percent of all clothing firms were Jewish owned. But for every success story, there were failures and businesses that ended in tragedy.

It was this dream that drew Levi Strauss, a Jewish peddler from Bavaria, to the West in 1853. Strauss was convinced that goods from the East would be in demand in San Francisco. He booked passage on a ship sailing from New York to San Francisco and brought merchandise with him. His ship was still anchored in San Francisco harbor when merchants rowed out and bought up most of his stock.

Soon Strauss himself was watching for arriving ships and rushing out to buy their merchandise so that he could resell it. As his business grew, he began transporting goods by train to merchants in smaller mining towns. By the early 1870s Levi Strauss & Company was a thriving business and Strauss was a millionaire.

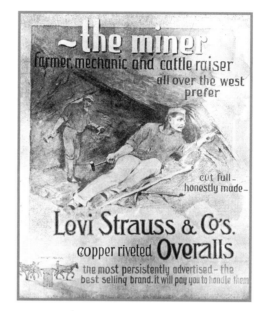

Levi Strauss used the theme of miners in this turn-of-the-century advertisement. Beyond the world of business, Strauss was also active in the Jewish community and a member of San Francisco's Temple Emanu-El.

Levi's Jeans

The story of Levi's jeans—an icon of American culture—dates to the gold rush, when Levi Strauss began selling a French denim cloth called *genes* (after the Genoese sailors who wore pants made from that fabric). One of his customers was Jacob Davis, a Jewish tailor in Reno, Nevada. Davis made pants from the cloth and sold them to miners.

When Davis received a complaint that the pockets were tearing, he strengthened them with metal rivets at the points of greatest stress. He wanted to patent his invention but didn't have the sixty-eight dollars required to file the papers. So Davis wrote to Strauss, suggesting that they become partners. "The secratt of them Pents is the Rivits," Davis wrote.

Strauss liked the idea and the two men became partners. On May 20, 1873, they received patent number 139121—and blue jeans were born.

Are Jeans Jewish?

Not only did two American Jews invent jeans, but the tradition of Jewish American designers of jeans is also alive and well today. Both Calvin Klein and Ralph Lauren (born Ralph Lifshitz) were Jewish boys who grew up in the Bronx, in New York City.

Strauss may have been the most famous Jewish pioneer, but he was hardly alone. Lewis Franklin found that out in September 1849, when he placed an ad in a San Francisco newspaper inviting Jews to his small store for Rosh Hashanah services. Immigrants from England, Germany, Poland, and Australia were among the thirty Jews who showed up. Together they conducted what is believed to have been the first public Jewish religious service in the Far West. By 1851 there were enough Jews in San Francisco to form two congregations. By the 1870s, Jews had fanned out to towns throughout the West.

Synagogues Sprout Up

The Jewish population of the United States grew from under 5,000 in 1820 to about 150,000 in 1860. Many Jews settled in growing eastern cities such as New York and

A Unifying Force

As Jews spread out across the United States, they wanted to be kept informed. National Jewish newspapers filled that need. Journals such as Isaac Leeser's *Occident and American Jewish Advocate* (1843–1869) and Isaac Mayer Wise's *American Israelite* (1854–present) reported on Jewish events nationally and internationally and promoted American Jewish culture.

The letters columns of such papers enabled Jews all over the country to debate the issues of the day.

In 1818 Rebecca Gratz founded the Hebrew Sunday School Society of Philadelphia. It was radically different from other Jewish religious schools of its time. Girls and boys were taught together, classes were held only once a week, lessons were presented in English, not Hebrew, and all the teachers and administrators were women.

Philadelphia. Others helped build new Jewish communities across the United States. As Jewish immigrants settled in cities with no Jewish residents and established businesses and families, they also established synagogues and communal organizations, such as B'nai Brith. These institutions provided Jews with a sense of unity and with support, for example, in the observance of life-cycle events, such as weddings, births, and burials.

When George Washington was inaugurated as president in 1789, only six Jewish congregations existed in the United States, all on the eastern seaboard. By 1860 there were over two hundred congregations spread across the entire country. Some were small enough to meet in private homes. But in cities with large Jewish populations, such as San Francisco, New York, and Philadelphia, Jews often established two or more congregations, usually along ethnic lines.

One example of a split along ethnic lines took place in New York. Shearith Israel, established largely by Sephardic Jews sometime between 1695 and 1704, was the first Jewish congregation in North America. In 1825, the congregation split in two. B'nai Jeshurun, the new congregation, was led by Ashkenazic Jews. It distinguished itself from Shearith Israel in its use of Ashkenazic rituals and prayer book.

The Civil War

The tense years leading up to the Civil War severely strained the unity of American Jews. As might be expected, Jews usually held opinions similar to those of their neighbors. Southern Jews tended to support slavery, whereas northern Jews opposed slavery and the breakup of the Union. There were some notable exceptions, such as Rabbi David Einhorn of Baltimore, who was run out of town for his opposition to slavery.

When the fighting began in 1861, some Jewish families literally split in two. Four sons of the Jonas family of Illinois fought for the South, and a fifth took up arms for the North. Alfred Mordecai, a Jewish West Point graduate and a general in the Union army, sat out the war rather than fight against the Confederacy, where most of his family lived.

The most famous Jew on either side was Judah Benjamin, a U.S. senator from Louisiana who served in President Jefferson Davis's cabinet as attorney general, secretary of war, and finally secretary of state. A total of almost eight thousand Jews served in the Union and Confederate armies. And while the war divided American Jews, it also helped strengthen many Jews' ties to their adopted land.

Reform Judaism Evolves

The Reform movement gained strength with the arrival of such religious leaders from Central Europe as Rabbi Isaac Mayer Wise. Although committed to Reform Judaism, Wise was a great believer in Jewish unity. He was willing to make compromises if he thought they could unite Jews.

Leading Congregation Beth El in Albany, New York, Wise broke with tradition by organizing a children's choir that included boys and girls. He also admitted that he did not believe in the Messiah or in the rising to life of the dead at the End of Days. Shocked, Beth El's president fired him. Wise's supporters then established a new congregation in Albany, Anshe Emeth, ("People of Truth").

Ernestine Rose was known as the Queen of the Platforms. She spoke out publicly on the major social issues of her day, including the emancipation of slaves and the right of women to vote. In 1869, Rose helped found the National Women's Suffrage Association, which advocated the rights of American women.

A Civil War Seder

Camped with his regiment in the mountains of West Virginia, Union army soldier J. A. Joel decided to conduct a Passover seder. A friend from home had sent him matzah and a haggadah. Joel gathered twenty Jews from the Twenty-third Ohio Volunteer Regiment. "We obtained two kegs of cider," Joel recounted, "a lamb, several chickens, and some eggs." For bitter herbs, they collected wild weeds.

The seder went well until the men ate the weeds, which were spicier than expected. Their mouths on fire, they gulped down the alcoholic cider. Joel reported, "We forgot the law authorizing us to drink only four cups, and the consequence was we drank up all the cider. Those who drank the more freely became excited, and one thought he was Moses, another Aaron, and one had the audacity to call himself Pharaoh."

After a brief interruption, the seder continued. "There, in the wild woods of West Virginia," Joel said, "away from home and friends, we consecrated and offered up to the ever-loving God of Israel our prayers and sacrifice."

In 1854, Wise moved to Cincinnati, where he led the Reform congregation Bene Yeshurun. A year later, he published a Reform prayer book, called *Minhag America* (*American Custom*), from which were deleted portions of the traditional prayer book that did not meet "the wants and demands of the time." For example, Wise excised all references to the rebuilding of the ancient Temple.

In 1873, Wise also inspired the creation of the first synagogue organization. Originally called the Union of American Hebrew Congregations (UAHC), it is now the Union of Reform Judaism (URJ). Two years later, Wise was instrumental in the opening of the first successful rabbinical school, Hebrew Union College (HUC), in Cincinnati, where Reform rabbis, cantors, and educators are still trained.

In 1885, Reform leaders held a meeting in Pittsburgh. There they adopted a radical platform that cut their ties to halachah. They reasoned that many halachic traditions, such as keeping kosher, lacked an ethical basis. The Reform rabbis also declared that they would no longer consider themselves members of a separate Jewish people or nation but only adherents of the Jewish *religion*. In effect, this proclamation broke the Reform movement's connection with the Land of Israel.

The Pittsburgh Platform did not represent the opinion of all Reform rabbis and was never officially adopted by the Reform movement. But it did strongly influence Reform Judaism in America for the next fifty years.

From Crisis to Strength

In spite of the American Jews' accomplishments, their self-confidence had given way to a sense of crisis by the late nineteenth century. Antisemitism appeared to be on the rise. In one famous incident, a wealthy Jewish banker, Joseph Seligman, was turned away at the Grand Union Hotel, a popular vacation spot in Saratoga Springs, New York. True, such social discrimination was a far cry from the legalized and violent antisemitism of Europe, but it was troubling nonetheless. Jews were also disturbed by evangelical efforts to add an amendment to the Constitution declaring the United States a Christian country. Finally, some Jews were concerned about rising rates of assimilation and intermarriage.

To the last concern, some Jewish leaders responded by promoting a revival of Jewish learning and observance. They hoped to renew interest in Judaism and strengthen Jewish self-confidence in the face of antisemitism. Like Reform Jews, they believed in adapting Judaism to American culture. But unlike the radical Reformers, the revivalists emphasized the ways in which Jews differed from their Christian neighbors.

Alphabet and Aleph Bet

For two hundred years, beginning about 1650, American girls learned to embroider by creating samplers. Using silk thread on linen fabric, they would stitch the alphabet and then add decorative designs. In this way not only did they learn to embroider but they also learned their letters. Jewish girls sometimes stitched both the English and the Hebrew alphabet, reflecting the desire to embrace American *and* Jewish traditions.

Ḥanukkah Joins the Major Leagues

Throughout Jewish history Jews have adapted to their surroundings while maintaining their core beliefs. A perfect example is the revivalists' effort to discourage Jews from celebrating Christmas. Recognizing that they could not fight the holiday's appeal, they sought to provide an alternative— the festival of Ḥanukkah.

Until the late nineteenth century, Ḥanukkah had been a minor holiday on the Jewish calendar. But gradually the customs of Ḥanukkah expanded to include gift giving and public celebrations. The traditional themes of Ḥanukkah, emphasizing the triumph of Jewish identity over assimilation, fit perfectly with the spirit and goals of the revival.

Like the Reformers, the revivalists strengthened their movement through the creation of organizations and institutions, many of which still exist today. A forerunner of the Young Men's Hebrew Association (YMHA) was founded in 1854 in Baltimore. The name was adapted from the Young Men's Christian Association (YMCA). But while the YMCA's activities were mostly religious and athletic, the YMHA's programs were much broader. They included literary groups, lectures, orchestras, glee clubs, libraries, and sometimes employment bureaus. By 1890 there were 120 YMHAs across the country, and by 1888 there were the beginnings of the Young Women's Hebrew Association (YWHA).

In 1886, the Jewish Theological Seminary (JTS) was established. Its response to the interest in reform was to adapt Judaism to modern life while preserving in America "the knowledge and practice of historical Judaism." Eventually, JTS became the intellectual, spiritual, and educational center of Conservative Judaism. Today it trains Conservative rabbis, cantors, and educators.

An early seal of JTS was designed by Victor Brenner in 1902. (Brenner would become well-known for his design of the U.S. penny, which was issued in 1909 to commemorate the one hundredth anniversary of Abraham Lincoln's birth.) The image on the JTS seal showed

FAMOUS FIGURES

Emma Lazarus

Emma Lazarus was one of the best-known participants in the revival movement. Born in 1849 to a family that traced its roots to the first Jewish settlers in America, Lazarus sought to balance her American identity with her Sephardic heritage and her commitment to the revitalization of Jewish life in America.

Encouraged by her father, Lazarus began writing poetry as a teenager. She is best known for "The New Colossus," which is engraved on a bronze plaque at the base of the Statue of Liberty. In the name of America and liberty, it beckons, "Give me your tired, your poor, your huddled masses yearning to breathe free."

Emma Lazarus wrote "The New Colossus" a few years before her death in 1887. Her poem helped create the vision of the United States as a safe haven for oppressed people.

From 1882 to 1883, Lazarus wrote a series of open letters, "An Epistle to the Hebrews," in which she presented her views on how to reinvigorate Jewish life through a cultural and national revival in the United States and the Land of Israel. Partly in response to the raging pogroms—the massacres of Jews—in Russia, she argued for the creation of a modern Jewish homeland in the Land of Israel (then still known as Palestine).

In contrast to the Reform leaders of her time, who focused on Judaism as a religious heritage, Lazarus saw Judaism as a national and cultural heritage.

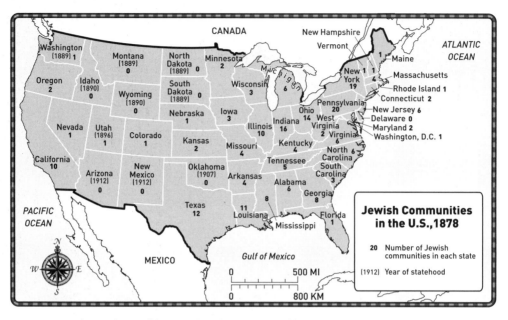

By 1880, the population of the United States was just over fifty million, and the Jewish population was 250,000. According to the Canadian census of 1881, there were 2,443 Jews in Canada.

the burning bush, from which God spoke to Moses, and the quotation from Exodus 3:2— "The bush was not consumed." The seal's message is that American Judaism will be kept strong through the Jewish learning and wide-ranging scholarship of JTS.

Building a Jewish Future

In barely a century, the Jews of the 1800s succeeded in building an American Jewish culture, a wide variety of Jewish institutions, and an American style of Judaism. America had lived up to its reputation as a land of opportunity.

The very ingredients that had made America inviting—the extraordinary degree of freedom and the enormous economic opportunity—also drew some Jews away from their religion. But most Jews cherished the view of themselves as links in the chain of Jewish tradition, a chain extending back more than three thousand years. They knew that Jews had always adapted to modern ideas and changing realities by creating new ways to celebrate their tradition and culture. This flexibility and diversity had been a source of strength rather than weakness. American Jews believed that they, too, would succeed in building a strong and exciting Jewish future.

Part Four
Antisemitism and Zionism

Chapter 15

Eastern European Jewry, 1881–1914
Turmoil and Transformation

The Big Picture

In every person's life certain events stand out as turning points: the day one receives a driver's license, marries, has a child, or suffers a great loss, like the death of a loved one. Whether the event is cause for celebration or sadness, somehow one never feels quite the same again.

So it is in the life of a people. Jewish history has key turning points, including the Maccabees' revolt in 167 BCE, the destruction of the Second Temple in 70 CE, and the expulsion of the Jews from Spain in 1492—the same year that Christopher Columbus set sail for America. For better or worse, each turning point separated all that had come before from everything that would happen after.

A great wave of antisemitic riots in 1881 and 1882 created just such a turning point in the life of the Jewish people. Known as pogroms, these attacks shook the foundations of Russian Jewry—which, at about five million, was the largest population of Jews in the world at that time. The pogroms made it clear to the Jews that they had to take matters into their own hands.

Hope for Greater Opportunities

When Alexander II became the czar of Russia in 1855, Russian Jews looked on with hope as they gained new freedom. Before Alexander, anti-Jewish prejudice had

TIMELINE

1855 Alexander II becomes czar of Russia, abolishes many anti-Jewish restrictions

1881 After the assassination of Alexander II, Alexander III issues anti-Jewish laws

1882 First Russian Jews establish a settlement in Palestine

World History
1896 *First modern Olympic Games are held in Athens*

1897 General Jewish Workers Union (the Bund) is formed

1900 Nearly half of all Jews in Eastern Europe are living in cities

1903 Antisemitic *Protocols of the Elders of Zion* is printed in Russia

1905 More than one thousand Jews are murdered in pogroms in Russia

Hundreds of Jews were killed or maimed in pogroms, and much of the property Jews owned was destroyed.

influenced Russian leaders to insist that all Jews live in the Pale of Settlement, the land that included much of present-day Lithuania, Poland, Belarus, Ukraine, and Moldova, so that the Jewish population would not spread throughout the Russian Empire. Now, under Alexander II, restrictions on Jewish settlement were loosened. In addition, Jewish children no longer were forced to serve in the Russian army.

Although many Jews maintained their traditional religious lifestyle, others were influenced by the ideas of the Haskalah, which emphasized secular learning and integration into the larger society. They began to attend government-sponsored schools and universities, studying Russian and other secular subjects. Eager to join the middle class, many looked forward to leaving their small towns and villages in search of greater opportunities in cities.

The Tides of Fortune Turn

But in March 1881, Alexander II was assassinated by anti-czarist revolutionaries, and Jewish hopes for a better life ended. Economic problems in the years before the czar's death had created resentment among the Russian people. Now they wanted a scapegoat. Anti-Jewish propaganda blamed the Jews for the czar's assassination even though only one of the revolutionaries who carried out the assassination was Jewish. Throughout the spring and summer of 1881 the Russian government idly stood by as a wave of pogroms violently swept through parts of the Pale.

Motivated by religious extremism, Russia's new czar, Alexander III, hated the Jews and wanted to isolate them from the rest of society. He issued laws that imposed limits on where Jews could live, how many could attend high schools and universities, and what jobs they could hold. As a senior member of the government is said to have admitted, the policies were designed so that "one-third [of the Jews] will die out, one-third will leave the country, and one-third will be completely absorbed into the surrounding population."

The Protocols of the Elders of Zion

In the mid-1890s, the czarist secret police produced a false document called *The Protocols of the Elders of Zion*. It claimed to provide a record of secret meetings at which Jewish leaders made plans to overthrow governments and seize world power.

Printed in a Russian newspaper in 1903, *The Protocols* was widely translated and circulated by antisemitic groups in Europe and the United States. Although in 1921 the London *Times* proved that *The Protocols* was a forgery, some people continued to use it to justify their antisemitic actions. It is still distributed by antisemitic groups today, circulating in the West as well as in parts of the Muslim world.

The anti-Jewish policies continued under Czar Nicholas II and new waves of pogroms broke out after a failed anti-czarist revolution in 1905. Six hundred and sixty communities were attacked, and over one thousand Jews were murdered. Determined to fight back against their attackers, Jews in some cities organized self-defense groups.

Unstable economic conditions fueled Russian antisemitism. Fears that Russia was falling behind the West prompted the government to strive to modernize and industrialize. New factories replaced traditional peasant industries. Factory-made clothes replaced handmade clothes, for example, and railroads replaced the traditional horse and buggy. At the same time, modern agricultural methods increased harvests so that fewer farmers were needed to work the land. Many farmers could no longer make a living. The government, church, and newspapers, recognizing that the changes had the potential to destabilize the government, encouraged the people to redirect their anxiety by channeling it into acts of antisemitism—by staging pogroms, for example.

Economic changes were also affecting many Jews. The growth of railroads and deterioration of Russia's peasant-based economy ruined the livelihood of Jewish merchants, peddlers, artisans, and innkeepers whose services were no longer needed. Peddlers suffered because trains brought goods to distant places faster than peddlers could travel, and in any case, fewer people in small villages could afford the goods. By the 1880s Jewish poverty was common in parts of Eastern Europe.

As a result of the pogroms, many Jews emigrated from the Pale of Settlement.

Socialism and the Bund

Among those most disappointed by events in Russia were the Maskilim, the Jewish intellectuals and professionals who had tried to integrate themselves into Russian society. They, too, now saw little hope that czarist Russia would ever grant Jews the full rights of citizens.

Some Jews became convinced that they would have to gain their own freedom. To do that, they believed, they had to revive Hebrew as their national language, return to their native Land of Israel, and rebuild the Jewish nation. In the 1880s the first groups of Russian immigrants began their journey to Palestine.

But the majority of Jews were determined to remain in Russia and improve their lives there. Many city dwellers joined with other Russians who were striving to better the conditions of working people. They formed trade unions and went on strike. The Jewish trade unions and intellectual groups combined the economic and political ideals of socialism with Jewish values of social justice.

In 1897 local Jewish organizations united to form a single socialist party, the General Jewish Workers Union, popularly known as the Bund. Bund-led strikes won improved working conditions. And when new waves of pogroms broke out between 1903 and 1905, the Bund took the lead in organizing Jews in local self-defense groups. It fired the imagination of tens of thousands of Jewish youths with its vision of a Russia free from the czars. By 1906 the Bund boasted over 40,000 members, a remarkable number given that the major Russian Socialist party had only 150,000 members.

I ♡ GR
even tho I
deny it always
— Gianni MIZ

FAMOUS FIGURES

Sholom Aleichem

Despite worsening conditions, the late 1800s and early 1900s were decades of Jewish cultural renewal in Eastern Europe. Yiddish stories, theater, and popular music found eager audiences.

Many of the most famous Yiddish authors lived at this time. Sholom Aleichem was the pen name of Solomon Rabinovitz, who lived from 1859 to 1916. Considered by many to be the greatest Yiddish humorist, he is often called the Jewish Mark Twain. Sholom Aleichem wrote in Russian and Hebrew, but his greatest successes were in Yiddish— including over forty volumes of fiction, short stories, and plays.

Sholom Aleichem is best known for his stories of everyday Jewish life in Russia. His most famous creation was Tevye the Dairyman, who remained firmly optimistic in the face of hardship. The modern American musical *Fiddler on the Roof* is based on the character Tevye.

Sholom Aleichem (holding book) with his family.

The Great Debate: Hebrew Culture Versus Yiddish Culture

Hebrew culture thrived alongside Yiddish culture at the beginning of the twentieth century. Supporters of Hebrew culture were determined to revive the Jewish holy language into a living language. The most famous of those supporters was Ḥayyim Naḥman Bialik, whose poetry not only expressed the anguish, despair, and shame that Jews felt in the face of the pogroms but also celebrated the beauty of Russian Jewish life.

Bialik, who lived from 1873 to 1934, began writing in Yiddish but soon abandoned it for Hebrew. Although he and other writers used both languages, and even Polish or Russian, to reach different audiences, the conflict between the Yiddishists and the Hebraists was often fierce. In choosing one language over the other, a writer made the political statement "I support the Bund" or "I support the return to Palestine."

In some cases the conflict threatened to tear apart families. Solomon Rabinovitz (Sholom Aleichem) chose to use a pen name because, as a Yiddish writer, he was afraid of angering his father, who supported the return to Palestine. The meaning of his pseudonym, "Peace be with you," was both a clever play on a Jewish greeting *and* a plea for tolerance.

Seeking New Homes

Meanwhile, many Jews were on the move, flocking to such cities as Warsaw, Vilna, Vienna, and Budapest. By 1900 almost half the Jewish population of Eastern Europe was living in a city. The Jewish population of Warsaw grew from 3,500 to 220,000, making Jews one-third of the city's population. Russia's five million Jews represented only 4 percent of the population, yet Jews made up a majority of the city dwellers in the Pale of Settlement.

Ever greater numbers of Jews left Eastern Europe and Russia altogether. Some moved to Western Europe. A few thousand settled in Palestine, and thousands more went to South Africa, Argentina, and Canada. But the vast majority went to the United States.

Chapter 16

The Great Migration
New Challenges to Jewish Tradition

The Big Picture

Abraham Cahan was a wanted man.

The year was 1881, and Abraham Cahan actively opposed the czar's regime. This twenty-one-year-old son of a Hebrew teacher yearned for greater freedom and social equality. He had just been graduated from Vilna's Teachers' Institute when the assassination of Alexander II brought a crackdown on anyone suspected of anti-czarist activities. With the secret police on his heels, Cahan sailed for America in 1882.

Abraham Cahan was one of more than two million Jews from Russia and Eastern Europe to make this journey between 1881 and 1914.

Difficult Decisions

Leaving home is never easy. For Abraham Cahan, it meant leaving all that was familiar, including friends and relatives, even his beloved parents. But like many others, he knew that there were too many mouths to feed, not enough money for food, and little hope that social and economic conditions would soon improve. In addition, young Jewish men in Russia once again faced the threat of conscription into the czar's army. Conditions in the army were harsh and discrimination against Jews was common. Finally, there were the brutal waves of pogroms, especially in 1881 and 1882, 1903, and 1905.

TIMELINE

1866	Samuel Gompers, a Jewish immigrant, becomes president of the American Federation of Labor (AFL)
1892	Ellis Island immigration center opens in New York Harbor
1893	Lillian Wald co-founds the Visiting Nurse Service and Henry Street Settlement in New York City

World History

1908	*Henry Ford introduces the Model T, the first car to be mass-produced*
1909	Clara Lemlich helps lead strike of women garment workers in New York City
1911	Fire at the Triangle Shirtwaist factory in New York City kills 146 women, many of them Jews and Italians
1914	At nearly three million the U.S. Jewish community is the second largest in the world after Russia's

If some factors *pushed* Jews away from Russia and Eastern Europe, others *pulled* them toward the United States. Railroads and steamships made long journeys easier, safer, and cheaper than ever before. And European Jews were hearing a lot about the freedom and opportunities in the United States.

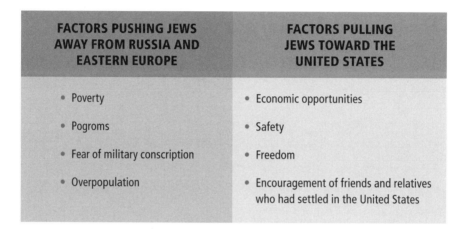

FACTORS PUSHING JEWS AWAY FROM RUSSIA AND EASTERN EUROPE	FACTORS PULLING JEWS TOWARD THE UNITED STATES
• Poverty	• Economic opportunities
• Pogroms	• Safety
• Fear of military conscription	• Freedom
• Overpopulation	• Encouragement of friends and relatives who had settled in the United States

Making a New Home

Jews faced challenges just leaving Russia. Like many other Jews, Abraham Cahan was not allowed to leave Russia legally. After sneaking across the border, he made his way to the port city of Hamburg, Germany. From there he went by ship to Liverpool, England, whence he sailed on the *British Queen* for the United States. Like most immigrants, Cahan could afford only a steerage ticket, which meant living in a foul-smelling cabin below decks for the thirteen-day transatlantic voyage.

After disembarking at Ellis Island, immigrants waited in large holding pens to be processed by immigration officials. They received quick medical exams and were asked a series of questions about where they came from, where they were going, and what they intended to do in the United States. If their health or responses were considered unacceptable, they were sent back to Europe.

This map appeared in the 1916 edition of John Foster Carr's *Guide to the United States for the Jewish Immigrant.* The names of states and their capitals and major cities are listed in English and transliterated using Yiddish letters.

There were more challenges, too, once Jewish immigrants set foot on dry land and passed through an immigrant center, such as Ellis Island in New York Harbor. The first might be finding a place to live. Many Jews moved into urban Jewish enclaves, near relatives or "*landsleit*," people from their hometown. The Jewish populations of New York City, Chicago, Boston, Philadelphia, Baltimore, and Cleveland spiked precipitously.

Manhattan's Lower East Side attracted more Jewish immigrants than any other neighborhood. It quickly became one of the most densely populated spots on earth. On the Lower East Side, immigrants crammed into five- and six-story brick buildings, often called tenement houses or simply tenements. Families of eight or more frequently shared tiny, sometimes windowless, tenement apartments.

A second challenge for immigrants was finding work. Some became peddlers, traveling great distances across the countryside or door-to-door in cities to sell their goods. Others found jobs in the fast-growing garment industry, which became New York City's biggest industry in the early 1900s. More than 80 percent of New York's clothing factories were owned by Jews and employed Jews. Thousands worked twelve- and fourteen-hour workdays in hot, cramped workshops known as sweatshops.

The arrival of hundreds of thousands of Jewish immigrants in a short period of time sometimes led to tension between the recent and the more established Jewish immigrants. Some Jews who had been in the country for a generation or more worried that the newer immigrants, who wore Old World-style clothing and spoke Yiddish, would embarrass them. Far more often, however, American Jews reached out to help the new arrivals adjust, providing English classes, free libraries, and the chance to learn practical job skills.

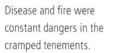

Disease and fire were constant dangers in the cramped tenements.

Many Jewish immigrants, like these striking shirtwaist makers, supported their families by working long hours in unsafe factories.

Jews and the Labor Movement

With thousands of Jews working in low-paying and often dangerous jobs, it is no surprise that Jews were among the leaders of the U.S. labor movement in the late 1800s. In 1866, Samuel Gompers, a Jewish immigrant from England, became the first president of the American Federation of Labor (AFL). The original membership of the AFL was estimated at about 140,000 workers from twenty-five national workers' unions.

By the time the labor leader Clara Lemlich was nineteen, she had been arrested seventeen times for organizing sweatshop workers into unions. On November 22, 1909, at a huge meeting of New York garment workers, the fearless Lemlich rose and declared, "I have listened to all the speakers. I would not have further patience for talk. . . . I move that we go on a general strike!"

Lemlich and others continued pushing for change, but it was the disaster at New York's Triangle Shirtwaist Company that brought national attention to workers' demands. On March 25, 1911, a fire started on the eighth floor of the factory, trapping workers who were locked inside and killing 146 people, most of them young Jewish and Italian women. The public was horrified, and labor unions finally began winning improvements in working conditions.

FAMOUS FIGURES

Lillian Wald

Lillian Wald was born into a wealthy Jewish family in Cincinnati in 1867. Although her wealth permitted her to choose a life of luxury, Wald became a nurse, dedicating herself to the relief of human suffering.

In 1893, Wald co-founded the Visiting Nurse Service of New York and the Henry Street Settlement. These institutions provided important services to immigrants and the poor, Jewish and non-Jewish alike, including home health care and instruction in hygiene, parenting, English, and the visual and performing arts. In addition, Wald fought for laws to protect the rights of women and children and was an active member of the Women's Peace Party. Wald died in 1940.

Lillian Wald.

JEWS IN RUSSIA	JEWS IN AMERICA
• Formed Jewish trade unions and went on strike to improve working conditions • Organized local Jewish self-defense groups in response to pogroms	• Helped organize labor unions to improve working conditions • Provided Jewish immigrants with financial aid and education to promote their integration into American society and help them earn a living

Like the Russian Jews, American Jews worked to improve their lives and the lives of other Jews in their community.

The Changing Map of World Jewry

More than two and a half million Jews settled in new countries between 1881 and 1914. Significant communities of Eastern European immigrants developed in Western Europe, Canada, Argentina, South Africa, and even far-off Australia, as well as the Land of Israel.

But by far the largest number—eight out of ten—ended up in the United States, changing the map of world Jewry forever. New York City suddenly was home to the largest Jewish

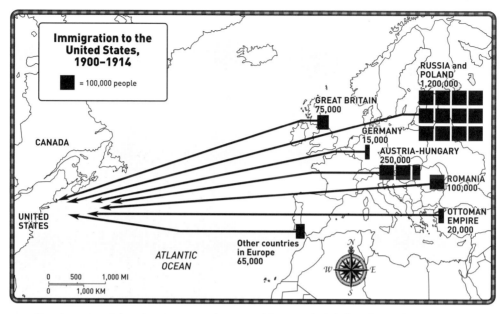

Escaping persecution and poverty, wave after wave of Jews, particularly from Eastern Europe, immigrated to the United States between 1900 and 1914.

community in the world. In fact, it had the largest Jewish community in the history of the world to that time. By World War I, the United States was home to nearly three million Jews, more than anywhere else except the Russian Empire, where almost seven million Jews still lived.

More than thirty thousand Sephardic Jews from Turkey, Greece, and the Middle East also settled in the United States during these years. Some spoke Arabic and others Greek, but most spoke Ladino. New York City, where most of the Sephardic Jews settled, became the most important Sephardic community outside the Ottoman Empire. A large Sephardic community also developed in Seattle, Washington.

By World War I, the great migration had dispersed Jews more widely than ever across the planet's six inhabited continents. For most, it led to a better life. In less than a decade, for example, Abraham Cahan learned English, helped found the leading Yiddish newspaper in the United States, the *Jewish Daily Forward*, and became its editor. The *Forward* helped its immigrant readers understand America and accommodate to it. In doing so, it served as a bridge between the old world and the new.

Chapter 17

Jewish Nationalism and Zionism
Imagining a Modern Jewish State

The Big Picture

The Jewish longing for the Land of Israel is as old as the Diaspora. The Bible describes the heartache of the Jewish exiles in Babylon, who wept for Zion after the destruction of the Holy Temple in 586 BCE. The Book of Psalms expresses their grief in these words: "If I forget you, O Jerusalem, let my right hand wither; let my tongue stick to the roof of my mouth if I cease to think of you, if I do not keep Jerusalem in my memory even in my happiest hour" (Psalms 137:5–6).

After the Second Temple was destroyed in 70 CE, Jews prayed for the rebuilding of Zion. Century after century they repeated those prayers at their Passover seders, on the fast of Tisha B'Av, and three times a day, in their recitation of the Amidah. Most Jews understood those prayers as an appeal for the speedy coming of the Messiah. But in the late 1800s a small group of passionate Jews committed their lives to turning the dream of a return to Zion into a reality.

A Recap: Palestine Before 1880

For almost two thousand years after the fall of the Temple in 70 CE, Palestine was controlled by a series of empires. Conditions were often difficult for the Jews who remained there and the few who returned, but their fortunes improved in the early sixteenth century, when the Ottoman Turks gained control. Although Jews were accorded second-class

TIMELINE

1882   First Aliyah begins bringing the first wave of Jews to Palestine in response to Zionism

1884   Students and workers found Ḥovevei Tzion to promote the establishment of a Jewish state

World History

1893   *New Zealand becomes the first nation in the world to allow women to vote*

1897   Theodor Herzl holds the First Zionist Congress, in Basel

1901   Jewish National Fund is founded

1905   Second Aliyah begins bringing a new wave of Jewish immigrants to Palestine

1909   Jewish settlers begin construction of the city that will become Tel Aviv

status under Muslim law, the Turks were tolerant rulers. Palestine became a refuge for many Jews who had been forced out of Spain at the end of the fifteenth century.

Legal reforms in the 1840s and 1850s brought the Jews greater equality and resulted in increased Jewish immigration. By 1880 about twenty thousand Jews were living in Palestine, making up about 5 percent of the population. The majority of the population was Muslim and Christian Arab. Most of the Jews were Sephardic but many of the newer arrivals were Ashkenazic Jews from Eastern Europe. Almost all the Jews lived in cities—Safed, Tiberias, Hebron, and Jerusalem—all particularly holy towns according to Jewish tradition. Most Jews lived in poverty, surviving on charity from the Diaspora.

Jews praying at the Western Wall, a supporting wall of the ancient Temple in Jerusalem, in about 1880.

The Dream of Jewish Nationalism

In chapter 13 we saw how the rise of nationalism affected Jews in Germany and France in particular. In fact, a wave of nationalism swept across much of Europe in the 1800s, provoked by the argument that every nation has a right to govern itself in its own homeland.

The influence of nationalism inspired a few dreamers to become *Jewish* nationalists. As antisemitism increased, more Jews were drawn to the idea of Jewish nationalism. Leon Pinsker, a Jewish doctor and author, believed that self-protection required Jews to free

The name Rishon L'tziyon was inspired by this biblical reference to the coming of the Messiah: "Behold, here they are, the first to bring the news of the Messiah to Zion—*rishon l'tziyon*" (Isaiah 41:27).

themselves and live in a country of their own. Jews, Pinsker wrote, "are everywhere as *guests*, and nowhere *at home*." Many of his followers were young students and workers in Russia, Austria-Hungary, and Romania. Organizing into small clubs, called Ḥovevei Tzion ("Lovers of Zion"), they held their first convention in 1884 and elected Pinsker as their chairman.

The First Aliyah

Pinsker cared that a Jewish state be created, but not *where* it would be created. In contrast, most of his followers believed that Jewish nationalism would be meaningless unless its goal were a return to the Land of Israel. Ḥovevei Tzion began raising money, sponsoring classes in Jewish history and Hebrew, and organizing self-defense groups. Its goal: *aliyah*—"going up" to and settling in the Land of Israel.

The first settlers started arriving in Palestine in the summer of 1882. And so began what is known as the First Aliyah, the first wave of Jews to immigrate to Palestine in response to the movement to create a modern Jewish state. The First Aliyah took place from 1882 to 1903. Some of the immigrants found work as artisans, shopkeepers, and farmhands. Others were poorly prepared to earn a living in Palestine and returned to Europe or moved to North America.

The Jews of the existing communities were very different from the Jews of the First Aliyah. Unlike the new arrivals, their connection to the Land of Israel was based on religion, and they were generally content to wait for the Messiah rather than build up the land.

The hardiest of the new settlers soon established farming colonies. The first of those was named Rishon L'tziyon. By 1905 there were about twenty such settlements. Today, many have become thriving towns and cities. But in the early years most struggled to survive. Threatened by malaria, poverty, and a lack of farming experience, the early Jewish colonists often lived on the edge of ruin.

A Journalist Sparks Excitement

Meanwhile, events in Europe gave new life to Zionism, the movement to create a modern Jewish state. In 1894, Theodor Herzl, a young Austrian Jewish journalist, was in Paris covering the Dreyfus affair when Alfred Dreyfus was unfairly convicted of spying. On January 6, 1895, Herzl witnessed the Jewish officer's humiliation as he was publicly stripped of his rank. It is said that Herzl listened in horror as the crowd of twenty thousand shouted, "Death to the traitor! Death to the Jews!

Responding to the injustice, Herzl published a short book in 1896 called *The Jewish State*. His message: emancipation has been a failure for the Jews; they still are not safe in Europe. Only a massive movement from Europe to their own land will put an end to antisemitism.

Herzl's ideas received an icy reception from leading Jews in the West. The Jews of Western Europe were full citizens and most were eager to demonstrate their patriotism to the nations in which they lived. But the Jews in Eastern Europe and Russia were not yet emancipated. Thus Herzl's ideas sparked great excitement among them.

On August 29, 1897, Herzl opened the First Zionist Congress in Basel, Switzerland. About two hundred delegates from Jewish communities in sixteen countries elected Herzl their leader and adopted his plan. They founded the World Zionist Organization (WZO) and made "Hatikvah" ("The Hope") the hymn of the Zionist movement.

So as not to offend the Ottoman Turks, the Congress avoided the term *state* in describing Zionism's goals, but in his diary Herzl declared: "In Basel, I created the Jewish State."

FAMOUS FIGURES

Theodor Herzl

Theodor Herzl was an unlikely father of Zionism. Born into a middle-class family in 1860 in Budapest, Hungary, he was a great admirer of German culture and spent most of his early life trying to fit into European high society. While studying at the University of Vienna, he joined a respected fraternity with few Jewish members.

Despite Herzl's best hopes, the antisemitism of his fraternity brothers forced him to quit the group in disgust. He suffered another painful blow when Vienna elected an openly antisemitic mayor. But it was the antisemitism in France, home of the ideals of liberty, equality, and brotherhood, that troubled Herzl most.

At first, antisemitism made Herzl ashamed of his Jewish identity. As late as 1893, he proposed the idea of a mass conversion of Jews to Catholicism. But Herzl changed his mind less than six months after Dreyfus was imprisoned on Devil's Island. By then, he had concluded that founding a Jewish state was the only solution to the problem faced by the Jews of Europe.

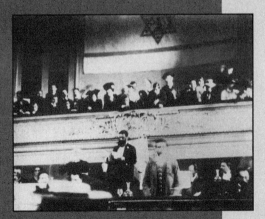

Theodor Herzl (standing left of center) addressing the First Zionist Congress.

Herzl's determination was reflected in his Zionist slogan: "If you will it, it is no dream." Herzl died in 1904; in 1949 his remains were reburied in Jerusalem.

To Be, or Not to Be, a Jewish State

For the next few years, Herzl traveled tirelessly from capital to capital, meeting with leaders of the great European powers, working to win support for the idea of a homeland for the Jews. Although he hoped that homeland would be in Palestine, his first concern was the political goal of establishing a state. Herzl wanted a state for the Jews, not necessarily a "Jewish" state. He had given a lot of thought to a future state's form of government and economy, but he was not especially concerned about the content of its Jewish culture. He assumed, for example, that the official language would be German, not Hebrew. So, when Herzl determined that the Ottoman rulers had no intention of parting with Palestine, he was open to other options. One option was the British offer of land in East Africa. That option became known as the Uganda plan.

But many Zionists believed that the creation of a modern Jewish culture and a Jewish state was essential to the Jewish people's survival. None was more passionate than Asher Ginsberg, a gifted Russian Jewish writer who was known by his pen name, Aḥad Ha'am ("One of the People"). Aḥad Ha'am believed that Jews needed to return to their historic center—the Land of Israel, Eretz Yisrael—and develop a modern, secular Jewish culture that would help unify the Jewish people.

Aḥad Ha'am knew that many Jews would remain in the Diaspora even if a Jewish state were created. He believed that a Jewish state and a national culture would enable Diaspora Jewry to survive and flourish: "From . . . [the Jewish] center [in Palestine] the spirit of Judaism will go forth . . . to all the communities of the Diaspora, and will breathe new life into them and preserve their unity."

Warning: Danger Ahead

Despite his passionate support of a Jewish state in the Land of Israel, Aḥad Ha'am voiced his deep concern that Palestine's majority Arab population would be hostile to Zionism.

Most Zionists ignored his concern. They convinced themselves that the Arabs would welcome the Jews. They expected the Arabs to be grateful to the Jews for bringing modern European culture to Palestine, including modern technology and modern medicine. The Zionists failed to imagine that the Arabs might develop their own nationalist feelings and resent becoming a minority in a land that they, too, considered their own.

As long as the Jewish population remained relatively small, few Arabs paid attention to the threat Zionism might pose for them. But as the Jewish population grew, Aḥad Ha'am's warning of conflict grew into a major concern.

The Second Aliyah

A new wave of immigrants emigrated from Russia between 1905 and 1914. Called the Second Aliyah, it was driven by the deadly pogroms of 1903 and 1905. It had a powerful effect on the Yishuv (meaning "Settlement"), as the Zionist community in Palestine came to be called. A number of Israel's future leaders, including its first prime minister, David Ben-Gurion, and its second president, Yitzhak Ben-Zvi, arrived during this period. Many came with only a knapsack on their back and the dream of a just and modern Jewish state in their mind.

JEWS IN RUSSIA	JEWS IN WESTERN EUROPE
• Jews were not permitted to live where they chose.	• Jews could live where they chose.
• Jews did not have the same rights as Christians.	• By the late nineteenth century, Jews in many countries had full rights.
• The Jews were subject to pogroms.	• For a while, antisemitism was on the wane.

Unlike the rulers of Western Europe, the czars refused to emancipate the Jews. So more Russian Jews than Western European Jews were motivated to support the creation of a Jewish state, where they would be free.

Unlike the earlier wave of immigrants, those who arrived during the Second Aliyah were committed to Socialist ideals. They dreamed of developing Eretz Yisrael with their own hands and experimented with forms of cooperative living and farming.

A key figure in the Second Aliyah was Aaron David Gordon, who arrived in Palestine in 1904. Gordon believed that life in the Diaspora had made the Jews weak because it had severed their connection to the soil. He wanted to create a modern Jewish society in Eretz Yisrael. Gordon believed that manual labor would not only help strengthen the Jews but also would enable them to rebuild their culture. He insisted that pioneers rely solely on "Hebrew labor" rather than hiring Arabs. Gordon and the pioneers of the Second Aliyah were trying to create "new Jews," Jews who would disprove the antisemitic stereotypes.

The founders of Tel Aviv in the spring of 1909, when the modern city was only a dream.

The newcomers acquired new lands to settle and cultivate by turning to the Jewish National Fund (JNF). Created in 1901, the JNF bought land in Palestine to be owned jointly by the entire Jewish people.

While this "back to the soil" movement inspired some of the new immigrants, many others settled in the cities. By 1908 the largely Arab port city of Jaffa was home to more than six thousand Jews. In 1909, with the help of the JNF, a group of settlers bought some nearby sand dunes and began construction. In time a city was built and became known as Tel Aviv, meaning "Hill of the Spring"—a name that was inspired by Ezekiel 3:15 and suggested rebirth. Just five years later Tel Aviv had over two thousand residents.

Most of the approximately fifteen thousand immigrants who arrived during the Second Aliyah soon became disillusioned and left Palestine. Daily life was extremely harsh. Food and other necessities were meager, and health conditions put the settlers at risk of becoming seriously ill. Gordon's wife was one of a number who died of malaria.

Many of the pioneers remained single and childless during their first years in the Yishuv. Their idealism and energies were focused on working the land and establishing political organizations and unions.

Many of the pioneers were committed to working the land. A popular folk song summed up their goals: "We've come to this Land to build and be rebuilt by it."

Foundation for the Future

In just a few decades, Zionists had built a solid movement and established over forty agricultural colonies and villages in the Land of Israel. The Jewish population of Palestine had grown to about sixty thousand—a little less than 10 percent of the total population. Hebrew had been reborn as a language for ordinary life, and the young suburb of Tel Aviv was on its way to becoming the first modern Jewish city.

But of all the Jews who left Russia betwee 1881 and 1914, only about 3 percent moved to Palestine. For the majority, Zionism and the Land of Israel were not a solution to the problems of economic hardship, antisemitism, and political oppression. For them, the United States—not Palestine—was the land of promise.

Chapter 18

World War I
Reaching Out Across the Diaspora

The Big Picture

Like the pogroms in Russia in 1881 and 1882, World War I changed the face of world Jewry. Fought from 1914 to 1918, it was the largest and deadliest war the world had ever known. Caught on both sides of the conflict, Jews served in the military of the United States and in the military of Germany, among other armies, and faced each other as enemies on the battlefield.

About one and a half million Jewish soldiers served in the war; 177,000 of them died. Another four million Jews lay directly in the path of the marching armies. Hundreds of thousands of Jews were forced to flee their homes, and centuries-old European Jewish communities were destroyed.

After the war, as a result of the destruction suffered by European Jewry, American Jewry held a new position of leadership in Jewish life. Great Britain, on the brink of wresting control of Palestine from the Ottoman Turks in 1917, announced its support for the establishment of "a national home for the Jewish people" in the Land of Israel. As another consequence of the war, in many parts of Europe the search for scapegoats led to an ominous rise in antisemitism.

TIMELINE

World History

1911 Manchu dynasty of China is overthrown; Sun Yat-sen is elected provisional president of Chinese Republic

1914 World War I begins

1915 Joseph Trumpeldor persuades British officers to form all-Jewish fighting unit

1916 Louis Brandeis becomes first Jewish justice of the U.S. Supreme Court

1917 Communists seize control of Russia; British government issues the Balfour Declaration, expressing approval of the creation of a Jewish homeland in Palestine

1918 Central Powers surrender to the Allies

Caught in the Fighting

World War I was fought between the Allied Powers—Russia, France, Great Britain, and later, the United States—and the Central Powers—led by Germany, Austria-Hungary, and the Ottoman Empire. From the start, a great sense of patriotism inspired Europe's Jews. To prove themselves devoted and loyal citizens, they joined the armed forces of their native countries in record numbers. National loyalties proved stronger than the ties linking Jews to one another.

If you were a young German Jewish man, you easily could have found yourself facing Jews from Russia on the battlefield. About 100,000 Jews served in the German army. As many as 650,000 Jews may have served in the Russian army. There were two all-Jewish units in the British army: the Zion Mule Corps and the Jewish Legion.

All-Jewish Fighting Forces

When World War I broke out there had not been an all-Jewish army since the Bar Kochba Revolt against Rome nearly eighteen hundred years before. Then, in 1915, Joseph Trumpeldor, a Russian Jew who had lost his left arm in the 1904–1905 Russo-Japanese War, persuaded British officers to form a Jewish fighting unit. Now, as deputy commander of the all-Jewish Zion Mule Corps, he was wounded again in the fierce fighting against the Turks at Gallipoli, a strategic peninsula in western Turkey.

Another Zionist leader from Russia, Ze'ev (Vladimir) Jabotinsky, helped form the Jewish Legion. Jewish Legion soldiers fought alongside the British as they drove the Turks out of Palestine. After the war, Trumpeldor, Jabotinsky, and many other Jewish veterans settled in Palestine. They formed the core of the fighting force that would one day defend the modern State of Israel.

Soldiers of the Jewish Legion next to the Western Wall in Jerusalem.

Many Russian Jews naturally felt uncomfortable fighting for the Russian czar while they and so many other Russian Jews were being persecuted. Those feelings became irrelevant, however, in the spring of 1917, when the czar was overthrown. The new government quickly granted Jews full legal equality. Jews who had opposed fighting alongside their Russian compatriots now viewed that prospect more willingly.

In the United States, about 250,000 Jews served in the military. Jewish chaplains helped the Jewish soldiers celebrate Jewish holidays and distributed Jewish Bibles and prayer books. As Jews withstood the rigors of combat together with Christians and distinguished themselves in battle, negative stereotypes diminished somewhat and greater trust developed between the two groups.

At the same time as Jews were serving in the military, millions of Jewish civilians were caught in the middle of the fighting. Hundreds of small, close-knit Jewish communities were destroyed. Hundreds of thousands of Jews became wartime refugees—uprooted, without food, jobs, and shelter. Many became widows and orphans.

The Aftermath

World War I ended on November 11, 1918, with the defeat of Germany. European Jewry had been greatly weakened. Eastern Europe was particularly devastated. Many Jews in Russia and Poland remained severely impoverished long afterward, kept alive only by donations from generous Diaspora Jews, especially those in America.

"The Joint"

With so many European Jewish communities destroyed, the American Jewish community assumed a position of leadership. American Jews quickly formed three relief organizations. One represented the mostly American-born Reform Jews of Central European descent. A second was formed by Orthodox Jews, mostly East European in origin. And a third was organized by trade union leaders and Socialists who represented poor immigrant Jews who sought to help but who could afford only small donations. The money from all three organizations was distributed through a committee that became known as the Joint—the American Joint Distribution Committee (JDC). The Joint was an outstanding example of Jews of different backgrounds pooling their resources to achieve greater success together than they could have by acting separately.

The czarist government of Russia had been overthrown, but the regime that replaced it did not last long. Under the leadership of Vladimir Ilich Lenin, Bolsheviks—radical Russian Communists—seized control in the October Revolution of 1917. A brutal two-year civil war followed with the Bolshevik Red Army battling the anti-Bolshevik White Army.

Although most Jewish organizations did not support Lenin, many Bolshevik leaders were Jewish. Thus for Bolsheviks' opponents, Jews among the Bolshevik leadership was an easy excuse for antisemitic attacks. Claiming that all Jews were Bolsheviks, the White Army butchered more than one hundred thousand Jews in pogroms. Communist supporters likewise murdered Jews—particularly those whom they considered "enemies of the people." Ironically Jews were murdered both because they were thought to be Communists and because they were thought to be anti-Communists.

In Germany, meanwhile, some leaders blamed Jews for their country's defeat in the war. Antisemites charged that Jews were weak and had refused to fight for their country— contradicting the fact that many German Jews had fought in the war, some of them winning medals for distinguished service and some dying. In addition, with the Bolshevik Revolution in Russia, a new antisemitic stereotype gained acceptance in Germany: Jews were portrayed as revolutionaries and Communists.

"A National Home for the Jewish People"

Increasingly it became clear that Jews needed a refuge, a place of protection where they could defend themselves from antisemitic attack. Zionists were determined to create that refuge in the historic Jewish homeland, the Land of Israel.

In the United States, Louis D. Brandeis boosted the Zionist cause. One of America's most famous and most respected lawyers, Brandeis had become a leader of the Zionist movement

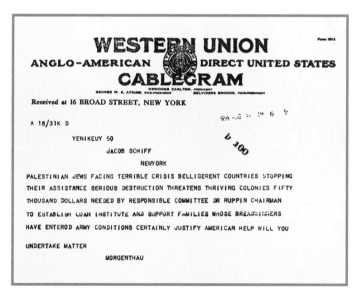

This cable was sent by Henry Morgenthau, the U.S. ambassador to Turkey, to Jacob Schiff, a German-born Jewish American banker and philanthropist, requesting help for the Jews of Palestine in 1914. It was the first appeal for aid and resulted in the founding of the JDC.

in 1914, tirelessly traveling around the country to speak in support of the cause. In 1916 he became the first Jew to serve on the U.S. Supreme Court. Brandeis won many supporters, helping to make Zionism a strong political force in the United States. His commitment to Zionism was especially influential among those American Jews who had feared that support of the Zionist cause might imply that their loyalties were divided.

Zionism was also gaining ground in Great Britain. One British Zionist leader was Chaim Weizmann. Weizmann believed that turning the Zionist dream into a reality required both practical work in Palestine and diplomatic efforts with major world powers. He focused his diplomatic efforts on British leaders, believing them to be the most likely to support the establishment of a Jewish state.

Weizmann's strategy paid off. In 1917 he helped persuade the British government to formulate an official statement in support of Zionism. Issued on November 2, 1917, the Balfour Declaration, as it came to be known, was a turning point in the history of the Zionist movement. It declared: "His Majesty's Government views with favour the establishment in Palestine of a national home for the Jewish people, and will use their best endeavours to facilitate the achievement of this object."

Louis Brandeis helped sway American Jewish opinion by asserting that "To be good Americans we must be better Jews, and to be better Jews, we must become Zionists."

FAMOUS FIGURES

Chaim Weizmann

The son of a timber merchant, Chaim Weizmann was born in the Belarusian village of Motol in 1874. When one of his teachers secretly taught the class science, a subject frowned on in many traditional Jewish communities, Weizmann discovered his love of and talent for it. He went on to study biochemistry in Germany and Switzerland and, after earning his doctorate, settled in England, where he taught and made important discoveries in the field of chemistry.

Weizmann's love of science was balanced by his passionate commitment to Zionism. He once said, "Miracles sometimes occur, but one has to work terribly hard for them." Weizmann served as the first president of the modern State of Israel and died in 1952.

Chaim Weizmann with his wife, Vera.

At first the British were not able to follow through on their promise—Palestine was still in the hands of Ottomans—but a month later Britain forced the Turks out and took control of the land. Because the Ottoman Empire had sided with Germany, the Allied Powers had blockaded Palestine and prohibited trade. The arrival of the British, especially given their promise of a "national home for the Jewish people," was seen as a hopeful sign for Palestine in general and the Jews in particular.

But the collapse of the Ottoman Empire had far-reaching negative effects on the 750,000 or so Jews who lived under Turkish and Arab rule. The Turkish city of Salonika, home to eighty thousand Jews in 1900, fell to Greece in 1912 and was devastated by fire five years later. Tens of thousands of its Jews emigrated after the war. At the same time, Arab communities from Morocco to Iraq came under European control, and the Jews of Syria and Iraq suffered greatly during the transition. Most important, World War I inspired nationalism among Arabs longing for self-government. Arab nationalism and Jewish nationalism would soon come into conflict.

A New Jewish World

After World War I, Eastern Europe declined as a center of Jewish life, and the two new centers—the United States and the Land of Israel—gathered strength. The Jewish community of Palestine was still small, yet it represented a place where persecuted Jews might settle and live in freedom. The Zionist movement continued to gain followers.

The American Jewish community had become the second-largest Jewish community in the world—and by far the best organized, the richest, and the most powerful. (The largest Jewish community was still in Russia.) American Jews began to play a critical role in world Jewish affairs, a role they continue to play to this day. 🦁

Chapter 19

At Home in the United States, 1920–1940
Creating an American Style of Judaism

The Big Picture

From 1880 to 1920, the Jewish population of the United States leaped from 250,000 to more than three million. This explosive growth was largely due to the massive wave of Jewish immigration from Eastern Europe. The situation changed, however, when in the early 1920s the U.S. government began closing America's doors. Anti-immigration attitudes were rising, and in response, Congress set strict limits on the number of immigrants allowed into the country, particularly from Eastern and Southern Europe. Jewish immigration to America suddenly was severely restricted.

With the doors of immigration almost completely shut by Congress in 1924, native-born Jews soon outnumbered the foreign-born. The typical Jew was now someone on the way to blending into the American middle class while maintaining a strong Jewish identity based largely on ethnic ties. Such Jews were called alrightniks. As more Jews became integrated into American society, they began to personalize their religious practices and develop a uniquely American style of Judaism.

A Jewish American First

"No thunder sounded, no lightning struck," noted Judith Kaplan as she recalled the controversy surrounding her

TIMELINE

1920 U.S. Jewish population reaches more than three million

World History
1921 *Canadian researchers discover insulin, the life-saving treatment for diabetes*

1922 First public bat mitzvah ceremony is held in the United States

1924 Immigration Act of 1924 limits immigration from Eastern and Southern Europe

1926 National Council on Jewish Education is formed to improve the quality of Jewish education in the United States

1927 Henry Ford apologizes for printing antisemitic articles in his newspaper

1937 Reform rabbis formally support the establishment of a Jewish homeland in Palestine

bat mitzvah celebration on March 18, 1922. It was a historic day: the first public bat mitzvah ceremony in the United States. Judith's father, Rabbi Mordecai Kaplan, a professor at the Conservative movement's Jewish Theological Seminary, was committed to advancing the religious equality of women. One way to do that was to conduct a bat mitzvah ceremony for his daughter in his new synagogue in New York City, the Society for the Advancement of Judaism.

Although public bat mitzvah ceremonies were not widely conducted until the 1960s, Judith Kaplan helped set the wheels in motion. She did so at a time when Jews were trying hard to Americanize yet hold on to their Jewish identity. Their many strategies included Americanizing Judaism itself. Thus, just as American women gained political power when they won the right to vote in 1920, so Judith and her father helped Jewish women take a step toward religious equality in 1922.

Moving Up

The economic status of American Jews improved along with that of millions of other Americans during the country's economic boom in the 1920s. Although that did not mean overnight middle-class comfort for immigrants, many of their children were able to take advantage of the educational and economic opportunities, entering professions such as teaching, law, and medicine.

The Pressure of Being First

Judith Kaplan was not as eager as her father to be a pioneer. As she remembered the occasion of her bat mitzvah, she had mixed feelings, "being perfectly willing to defy my grandmothers [who opposed the ceremony], pleased to have a somewhat flattering attention paid me, and yet perturbed by the possible effect this might have on the attitude of my own peers, the early teenagers who . . . could be remarkably cruel to the 'exception,' to the non-conformist."

Rose Schneiderman, the daughter of poor Jewish immigrants, was a garment worker, a leading union organizer, and a feminist. Her influence went as far as the White House, where she was befriended by President Franklin Roosevelt and his wife, Eleanor. Schneiderman is seen here speaking at a women's suffrage meeting.

Jews also started their own businesses, especially in new and growing industries like music, radio, and motion pictures. Young Jewish composers, such as George Gershwin and Irving Berlin, were among the most popular songwriters in America. David Sarnoff, a pioneer of the radio industry, established the first national radio network, the National Broadcasting Company (NBC), in 1926. And in Hollywood, Jews founded most of the major American movie studios.

Old Problems in a New Land

Even as the Jews were successfully adapting to life in America, familiar problems arose. Although antisemitism was not as strong or as dangerous in America as it was in Europe, it did become more widespread after World War I. Prejudice intensified among some Americans, especially in lower-middle-class communities in small towns. America was changing quickly, becoming more urban, more culturally diverse, and more involved in the affairs of the world, and those Americans who were not keeping up with the changes felt that their way of life was threatened, that immigrant Jews (and Catholics) were destroying American society.

Poster for a 1929 silent film with Yiddish subtitles, *East Side Sadie*.

As small-town Americans watched their familiar way of life slipping away, many wanted to turn back the clock. They accused the Jews in the entertainment industry of producing movies and writing songs designed to destroy traditional American culture and values. They imagined that the Jews were secretly trying to bring about a Communist revolution in the United States, yet they also believed that Jews controlled major capitalist interests.

Judaism American-Style

As Jews became increasingly middle class and Americanized, they reshaped Judaism. In the years after World War I, for example, American Jews transformed the celebration of Jewish holidays. Passover, with its theme of freedom, was especially significant to American Jews and thus the holiday soon became the most observed festival on the Jewish calendar. In time, big food companies began directing advertisements to Jewish customers and manufacturing a variety of kosher foods and even Passover haggadahs, influencing Jewish life and observance.

Henry Ford's Antisemitism

One powerful American who spread antisemitic propaganda in the 1920s was the automaker Henry Ford. Ford owned a newspaper, the *Dearborn Independent*, in which he ran a series of articles, "The International Jew: The World's Foremost Problem," based on *The Protocols of the Elders of Zion*. Ford made sure his newspaper was available at all his automobile dealerships.

Jewish leaders took action, organizing a boycott of Ford automobiles by American Jews. In 1927, under economic and legal pressure, Ford apologized to the American Jewish community for the articles and stopped printing them. Although he offered Jews his "future friendship and good will," he never gave up his antisemitic beliefs and later accepted a medal from Adolf Hitler's government.

Antisemitism was not confined to small-town America. Many universities set quotas on the number of Jews who could enroll, and many businesses refused to hire Jews. Certain wealthy neighborhoods were off-limits to Jews, and Jews were excluded from many social clubs and resorts.

Jews responded to antisemitism in a variety of ways. Some sought to escape their Judaism completely and blend into the larger American society. Others adopted strategies designed to minimize or mask their Jewish identity in public. Changing one's name was one such strategy. The actress Betty Perske, for example, became Lauren Bacall. The songwriter Israel Baline, who composed two of America's best-known holiday classics, "White Christmas" and "Easter Parade," became Irving Berlin.

But generally Jews simply found ways around the challenges of antisemitism. When quotas prevented Jews from enrolling in private universities, they turned to schools that had no quotas. Brandeis University was founded, in 1948, in part as a response to quotas that denied Jews entrance into elite universities. Similarly, rather than try to earn a living in a place that did not welcome them, many Jews started their own businesses, law firms, and medical practices. They also created their own country clubs and resorts.

Jewishness Without Judaism

Many Jews imagined that the move to middle-class neighborhoods would lead to greater interaction with non-Jews. For the most part, however, they were wrong. As Jews moved in, white Protestant residents moved out. In many cases the Jews' new communities became as Jewish or more heavily Jewish than the neighborhoods they had left. Signs of Jewishness were everywhere—from storefront synagogues to corner-store delicatessens.

By the 1920s many Jews had given up attending synagogue and strictly observing Jewish laws and rituals. In 1919, less than a quarter of the Jews in the United States were members of a synagogue, and many limited their attendance to High Holidays and the anniversaries of family members' deaths. For a large number, their connection to Judaism involved only the cultural activities they enjoyed, such as attending Yiddish theater and Yiddish music hall concerts—or political activism, such as organizing labor unions or Zionist clubs. The popularity of Jewish secularism alarmed religious leaders. Most agreed that Judaism urgently needed to respond to the challenges posed by American life; it needed to become meaningful to the upwardly mobile American Jews.

The Americanization of Jewish Religious Life

As the twentieth century progressed, more and more Eastern European Jews found a home in the Reform movement. By 1931, half of the Reform synagogues' membership traced its roots to Eastern Europe. In 1937, Reform rabbis adopted a platform that supported Zionism. That platform also supported the reintroduction of more traditional Jewish rituals and ceremonies. Bar mitzvah ceremonies were reintroduced, as was the use of Hebrew in prayer services.

But most American Jews of Eastern European origin found Reform Judaism too foreign to adopt. Instead, some adapted Orthodox Judaism to American life. In 1928, for example, Orthodox Jews inaugurated the upper Manhattan campus of Yeshiva College, which emphasized secular as well as Jewish studies. America's Modern Orthodox Jews were likely to discuss sports scores and the latest movies as well as the weekly Torah portion. Only the most strictly Orthodox Jews resisted American culture. In doing so, they established a network of yeshivas, Orthodox schools designed to carry on traditional learning and Old World values.

A Shul with a Pool

Jews were beginning to feel more like Americans by the 1930s, a feeling reflected in their synagogues, called *shuls* in Yiddish. Eastern European congregations with Yiddish-speaking rabbis increasingly hired English-speaking associate rabbis to preach to younger members who were not fluent in Yiddish. Rabbis like Herbert Goldstein and Mordecai Kaplan also popularized the concept of the synagogue center, the "shul with a pool." Such centers expanded the programs of the traditional synagogue to include educational and social activities and even athletic facilities. Multipurpose synagogue buildings were built in Jewish communities all over the United States.

The fastest-growing movement during this period was Conservative Judaism. In 1919 only 22 congregations identified themselves as Conservative. By 1929 the number had jumped to 229. The Conservative movement generally steered a middle course. Balancing tradition and change, it embraced the traditional order and form of prayer services while accepting such innovations as seating men and women together during the services.

Most teachers at the Conservative movement's Jewish Theological Seminary were primarily concerned with maintaining Conservative Judaism's commitment to Jewish law and tradition. An important exception was Mordecai Kaplan, who believed that Judaism would not survive unless it was adapted to American life and values. In keeping with that conviction, he rejected the traditional idea of the Jews as "the chosen people" because it conflicted with American ideals of democracy and equality.

Influenced by modern scientific advances, Kaplan understood God as a force or power for good but not as a supernatural being capable of reversing the laws of nature and performing miracles. He saw the Torah as sacred but not as a literal record of God's words to Moses. And he believed that in America, Jews live in two civilizations, one reflecting American traditions and ways of life and the other reflecting Jewish traditions and ways of life.

Kaplan's system of ideas and beliefs, which he called Reconstructionism, influenced many Reform, Orthodox, and, most especially, Conservative Jews. Reconstructionism remained within Conservative Judaism until after World War II when it became a separate movement. The Reconstructionist Rabbinical College was founded in 1968.

Politics and World Events

The Great Depression in the 1930s was marked by widespread economic hardship and Jews suffered along with all other Americans. With the failure of the New York Bank of the United States, many Jews saw their life savings all but disappear. Jewish garment workers, who made up one-third of New York's Jewish population, were devastated when they lost their jobs. For young Jews entering the labor market, the discriminatory hiring practices of many businesses made already scarce jobs almost nonexistent.

Kid-Friendly Judaism

As Judaism Americanized, it also became more child centered. Synagogue sisterhoods taught mothers how to make their homes more Jewish and how to capture the interest of their children with Jewish-themed games, activities, and foods. Instructions were given, for example, on how to make Bible dolls and how to make "Maccabean sandwiches." Jewish children's books were published in greater number, and the celebration of Hanukkah became increasingly widespread as an alternative to Christmas.

Efforts were also made to modernize afternoon religious schools, the Talmud Torahs. In the first decades of the twentieth century, many boys received little more than bar mitzvah training, and girls rarely received any Jewish education. With the help of Mordecai Kaplan, the Jewish educator Samson Benderly led an effort to instill in its pupils an American-style Judaism. Students sang Jewish songs, studied Jewish current events, and created Jewish art projects and cultural presentations. In addition, they learned about Zionist culture and studied modern Hebrew.

FAMOUS FIGURES

Mordecai Kaplan

Mordecai Kaplan was born into an Orthodox family in Lithuania in 1881. When he was eight years old, the family moved to New York City. As a teenager, influenced by secular and religious studies, Kaplan saw Judaism in a new way. After completing his university studies, he was ordained by the Conservative movement's Jewish Theological Seminary.

Zionism was central to Kaplan's vision of Judaism. He saw Palestine as the birthplace of Jewish civilization. By civilization, Kaplan meant everything from Jewish religion to Jewish music, art, literature, and food. He believed that a strong and creative Jewish civilization in the Diaspora along with an equally thriving Jewish civilization in the Land of Israel, would help Judaism develop and grow.

Kaplan did not hold Jewish law to be absolute; rather, he was famous for saying, "Halachah [Jewish law] should have a vote but not a veto." Kaplan, who died in 1983, taught that each Jew must study Jewish tradition in order to figure out what it means to him or her to be a Jew.

Mordecai Kaplan.

Sign in a Jewish store during the Depression announcing that relief tickets could be exchanged for food.

The 1930s also saw much of the Jewish community identifying with the Democratic Party. Most Jews supported President Franklin Roosevelt's New Deal policies, which created programs to give relief, create jobs, and stimulate economic recovery. Many felt indebted to Roosevelt because he opened government jobs to Jews and had an unusually large number of Jewish advisers within his inner circle.

But Jews were not able to convince Roosevelt to ease the strict quotas on immigration from Europe. This issue was becoming increasingly important because Adolf Hitler had come to power in Germany; conditions for German Jews as well as Jews in Poland and other Eastern European countries were rapidly worsening. American Jews responded by supporting the development of the Jewish homeland and the resettlement of refugees in Palestine. Membership in Zionist organizations began to grow rapidly in the mid-1930s.

Chapter 20

The British Mandate
Zionist Achievements and Arab-Israeli Conflict

The Big Picture

On the morning of December 9, 1917, the residents of Jerusalem woke to find that their city had a new ruler. The British army, commanded by General Edmund Allenby, had defeated the Ottoman Turks, and the British now controlled Jerusalem. Crowds of residents, both Jews and Arabs, flooded the streets to greet the British as liberators.

A month earlier, Britain's Balfour Declaration had promised support for a Jewish homeland in Palestine. To many Jews, Britain's victory over the Turks and its promise to establish a Jewish national homeland seemed like a modern-day Ḥanukkah miracle.

A time of great growth and achievement was beginning for the Zionists of Palestine, and a new identity of the Jew as a courageous and powerful pioneer and soldier was developing. But it was also a period in which the seeds of conflict were sown between the Jews and the Arabs.

The Roots of the Conflict

Like the Jews, the Arabs were filled with hope, for the British had promised them that they would receive an independent state in return for staging a revolt against the Turks. But the British had also signed a secret agreement with France, in which each pledged to take a piece of the Ottoman Empire for itself and jointly rule most of Palestine.

TIMELINE

1917 British army takes control of Jerusalem

1919 Third Aliyah begins, eventually bringing forty thousand Jews to Palestine

1920 Jews form the Haganah to protect the Zionist community of Palestine

World History
1922   *Mussolini forms the Fascist Party in Italy*

1924 Fourth Aliyah begins, eventually bringing eighty thousand Jews to Palestine

1929 Arab riots occur throughout Palestine

1936 Palestinian Arabs begin the Great Uprising

1939 British issue the White Paper, ending their commitment to the establishment of a Jewish homeland in Palestine

Hashomer ("The Guard") was responsible for the security of many Jewish settlements in Palestine from 1909 to 1920. The organization required that the settlements employ only Jewish workers.

The British made these conflicting promises because they were determined to win the war with the Turks. They hoped their promises would gain the cooperation of the various groups. Their strategy worked, but when the war ended it became clear that Britain could not possibly keep all its promises.

Britain and France carved up the region much the way they had planned, forming mandates, colony-like territories that the two countries would govern until they determined that the population was ready for independence. The borders of the mandates were designed more to satisfy the interests of the British and the French than to address the needs and interests of the Arabs and the Jews.

Believing that the European powers had no right to rule over them, the Arabs opposed the creation of the mandates. They also opposed the Balfour Declaration and the Zionist desire to build a Jewish nation in Palestine. Palestine, they argued, already had an Arab population, and that population had no desire to become a minority in a Jewish state.

The roots of the conflict over Palestine lie in the struggle between two peoples for the same small piece of land. Britain's effort to build a Jewish national home without raising Arab opposition was doomed from the start.

The Outbreak of Violence

Violence between Jews and Arabs first flared in March 1920. Jews living in an isolated group of settlements in the far north of Palestine found themselves in the middle of a battle between Arab nationalists and French troops. Despite the Zionists' efforts to remain neutral, the Arabs were convinced that the Jews were aiding the French.

Zionist leaders encouraged the settlers to leave the area. Many did, but the members of two settlements, Tel Ḥai and K'far Gil'adi, chose to stay. On March 1 several hundred Arabs arrived at Tel Ḥai looking for French soldiers. A firefight erupted. The settlers temporarily drove out the Arabs, but in the end the settlers were forced to leave.

A month later, anti-Jewish riots broke out in Jerusalem. Protesters descended on Jews with clubs, knives, and stones.

In the Diaspora, Jews often seemed powerless and defenseless. Those images troubled the "new Jews" of Palestine. So in 1920 they formed a militia, called the Haganah ("Defense"), to protect the Yishuv. Under the leadership of Ze'ev Jabotinsky, the Haganah helped evacuate some Jewish families from the center of the rioting, the area in East Jerusalem known as the Old City. To ensure that the rioting did not spread, Haganah members also patrolled the streets of West Jerusalem, the New City.

The Pioneer Spirit

Another wave of Jewish immigration to Palestine known as the Third Aliyah, occurred after World War I. A core of the latest immigrants was devoted to working the land and exemplifying Socialist ideals. These immigrants called themselves *ḥalutzim*, a term based on the biblical word for a frontline soldier or pioneer. In many ways the *ḥalutzim* followed in the footsteps of the Second Aliyah. They, too, were committed to "Hebrew labor," the Hebrew language, self-defense, and social justice.

The *ḥalutzim* set up the first settlements formally known as *kibbutzim*, collective communities that combined many of the ideals of Socialism and Zionism. Kibbutz members lived and worked together, owned all property together, and kept a communal treasury. Many *kibbutzim* included factories as well as farms. Kibbutz members prided themselves on the equal treatment of men and women. Women performed tasks as diverse as cooking, child rearing, tractor driving, and fruit harvesting.

By the late 1920s, about four thousand people lived on approximately thirty *kibbutzim*. A number were built in outlying areas to provide security and widen the borders of the growing Jewish national home. Although residents of *kibbutzim* accounted for only a small percentage of the total Jewish population, they had a large impact on the Yishuv. Beyond their role in securing the land, many leading military figures, politicians, and intellectuals were drawn from the *kibbutzim*.

The Labor Brigade

The pride of the Third Aliyah was the Joseph Trumpeldor Labor Brigade, named for Tel Ḥai's fallen hero. Almost two thousand *halutzim* were members of the brigade at one time or another. Its members hired themselves out to new settlements. They built roads and drained swamps while living in tent camps and braving harsh conditions.

The Growth of Urban Jewish Centers

As in earlier years, the majority of Jewish immigrants who arrived during the Third Aliyah settled in cities. In Haifa an entirely Jewish community, Hadar Hacarmel, was established. By the mid-1920s it had over three thousand residents and the Technion, the Israel Institute of Technology, opened. Both Jews and Arabs flocked to Haifa as its fortunes continued to rise. In the 1930s the British built a modern port and completed an oil pipeline to Iraq.

Jerusalem, too, was growing. New middle-class Jewish neighborhoods were constructed in West Jerusalem. In East Jerusalem, Mount Scopus became the site of the Hebrew University, a center for Jewish scholarship.

The fastest-growing city by far was Tel Aviv. Between 1920 and 1939 its population exploded from 2,000 to 160,000. With its seaside promenade, sidewalk cafés, broad avenues, public squares, and neighborhood parks, Tel Aviv seemed like a European city with a Mediterranean flavor. It became known for its modernity, sophistication, and secular Jewish culture.

FAMOUS FIGURES

Henrietta Szold

Born in Baltimore in 1860, Henrietta Szold made her first visit to Palestine in 1909. Troubled by the unhealthy conditions of the children living there, Szold formed Hadassah, the Women's Zionist Organization of America, upon her return home. Until her death in 1945, Szold worked to improve health care and education for Palestine's Jews and Arabs.

Hadassah sent American-trained nurses and, later, entire medical units to Palestine to combat the primitive health conditions. It worked to improve maternity and infant care and set up training programs for nurses, health clinics, and hospitals.

Today Hadassah Hospital, located in Jerusalem, is considered one of the finest hospitals in the Middle East. It continues Szold's commitment to providing quality medical care to Jews and Arabs.

Henrietta Szold.

Separate Lives

The Fourth Aliyah, from 1924 to 1928, brought another eighty thousand Jewish immigrants to Palestine, including middle-class shopkeepers and artisans. The Palestinian Arab population was growing quickly, too, mostly because the British improved health conditions, road and rail networks, and sewage systems. The decline of the rural economy brought many peasants to the cities. Urban Arabs created a rich intellectual and cultural life, and newspapers and political parties introduced many Arabs to the principles of Arab nationalism.

Arabs and Jews often led separate lives, even in mixed cities like Haifa and Jaffa. Zionists created their own economy and cultural institutions, organizing their own trade union and priding themselves on hiring only Jews.

The 1929 Riots

The Arabs became alarmed as Jews continued to buy up land in Palestine. The JNF preferred to buy uninhabited tracts of land, but as such territory became scarce, Jews bought land from Arabs that was leased to other Arabs. Many of the tenants had lived on and farmed the land for generations. Evictions by the new owners fueled the Arab's resentment.

Arabs' fears of a growing Jewish population buying more and more land set off a new round of riots in 1929. The worst violence took place in the cities of Safed and Hebron. In Hebron, rioters attacked the yeshiva, and in both cities they attacked Jewish homes. Sixty-six Jews were killed.

Jews in larger cities were better able to defend themselves. Haganah squads patrolled the streets and fired on rioters. The British army and police tried to put down the violence. Low-flying British aircraft even fired at a band of Arab villagers on their way to attack Jews in Haifa. But there were only 292 policemen and fewer than a hundred soldiers in all of Palestine. In total, 133 Jews and 116 Arabs were killed.

The riots convinced the high commissioner of Palestine that the Balfour Declaration was "a colossal blunder." He urged the British government to back away from its promises to the Jews. In London, British officials were beginning to wonder whether the mandate in Palestine was more trouble than it was worth.

The Arab Revolt

The rise to power of Adolf Hitler in Germany caused yet another wave of Jewish immigration to Palestine. Between 1933 and 1936 about 165,000 immigrants arrived from Europe. By

1936, Jews made up almost one-third of the population of Palestine. Jewish dreams and Arab fears of a Jewish majority in Palestine seemed on the verge of becoming a reality.

The Habimah Theater

Despite the difficult times, Hebrew culture managed to thrive. The Habimah Theater, which was founded in Russia in 1917 and was committed to producing plays in Hebrew, moved to Palestine in 1931. In 1945 it moved into a building in the heart of Tel Aviv and, thirteen years later, became the National Theater of Israel.

Meir Rosenblatt (center) in 1933 shortly before he immigrated to Palestine from Botoshani, Romania. Like many other elderly immigrants, Rosenblatt, a *shohet* (ritual slaughterer) and scribe, was motivated by the wish to be buried in Jerusalem. His sons Baruch (left) and Jacob (right) remained in Botoshani. After the Holocaust, their surviving descendants immigrated to the newly established State of Israel.

Youth Aliyah

After Hitler came to power in Germany, in 1933, thousands of Jewish children from Germany were sent by their parents to Palestine. They were part of Youth Aliyah, a project directed by Henrietta Szold to help young Jews escape from Germany. About five thousand teenagers arrived in Palestine before World War II, and more than fifteen thousand more youngsters emigrated after the war.

In April 1936 an organized Arab revolt began, aimed at stopping the Zionist nation-building project and ending British rule. The Arabs declared a general strike. Shops were closed, and many Arabs refused to pay their taxes.

The Great Uprising, as the Palestinian Arabs called it, enjoyed popular support among the Palestinian Arab population. Grand Mufti Haj Amin al-Husseini, who eventually took charge of the revolt, announced that the strike would end only when Jewish immigration was halted. Arab rebels bombed the oil pipeline, railway lines, and trains, assassinated British officials, and committed acts of terrorism against Jews. The British brought in twenty thousand troops and put down the rebellion.

The Plan for Partition

In November 1936, a British commission, known as the Peel Commission, arrived in Palestine to determine the causes of the revolt and recommend a solution. The commissioners spoke with Jewish and Arab leaders, including Ben-Gurion, Weizmann, and al-Husseini. In July 1937 the commission issued a 404-page report, which concluded that Jews and Arabs could never live peacefully in one state. The only solution was a plan that would divide Palestine into two states.

The report suggested that the Jews receive the Galilee, the Jezreel Valley, and most of the coast. The Negev, the Gaza Strip, and the West Bank would be given to the Arabs. Jerusalem and some other towns with Arab-Jewish populations would remain in British hands. The proposed map gave the Jews only one-fifth of Palestine. The leadership of the Yishuv accepted the plan, however reluctantly. In Weizmann's words, "The Jews would be fools not to accept it even if . . . [the Jewish State] were the size of a tablecloth." The Arabs, however, rejected the idea of a partition. In their minds, the only just solution to the problem was an independent Arab-majority state.

The White Paper

After a lull in hostilities while the Peel Commission was meeting, the revolt started again. The British stepped up their actions against the Arabs, and by early 1939 the Revolt had collapsed. But the human toll of the uprising was enormous: More than five thousand Arabs, five hundred Jews, and two hundred Britons were dead. Al-Husseini fled to Germany and supported the Nazis during World War II.

Flyer printed to raise support and funds for forty-three members of the Haganah who were arrested by the British in 1939.

The Haganah and the Irgun Respond to Violence

The violence shook the Yishuv, convincing many Jews that it was impossible to live with the Arabs. But Ben-Gurion and other leaders did not want to provoke the British. For that reason at first the leadership followed a policy of restraint. In the early months of the revolt, most of the Haganah's actions were defensive—patrolling settlements, for example. Jabotinsky's followers opposed the policy of restraint but their underground militia, the Irgun Tz'vei Leumi, known simply as the Irgun and headed by Menaḥem Begin, went along with it.

As Arab violence increased, many Jews who had resisted taking up arms came to believe that there was no alternative but to fight for the community's survival. Their rallying cry was *"Ein b'reira!"* ("There is no choice!") The British army and the Haganah organized joint night squads, which ambushed Arab fighters and attacked the villages they used as bases. Irgun fighters conducted scores of attacks on Arab civilians in marketplaces, cafés, and buses, killing more than 250 people.

What, wondered the British government, was the solution to the Palestine problem? In Europe the threat from Germany was intensifying, and war seemed inevitable. Therefore, maintaining twenty thousand troops in Palestine was out of the question for the British, and securing Arab cooperation in the coming conflict with Germany was essential. The British knew they could count on Jewish cooperation because the Zionists would want to help defend the Jews of Europe. So the British chose to withdraw the promises made in the Balfour Declaration.

In May 1939, Britain issued its long-awaited White Paper, or official government report. Palestine, the White Paper declared, was to become an independent state allied with the British Empire. To ensure that the Arabs remained a majority in Palestine, Jewish immigration was to be limited to seventy-five thousand people over the next five years. Arab permission would be required for Jewish immigration and land sales to Jews were to be severely restricted.

ARAB AND JEWISH POPULATION IN PALESTINE, 1914–1946		
YEAR	ARAB POPULATION	JEWISH POPULATION
1914	738,000	60,000
1922	730,000	85,000
1931	880,000	175,000
1939	1,070,000	460,000
1946	1,269,000	608,000

The Zionists were outraged. All they had worked for in Palestine was at risk, as was the fate of the Jews of Europe. With other countries enforcing strict immigration quotas, unrestricted immigration to Palestine had been the best hope for saving the Jews of Germany and Eastern Europe.

The leaders of the Yishuv faced a dilemma: They could refuse to cooperate with the British authorities in Palestine, or they could ally with the British to defeat Hitler. They decided to do both. Their policy was summed up by Ben-Gurion, who declared, "We shall fight the war as if there were no White Paper and we shall fight the White Paper as if there were no war."

Chapter 21

Europe Between the Wars
Rising Antisemitism and Jewish Diversity

The Big Picture

In February 1921 a group of American Jews traveled to Warsaw, bringing food, medical supplies, and money. Many of Poland's Jews lived in poverty. The Warsaw Jews welcomed the Americans, but as Boris Bogen, a member of the relief mission, recalled, "No sooner was the cheering over than they divided into many voices."

This was typical of much of European Jewry during the years after World War I. Still treated as outsiders in their home countries, Jews developed many ideas about how to improve their living conditions. The Jewish population was diverse, including those who were Orthodox and those who were Zionists, Jews who supported revolutionary change and Jews who wanted to assimilate into European culture.

But with each new outbreak of antisemitism, the differences mattered less. Blaming the Jews for the problems of Europe, Adolf Hitler rose to power in Germany in 1933. He claimed that Jews were an inferior and dangerous race that should never be permitted to assimilate into German life.

European Jewry at a Glance

European Jews were now heavily urban. Two-thirds of Germany's Jews lived in cities of over one hundred thousand,

TIMELINE

1920	Franz Rosenzweig opens the Frankfurt Free Jewish Lehrhaus to encourage Jewish education
1921	Albert Einstein wins the Nobel Prize in Physics
1925–1927	Adolf Hitler publishes a detailed plan to seize power and rid Germany of Jews
1928	Joseph Stalin gains power in the Soviet Union
World History	
1932	*Amelia Earhart becomes the first woman to fly solo across the Atlantic Ocean*
1933	Adolf Hitler becomes chancellor of Germany
1935	Nuremberg Laws officially strip German Jews of their basic rights

and three-quarters of Poland's Jews lived in urban areas. The three hundred thousand Jews of Warsaw formed the largest Jewish community in Europe. Far more Jews now earned their living from urban industries and trade than from agriculture.

But European Jews were divided over how to respond to developments in modern science, culture, and industry. In Western Europe, where Jews had experienced emancipation and had been influenced by the Haskalah, modern ways of life were generally embraced. Jews dressed similarly to non-Jews, spoke the national language, had small families, lived in cities, and were able to move up economically to the middle class. Some Jews became leading figures in European culture, such as Sigmund Freud, Albert Einstein, and the painter Max Beckmann. Growing numbers of Jews were drawn to Reform Judaism rather than to traditional Orthodoxy, and more and more Jews intermarried with non-Jews.

In contrast, Eastern European Jews faced greater legal restrictions and had less access to modern advances than Western European Jews. Living in comparatively underdeveloped countries, they struggled to earn a living as laborers and small-scale merchants. Some still lived in small towns and villages. Many dressed differently from their non-Jewish neighbors, primarily spoke Yiddish, had large families, and remained Orthodox. Many also continued to observe traditional ways of life, including, in the case of men, keeping their sidelocks (*payos* in Yiddish) uncut and wearing a long beard and, in the case of married women, keeping their head covered in public.

In the years after World War I, however, even the most modern Jews of Europe often found themselves treated as outsiders. They may have considered themselves Poles, Latvians, Lithuanians, Germans, or Hungarians but in the eyes of many of their nationalist neighbors, they were simply Jews. This sentiment would lie at the heart of the coming wave of European antisemitism.

Facing the "Jewish Problem"

In the years after World War I, many Europeans spoke about Jews as a "problem." By this they meant that Jews were both different and disliked. They did not believe that Jews could ever become true citizens of their nations—Jews would forever be distinguished by religious and racial differences.

FAMOUS FIGURES

Albert Einstein

Although many European Jews achieved great success in the early 1900s, they were not accepted as equals in most countries. The experience of Albert Einstein was typical. Born in the German town of Ulm in 1879, by the time Einstein was in his mid-twenties, he had written a series of scientific papers that forever changed the way we understand the universe and the laws of physics. Recognized as one of the world's great scientists, he was awarded a Nobel Prize in 1921.

Yet when Adolf Hitler came to power in Germany in 1933, he ordered the burning of "subversive" books, including Einstein's work. Einstein, who was visiting the United States at the time, renounced his German citizenship and never returned. He settled in the United States and continued his research. A resident of Princeton, New Jersey, Einstein also worked as a human rights activist, a champion of nuclear disarmament, and a fund-raiser for the establishment of the modern State of Israel. He died in 1955.

Einstein asserted that "the life of the individual has meaning only insofar as it aids in making the life of every living thing nobler and more beautiful."

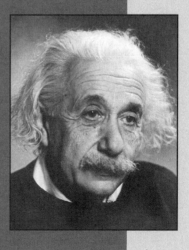

Albert Einstein.

Jews in the Soviet Union

The Jews of Russia experienced one moment of hope after World War I. In 1917, when the Communist Party took power, it outlawed discriminatory laws based on religion, and it banned antisemitism. The government set up a special department to inculcate Yiddish-speaking Jews with the ideals of the new Soviet Union.

It soon became clear, however, that the Communist Party's goal was not to ensure equality for Jews but rather to stamp out Judaism in the Soviet Union. Synagogues were closed down, and the publication and distribution of religious books were banned. Zionists were arrested.

Conditions for Jews worsened with Joseph Stalin's rise to power in the late 1920s. Stalin considered Jews outsiders and persecuted them. Jews were placed under the authority of his secret police, and once again antisemitism became government policy.

The Jews of Europe developed four responses.

Remain Separate

Orthodox Jews believed that the Jews are a people—a nation in exile awaiting the Messiah, united by a shared commitment to God's law, as written in the Torah. Following the teachings of the ancient rabbis in *Pirkei Avot* (*Ethics of the Sages*), they prayed for the welfare of their nation's governments and did not call for political change. They were happy to live and work separately from non-Jews. All they asked was the right to earn a living and practice Judaism in peace—and to use Jewish law to address community issues, such as marriage and divorce.

Integrate

By contrast, integrationists insisted that Jews should differ only in religion from the people among whom they lived. In other words, they should be Poles, Germans, or French citizens of the Jewish faith. They believed that the more ways in which Jews were similar to their non-Jewish neighbors, the more likely they were to win acceptance. For integrationists, Judaism was a religious faith only, not an ethnic or national identity.

Return to the Jewish Homeland

The Zionists agreed with the Orthodox vision of the Jews as a people, but they disagreed with the idea of remaining in Europe. Zionists argued that Jews needed to return to the Land of Israel, where they could speak Hebrew, develop their own culture, and govern themselves. They did not believe that Jews would ever be accepted as equals in Europe.

Zionists like these young Jews in Kosow, Poland, in 1922, believed that the only place where Jews could feel at home was their own homeland, the Land of Israel.

Support the Socialist and Communist Revolutions

Radical Jews offered a fourth idea: "The Jewish problem" was actually part of a larger social problem that could be solved only through social revolution and the overthrow of oppressive leaders. Many radical Jews opposed nationalism and religion, instead supporting equality and harmony among all people. Under Socialism or Communism, they believed, economic classes and national differences would eventually disappear.

In the end, all four solutions failed to keep Jews safe as economies collapsed around the world during the Great Depression of the 1930s. Jews throughout Europe, especially in

Poland and Germany, found themselves excluded from society and treated as scapegoats. In Poland, Jews were forced out of public life and barred from government jobs. Special taxes were levied on them, and they were required to purchase expensive work licenses simply to practice their trade. By the late 1930s, the limited number of Jews who were still being accepted by universities were made to sit apart from other students on special "ghetto benches."

Meanwhile, in Germany, economic depression forced banks and factories to close. As the Great Depression continued, increasing numbers of desperate Germans turned to a new political party: the National Socialist German Workers' Party, known as the Nazi Party. Its leader was Adolf Hitler.

The Rise of Adolf Hitler

Born in Austria in 1889, Hitler was a failed art student who lived on the fringes of society. After fighting in the German army in World War I, he expressed outrage at those whom he believed had caused Germany to lose the war. Hitler claimed that Communists and Jews were especially to blame, and he directed particular fury toward the Jews, whom he considered "a non-German, alien race." His autobiography, *Mein Kampf* (*My Struggle*), spelled out his plan to seize power and rid Germany of its Jews.

Promising Germans that he could erase the painful memories of their defeat in World War I and return Germany to economic prosperity, Hitler quickly built a following for his extreme right-wing party. In 1930 the Nazis received over 18 percent of the vote, entitling them to 107 of the 577 seats in the Reichstag, Germany's parliament. This made them the country's second-largest political party.

Hitler's followers were aggressively antisemitic, attacking Jews on the street, disrupting religious services, and desecrating synagogues and cemeteries. The Nazis continued to gain ground, and in January 1933 Hitler was named the nation's chancellor. Using intimidation and violence, he eliminated competing political parties. He also sent many political rivals to Dachau, Germany's first concentration camp, established for people who were considered enemies of the party. By the summer of 1933, Hitler had become dictator, holding absolute power over the German government and people.

Jewish Learning and Culture Thrive

Following World War I, even as antisemitism grew, more and more Jews sought to explore and understand Judaism. In Germany, for example, some young Jews developed a new interest in Jewish spirituality and mysticism. Franz Rosenzweig, a philosopher who had once considered converting to Christianity, opened in Frankfurt the Free Jewish Lehrhaus ("house of learning"). Jewish libraries and adult education programs multiplied throughout Germany.

In Poland, Jewish literature, theater, rabbinic scholarship, and dozens of Jewish newspapers flourished in Yiddish, Hebrew, and Polish. To increase popular knowledge of the Talmud, Rabbi Meir Shapira began a program in which Jews throughout Poland would study a page of the Talmud each day (with everyone on any given day studying the same page). To this day, Jews around the world follow this program, called *daf yomi* in Hebrew.

Deprived of the freedom to study or work in their chosen field, Jews sought to earn a living in new ways. Charitable organizations, like the United Jewish Appeal, provided money for professional retraining and for the settlement of Jews in Palestine.

Living conditions for Jews in Germany immediately worsened. New laws expelled Jews from all government positions and from many professions, including teaching. On April 1, 1933, the Nazis declared a general boycott of all Jewish shops, goods, lawyers, and doctors. Some Jews were kidnapped, beaten, or shot. Others were imprisoned in concentration camps. (Fifty such camps had been established in Germany.) On September 15, 1935, the Nuremberg Laws officially stripped Jews of their basic rights, including German citizenship. 🦁

Part Five
Devastation and Rebirth

Chapter 22

The Holocaust
The Monstrous Cost of Intolerance and Indifference

From the moment he took power in Germany, Adolf Hitler made the rebuilding of the German military a top priority. Hitler quickly constructed one of the most powerful war machines the world had ever seen and began building an empire. With each new conquest, a larger percentage of Europe's Jews fell under his control. First, in 1938, Germany annexed the neighboring country of Austria with its two hundred thousand Jews. Then, in 1939, it seized Czechoslovakia, home to three hundred and sixty thousand Jews.

World War II began on September 1, 1939, when German forces struck east into Poland, home of Europe's largest Jewish community—more than three million Jews. In 1940 Hitler conquered Denmark, Norway, Holland, Belgium, and France. The next year he drove deep into the Soviet Union. By the end of 1941, Hitler controlled the fate of nearly nine million Jews. He had vowed "to settle the Jewish problem." Now it was within his power to fulfill this chilling promise.

The Night of Shattered Glass

On November 9, 1938, at 7 AM in Cologne, Ann Schwarz was awakened by screams. Hearing someone shout, "The synagogue is burning," she quickly rose and went outside. Nazi storm troopers were smashing the windows of her

TIMELINE

1938	Kristallnacht attacks against Jews take place throughout Germany
1939	World War II begins in Europe
1940	Nazis establish the Warsaw Ghetto
1941	At Babi Yar, 33,000 Jews are massacred; United States enters World War II after the Japanese bomb Pearl Harbor
1943	Warsaw Ghetto Uprising is planned and executed

World History

1944	*Harvard Mark I computer, the first large-scale digital computer in the United States, is invented*
1945	Germany surrenders to the Allies; Japan surrenders after the United States drops atomic bombs on Hiroshima and Nagasaki; World War II ends

family's bakery. Shattered glass was flying and the storm troopers completely destroyed the store. Ann went to the police station and was told, "Go home. We can't help you."

This government-supported pogrom was one of many similar attacks against Jews throughout Germany on what has become known as Kristallnacht, "night of shattered glass." Synagogues and homes were destroyed, stores were looted, and thousands of Jewish men were rounded up and taken to concentration camps.

Those Jews who could left Germany immediately. They sought refuge elsewhere in Europe, in Palestine, or in the United States. Those who did not get far enough away would meet up with Hitler again as he conquered neighboring lands and set in motion the Holocaust, or Shoah, as it is known in Hebrew—the Nazi's deadly international campaign against the Jews.

World War II

Before World War II began, Germany and the Soviet Union had agreed not to go to war against each other. Hitler had had no intention of keeping his pact with Joseph Stalin; he simply wanted to defeat other European armies before confronting the Soviets. Indeed, the German military quickly conquered most of Europe in 1939 and 1940. By early 1941 Great Britain stood alone against Hitler. Then, in June 1941, Hitler broke Germany's pact with the Soviet Union and attacked Russia.

Hitler had already joined forces with Italy and Japan, forming the Axis Powers. After Japan attacked the United States at Pearl Harbor in December 1941, the United States entered the war. Hitler now faced three great foes simultaneously—Great Britain, the Soviet Union, and the United States, known collectively as the Allied Powers. But the Allied forces were not then strong enough to attack Nazi-controlled Europe: Hitler ruled the continent, and that dominance allowed him to carry out his plan to eliminate the Jews of Europe.

As soon as the war began, the Nazis moved rapidly and methodically against the Jews. First, they evicted Jews from their homes, taking most of their belongings from them. Then, in an effort to isolate them, they packed many of them into overcrowded ghettos. Other Jews were forced into concentration camps, which had been quickly built all over German-held Eastern Europe. Jews healthy enough to work were used as slave labor for German war industries. Others were beaten, starved to death, or simply shot.

Jews were rounded up and marched through the streets as bystanders looked on.

Jews were not the only victims of the Germans: Romanies (often called gypsies), homo-sexuals, Communists, and anyone else considered an opponent of the state were also targeted. The Jews, however, were attacked with special ferocity. Even non-Jewish de-scendants of Jews were considered to be Jews by "race" and were persecuted.

Special mobile killing forces traveled behind the German army as it stormed into the Soviet Union. After the Germans conquered an area, the killing units would gather all the Jews and murder them. Sometimes the Nazis used gas vans—mobile gas chambers mounted on cargo trucks—to kill their victims; more commonly they collected the Jewish population of an entire town, drove the people into the woods, had them dig a mass grave, and shot them dead on the spot. In a period of less than forty-eight hours at Babi Yar, a ravine northwest of Kiev, thirty-three thousand Jews were robbed of their valuables, stripped, lined up, and shot, their lifeless bodies falling into the pit.

Historians estimate that by the end of 1941 the Nazis had worked to death, starved, shot, or gassed about one million Jews. But even that rate was not fast enough for Hitler.

In 1939 about 950 Jewish refugees left Germany on the ocean liner *St. Louis*, hoping to find a safe haven from Nazi persecution. But most were turned away from Cuba and the United States, and forced to return to Europe. Many of them eventually died in Nazi concentration camps. Here we see Jewish residents of Cuba helplessly watching as friends and family depart on the *St. Louis*.

Dreams of Escape

Jews throughout Europe sought escape—to America, to Palestine, to any place that would take them. Thousands of Jews did manage to escape, but far more were trapped. Most of the nations of the world, including the United States and Canada, had quotas limiting the number of Jews they permitted to enter.

The American economy was still suffering from the Depression, and antisemitism was on the rise. Two-thirds of Americans in 1938 believed that Jewish refugees should be kept out of the country. Even a bill to admit twenty thousand refugee children was defeated. When asked how many Jews should be admitted to Canada, Frederick Charles Blair, the director of the Immigration Branch of the Canadian Department of Mines and Resources, responded, "None is too many."

Other countries were no better. England refused to allow Jewish refugees to enter Palestine. Latin American nations admitted some but then closed their doors. Cuba actually revoked the entry permits of many Jews already in Cuba.

The Final Solution

When Hitler saw that no country would accept masses of Jewish refugees, he became even bolder in his plans. In 1941, after the invasion of the Soviet Union, he and other high-level Nazi officials began discussing what they eventually called the "final solution" to the Jewish problem: a plan to murder all European Jews.

By the spring of 1942 the Nazis had built a series of extermination camps in such places as Sobibor, Treblinka, and Auschwitz. These death camps were designed as efficient factories of mass murder. Railroad tracks ran directly to the camp entrances. Huge gas chambers were built, enabling camp officials to use poison gas to murder hundreds of Jews at once.

The Germans preferred the extermination camps to any other methods of mass murder: The camps produced the most efficient results. Most of the Jews of Greece—Sephardic Jews—were deported to Auschwitz in the spring of 1943 and killed. A year later some 437,000 Jews from Hungary were sent to Auschwitz in just two months. Most of them were murdered, too.

Liberation

By 1944, Germany was clearly losing the war. In June, after the unprecedented landing at Normandy, Allied forces began driving east toward Germany. Soviet forces, meanwhile, had pushed the Germans out of Soviet territory and were rolling west toward Germany. On April 30, 1945, with the Soviet army closing in on Berlin, Hitler shot and killed himself. Germany surrendered on May 7.

Resistance

Although Jews were practically powerless in the face of the German war machine, there were those who resisted. For some, resistance meant struggling to survive in the camps. For others, it involved a spiritual act: practicing Judaism in the face of the Nazi threat. For still others, resistance meant taking up arms. Beginning in 1942, as Jews learned more about the Nazi death camps, some escaped to the forests of Europe to join the underground movement. Others, determined to fight to the death, gathered weapons in Jewish ghettos.

In Warsaw a German effort to deport Jews to concentration camps on the eve of Passover 1943 met with massive resistance. Most of the resisters died and the ghetto was destroyed, but the story of the Warsaw Ghetto Uprising inspired Jews and non-Jews alike.

In another act of resistance, at Auschwitz on October 7, 1944, Jews dynamited one of the crematoriums and killed several guards. More than twenty-three other Jewish uprisings in ghettos, labor camps, and death camps have been documented.

FAMOUS FIGURES

Anne Frank

Anne Frank was born in Germany in 1929. Her family fled to Holland to escape the Nazis when she was four years old. Their safety was short-lived, however, because the Nazis took control of the Netherlands in 1940 and began sending Jews to concentration camps in 1942. Unable to secure exit visas, Anne's family chose to go into hiding. They found refuge in a secret set of rooms adjacent to Anne's father's business in Amsterdam. There they lived with several other Jews— Fritz Pfeffer and the Van Pels family—until August 4, 1944, when the police discovered them and sent them to a concentration camp. Anne died less than a year later, at age fifteen.

From June 12, 1942, to August 1, 1944, Anne kept a diary. In it she wrote that after the war she would publish a book based on the diary. Although Anne did not live to fulfill her dream, her father, Otto Frank, did survive the war and published the diary.

On Thursday, July 6, 1944, Anne wrote: "We're all alive, but we don't know why or what for; we're all searching for happiness; we're all leading lives that are different and yet the same. . . . Earning happiness means doing good and working."

Anne Frank.

The War Against
the Jews

- ▣ Concentration camps
- ◼ Extermination camps
- ● Large-scale massacres
- ◯ Large ghettoes
- ◉ Large ghetto; large-scale massacre

Before the Holocaust, more than nine million Jews lived in Europe. By the end of the Holocaust, only about three million were still alive.

As the Germans retreated, they tried to destroy evidence of their crimes, blowing up gas chambers and burning documents. But they didn't have time to complete the massive task. The first extermination camp to be liberated by the Allies was Majdanek, in Lublin, Poland, in July 1944. Over the following year, the rest of the camps were liberated.

At least six million Jews were dead: gassed, shot, starved, beaten, left to die by disease and exposure, or killed on the death marches as Allied troops closed in on Germany late in the war. Roughly three million European Jews survived: Some had managed to escape the continent. Others had been saved by non-Jews who hid and otherwise assisted them. Still others were found alive in the death camps themselves.

Jewish underground fighters.

Righteous Gentiles

Amid the terror and tragedy of the Holocaust, there were heroic non-Jews, known as Righteous Gentiles, who showed great courage and humanity by risking their lives to save the lives of Jews. In Budapest a Swedish diplomat named Raoul Wallenberg issued Swedish citizenship papers to Hungarian Jews. Sweden was neutral in the war, making Swedish citizens off-limits to Nazi forces. Wallenberg also set up "Swedish houses," buildings flying the Swedish flag, where Jews could live in safety. His efforts saved tens of thousands of Hungarian Jews.

Similarly, tens of thousands of Jewish children, known as hidden children, were saved by Righteous Gentiles. The children were hidden in such places as convents or were "adopted" by Christian families who pretended that they were their own children.

DEATH TOLL OF EUROPEAN JEWS			
Poland	2,700,000	Yugoslavia	51,400
Soviet Union	2,100,000	Austria	48,767
Hungary	559,250	Belgium *(including people of other nationalities)*	28,000
Germany	144,000		
Czechoslovakia	143,000	Bulgaria	7,335
		Italy	5,596
Romania	120,919	Norway	758
Netherlands	102,000	Luxembourg	720
France *(including people of other nationalities)*	76,000	Albania	591
Greece	58,443	Denmark	116

After the war, Europe was no longer the spiritual center of world Jewry; far more Jews now lived in North America. Many of the surviving European Jews left for non-European Jewish communities, especially in the United States, Canada, and Australia. Those Jews who did return to their homes found themselves part of much smaller Jewish communities or, in fact, found nothing at all. Yet other survivors left for Palestine, convinced that the Jewish future lay in the Land of Israel.

Chapter 23

The Birth of the Modern State of Israel
From Dream to Reality

The Big Picture

People liked to say he was the first Jewish general since Judah Maccabee. New Yorker David "Mickey" Marcus had shown little interest in Zionism until he came face-to-face with Nazi atrocities upon visiting the Dachau concentration camp shortly after it was liberated. Marcus's interactions with its survivors convinced him that the Jews needed a homeland of their own. Three years later he was in Palestine helping to turn the underground Haganah into a disciplined, modern army and playing a critical role in the War of Independence.

Mickey Marcus was motivated by a strong sense of Jewish unity. This same spirit gave the Jews of Palestine the courage to stand up to the British and the determination to defeat the Arabs. It motivated their concern for Jews in distress and inspired lifesaving efforts, like the airlifts of Jews from Iraq and Yemen that were organized by the newly established State of Israel.

The Survivors

Europe was in shambles. Millions of people had been displaced by the war, including hundreds of thousands of Holocaust survivors. The Allied armies and the United Nations Relief and Rehabilitation Administration (UNRRA) provided aid for the displaced persons (DPs), helping to return them to their countries of origin.

TIMELINE

1946	Irgun bombs the King David Hotel in Jerusalem

World History

1947	*Jackie Robinson plays for the Brooklyn Dodgers, ending segregation in Major League Baseball*
1947	The *Exodus 1947* sets sail for Palestine carrying more than 4,500 Jewish refugees; UN General Assembly votes to partition Palestine into Jewish and Arab states
1948	Independent modern State of Israel is established
1949	Israel holds its first election; Operation Magic Carpet begins, bringing about 47,000 Jews from Yemen to Israel

But many Jews refused to go home. Most of their loved ones were dead, and the lives they had known before the war were shattered beyond repair. Other Jews returned to their towns and villages only to find they were not wanted. In Poland, antisemitism was so virulent that some Jews were brutally attacked by their former neighbors.

Jewish underground soldiers and soldiers from the British army's Jewish Brigade secretly helped move many survivors across the Polish border to DP camps, or refugee camps, in Germany, Austria, and Italy. Some camps were located on the sites of former concentration camps, such as Bergen-Belsen. By 1947, the camps were teeming with refugees, including 250,000 Jews. At first there were terrible shortages of food and clothing. The UN and various nongovernmental organizations worked to improve conditions. The American Jewish Joint Distribution Committee provided the survivors with food, clothing, school supplies, books, and religious articles such as Bibles.

Underground Resistance

The Jewish underground militias in Palestine used force to pressure Britain to change its policies. For eighteen months the Haganah, Irgun, and Lehi (Loheim Heirut Yisrael, Fighters for the Freedom of Israel) sabotaged railway tracks and attacked police posts, airfields, and radar installations. The British sent eighty thousand troops to Palestine to quash the violence and round up the attackers.

Cooperation among the Jewish militias fell apart after the bombing of the British military and civilian headquarters in Jerusalem's King David Hotel on July 22, 1946. About ninety people—Britons, Arabs, and Jews—were killed. The plot's mastermind, Irgun leader Menahem Begin, claimed that warnings had been given.

The attacks and British retaliations continued, but the hotel bombing soured much of the Yishuv on the use of terror. Yishuv leaders did not want an all-out war with the British and even urged parents to turn in their own children if they joined one of the militias.

The Jewish Refugees

Even after the war the British refused to abolish the White Paper of 1939 and allow DPs to immigrate to Palestine. Dependent on Middle Eastern oil, the British did not want to anger the Arabs. In order to increase pressure on the British, the Haganah brought thousands of DPs to southern Europe, whence they set sail for Palestine. But in 90 percent of the cases the British stopped the ships before they reached Palestine, sending the Jews to detention camps instead.

In January 1947, hurting from severe economic problems and unable to effectively address the competing demands of the Arabs and Jews, Britain handed over the problem in Palestine to the UN, which created the United Nations Special Committee on Palestine (UNSCOP). Composed of representatives of eleven neutral countries, UNSCOP was assigned the job of investigating the situation and reporting on it to the UN General Assembly.

Exodus 1947

While the UN was beginning its work, the Haganah continued its efforts to bring refugees to Palestine. The *Exodus 1947*, a former American passenger ship that the Haganah had acquired and renamed, set sail for Palestine from France in July 1947 with over forty-five hundred Jewish refugees aboard, including 655 children. As the ship neared Palestine, British destroyers rammed it, and crew members boarded it. The passengers tried to defend themselves and a short battle ensued: two refugees and one Jewish crew member died, and thirty people were injured.

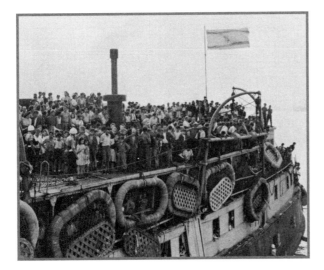

Passengers on the *Exodus 1947*. A year after being turned back to the DP camps in Germany, more than half the *Exodus 1947* passengers attempted *aliyah* again and were successful. The remaining passengers settled in Israel after the establishment of the nation in 1948.

The British towed the ship to Haifa's harbor, forced the refugees onto British navy transports, and returned them to Europe. When the transports arrived in France, the passengers refused to disembark and declared a hunger strike. Nonetheless, the British forced them to return to DP camps in Germany.

UNSCOP members in Palestine on a fact-finding mission witnessed the events in Haifa harbor with horror. Newspapers gave the story front-page coverage, calling the *Exodus 1947* a "floating Auschwitz." The incident helped sway world opinion in favor of the Zionists.

The UN Plan

The UNSCOP report, presented in August 1947, recommended the cessation of the British mandate. A majority of the committee members backed the partition of Palestine into separate states—one Jewish, the other Arab—with Jerusalem under international authority.

The Arabs were outraged and threatened war. They outnumbered Jews two to one in Palestine yet were to receive only about 45 percent of the territory. Why, they protested, should they pay the price for Europe's persecution of the Jews? The Jews, who believed they had been promised a much larger territory by the Balfour Declaration, nevertheless accepted the partition plan, which promised them self-rule and unlimited immigration.

On November 29, 1947, the UN General Assembly voted on the partition plan. The final vote was 33 in favor and 13 against, with 10 abstentions. The British announced they would leave Palestine in May 1948.

As crowds of Jews celebrated the news in Jerusalem's streets, they were addressed by Golda Myerson, the leader of the Yishuv: "For two thousand years we have waited for our deliverance. . . . Now that it is here it is so great and so wonderful that it surpasses human words. Jews, *mazal tov!*" David Ben-Gurion was less sanguine. "I could not dance, I could not sing that night," he later recalled. "I looked at them so happy dancing, but I could only think that they were all going to war."

Israel's War of Independence

Finally, on the morning of May 14, 1948, the British lowered their flag at the Government House in Jerusalem. At 4 PM, Jewish leaders gathered in the Tel Aviv Museum under a portrait of Theodor Herzl. Ben-Gurion banged his gavel to bring the gathering to order, and the crowd spontaneously began singing "Hatikvah." Ben-Gurion then read the Scroll of Independence, proclaiming, "We, members of the People's Council, representatives of the Jewish community of Eretz Yisrael and of the Zionist movement . . . hereby proclaim the establishment of a Jewish State in Eretz Yisrael, to be called the State of Israel."

But there was little time for celebration. Before dawn on the next day, Egyptian fighter planes attacked Tel Aviv. Arab armies from neighboring countries launched an invasion on three fronts, but by early June the Israelis had gained strength, stopping the Egyptian advance in the south and repelling attacks from the Syrians and Iraqis in the northeast.

Israel made important gains in the later stages of the war, capturing the Negev in the south and widening the narrow corridor of land between Jerusalem and Tel Aviv. By the time the

Fighting for Control of Palestine

Between December 1947 and May 1948, as the British looked on, hostilities raged between the Zionists and the Arabs. In the early months of the fighting, the Jews were on the defensive. The road between Tel Aviv and Jerusalem was cut off, and the Jewish community in Jerusalem was under fire. In mid-March, an arms shipment from Czechoslovakia helped the Haganah gain the offensive. By early May it had captured Haifa, Jaffa, and most of the Galilee.

Meanwhile, Arab militias and the Irgun and Lehi engaged in a tit-for-tat campaign of terror. Houses, buses, office buildings, oil refineries, and hotels were bombed and ambushed. Hundreds of Jewish and Arab civilians were killed. In mid-April, Irgun and Lehi fighters attacked the Arab village of Deir Yassin, along the Tel Aviv–Jerusalem road, killing more than one hundred civilians. Hearing of the violence, many Arabs in surrounding areas fled. Days after the Deir Yassin attack, Arab militiamen ambushed a ten-vehicle convoy of Jewish doctors and nurses headed for Hadassah hospital, murdering more than seventy Jews.

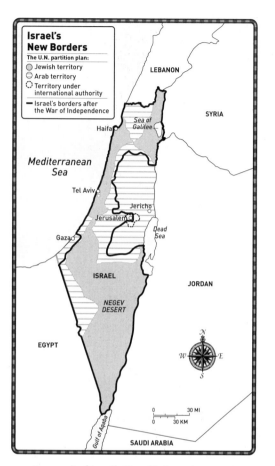

Israel's New Borders

The U.N. partition plan:
- Jewish territory
- Arab territory
- Territory under international authority
- Israel's borders after the War of Independence

LEBANON

SYRIA

Sea of Galilee

Haifa

Mediterranean Sea

Tel Aviv

Jericho

Jerusalem

Gaza

Dead Sea

ISRAEL

JORDAN

NEGEV DESERT

EGYPT

N
W — E
S

0   30 MI
0   30 KM

Gulf of Aqaba

SAUDI ARABIA

As a result of Israel's War of Independence Israel's borders were expanded.

fighting ended, Israel controlled 80 percent of Palestine. Jordan controlled the West Bank and East Jerusalem, including the Old City, and Egypt controlled the Gaza Strip.

Casualties were heavy on both sides, but there was no doubt that Israel had won the war and gained its independence. Early on there were signs that the Arab states might negotiate permanent peace treaties with Israel. The Israelis considered Arab demands for territory too high, however. "The neighboring states do not deserve an inch of Israel's land," insisted Ben-Gurion. "We are ready for peace in exchange for peace." In the end, no peace treaties were signed.

On January 25, 1949, Israel held its first election. Ben-Gurion's Labor Party won the most seats and formed the first government with Ben-Gurion as prime minister.

The Palestinian Refugees

What Israel calls the War of Independence is known in Palestinian history as the *Naqba,* or "Catastrophe." During the war, more than 700,000 Arabs fled or were forced from their homes in the territory that became the State of Israel and when the war was over, the Israeli government would not allow them to return. The Israelis feared that the Arabs would not support the Jewish State and might eventually become the majority, thereby posing a threat to the Jewish character of Israel. Many Palestinian refugees never gave up the hope of returning to their former homes.

The more than 150,000 Arabs who remained in Israel, meanwhile, were officially granted equal rights under Israel's Scroll of Independence. But in practice the government was suspicious of their loyalties. Military rule was declared over many Arab towns and villages

FAMOUS FIGURES

Golda Myerson Meir

Golda Mabovitch was born in Kiev in 1898, immigrated to the United States with her family, and became a schoolteacher and passionate Zionist. In 1921 she and her husband, Morris Myerson, settled on Kibbutz Merḥavyah in Palestine.

Golda Myerson quickly became active in Zionist politics. Among her many contributions were the secret negotiations she conducted with Jordan's King Abdullah, which helped limit Jordan's involvement in Israel's War of Independence. In 1956 at Prime Minister Ben-Gurion's request, she changed her name from Myerson to Meir, a Hebrew name. She was foreign minister of Israel from 1956 to 1966 and became Israel's fourth prime minister in 1969. She died in 1978.

Meir was one of only two women to sign Israel's declaration of independence. She later recalled: "After I signed, I cried. When I studied American history as a schoolgirl and I read about those who signed the Declaration of Independence, I couldn't imagine these were real people doing something real. And there I was . . . signing a declaration of independence."

Golda Meir.

near Israel's borders and was lifted only in 1966. Studies indicate that discrimination against Arab communities and individuals continues to this day.

A Flood of Newcomers

With the hostilities over, chief among Israel's challenges was absorbing the waves of immigrants flooding the country. They came from Europe and the Middle East, by boat, by airplane, and even on foot. Between 1948 and 1951, almost 700,000 Jews arrived in Israel, substantially increasing the size of its Jewish population.

Holocaust survivors continued to immigrate to Israel into the 1960s. Many came from Communist countries, where it often took years to obtain an exit visa. This young soldier, Elimelech Wasserman, and his parents, who were survivors, waited twelve years for permission to immigrate. Like many new immigrants, Wasserman's stint in the army facilitated his absorption into Israeli society.

Nearly half the newcomers were Holocaust survivors, including 136,000 DPs. (The remaining 115,000 mostly immigrated to the United States, Canada, Australia, and South Africa.) The other immigrants arrived from Middle Eastern and North African countries—some of the oldest Jewish communities in the world. These Jews are referred to as Eidot Hamizrah ("Congregations of the East"), or Mizrahi ("Eastern") Jews.

With conditions for Jews in many Arab countries having deteriorated after the creation of the State of Israel, many Mizrahi Jews left their homes eager to start a new life in Israel and such Western countries as France, the United States, and Canada. But others, especially in North Africa, were attached to their homes and their cultures and were less willing to leave. Continuing Arab-Israeli tension, particularly in the 1960s, eventually forced most of them to evacuate. By 1974, more than 600,000 Mizrahi refugees had settled in Israel.

In a secret airlift called Operation Magic Carpet, about 47,000 Jews from Yemen were brought to Israel. Many walked hundreds of miles across rugged terrain to the British

Palestinians as Pawns

Using the Palestinian Arab refugees as pawns in a game of politics served the purposes of both the Arab and the Israeli governments. Arab governments, with the exception of Jordan, refused to accept the refugees as citizens of their own countries because they wanted the refugee problem to be a thorn in Israel's side. So they kept the Palestinians in refugee camps along their border with Israel, where the Palestinians' anger and frustration would grow and their plight would be on display for the world to see. Israel, for its part, wanted to pressure the Arabs to negotiate a peace treaty. So it refused to compensate the Palestinians until a more comprehensive agreement could be worked out.

colony of Aden, where the Joint Distribution Committee cared for them until American planes could fly them to safety. Between 1950 and 1951, 120,000 Jews were evacuated to Israel from Iraq in Operation Ezra and Nehemiah. Tens of thousands of Jews arrived from Morocco and Libya.

Helping these immigrants learn Hebrew, find homes, and earn a living was a huge task. Half were between the ages of fifteen and forty-five and were able to enter the army or the workforce, but only half of the immigrants in that group were skilled in a trade or a profession, and only 16 percent had a high school or higher education. Housing, in particular, was a major problem. Immigrants were arriving faster than homes could be

Most passengers on Operation Magic Carpet had never *seen* a plane before, let alone *flown* in one.

built. Many of the earliest immigrants, mostly survivors from Europe, moved into houses that had been vacated by fleeing Arabs. When that supply of housing was exhausted, many immigrants lived temporarily in tent camps and *ma'abarot*, makeshift shantytowns.

The Challenges of Diversity

Many long-established Israelis looked down on Mizraḥi Jews, showing little regard for their customs and traditions, and government policies encouraged Mizraḥi Jews to shed their cultural distinctiveness and assimilate into Israeli society. Such policies engendered mistrust, anger, and resentment in the immigrants.

One government official warned in 1949 that the Mizraḥi immigrants were becoming "a kind of second nation." As time went on, the second-class status of the Mizraḥi Jews became set. In general, the Mizraḥi Jews were more poorly educated, held lower-paying jobs, and were overrepresented in prisons and underrepresented in government.

In Israel, as in the United States and other democracies, the challenge to offer equal opportunity and balance national unity with respect for diversity continues.

A Foundation of Challenges and Achievements

By the early 1950s, major problems that continue to confront Israel today were already clear—in particular, social inequality, the status of Israeli Arabs, the conflict with Israel's Arab neighbors, and the problem of the Palestinian refugees. But the founders of the modern State of Israel also had achieved many successes. After two thousand years they had reestablished an independent Jewish state. Moreover, in just a few years Israel had doubled its population and had transformed diverse groups of people, each with its own culture, language, and set of views, into a single people working toward a common future.

Chapter 24

Making It in America, 1945–1965
Golden Decades

The Big Picture

Baseball has long been a symbol of American culture. So it makes sense that American Jews swelled with pride as they cheered for Hank Greenberg, baseball's first Jewish superstar. Greenberg's success in the 1930s and 1940s became a symbol of the Jews' success in America.

The child of immigrants, Greenberg never tried to hide his Jewish identity by changing his name. In fact, he wore it as a badge of honor. "I just had to show that a Jew could play ball," Greenberg once explained. "I came to feel that if I, as a Jew, hit a home run, I was hitting one against Hitler."

That a Jew could master America's favorite pastime seemed to prove that Jews were no longer outsiders. Indeed, the years between 1945 and 1965 are sometimes referred to as the Golden Decades in American Jewish history. Jews joined synagogues in record numbers and became prominent political and civil rights activists as expressions of both their American and their Jewish identities.

Postwar Opportunities

Americans were eager to make a fresh start after World War II. Returning soldiers were especially eager to settle down and put their energy into work and family. In 1944, Congress created a program, popularly known as the GI Bill of Rights, to help soldiers pay for a college education

TIMELINE

1947 William Levitt begins building the suburban community of Levittown

1950 Julius and Ethel Rosenberg are arrested on charges of spying for the Soviet Union

1951 Olin-Sang-Ruby Union Institute (OSRUI), the first Reform summer camp in United States, is founded

1954 Jews have been living in North America for 300 years

World History

1957 *Soviet Union launches the space satellite Sputnik I*

1964 Two Jewish civil rights workers are murdered by members of the Ku Klux Klan in Mississippi

1965 One third of the American Jewish community is now living in the suburbs

Growing interest in the American Jewish consumer is seen in this 1940s Yiddish brochure for Tide laundry detergent.

and buy a home. Thousands of Jewish veterans who could not have afforded college before the war now could. At the same time, many universities were abolishing the quotas that had limited Jewish enrollment.

Young families were eager to move from the inner cities to the suburbs. Larger disposable incomes and the growing network of highways helped make this dream possible. William Levitt, a Jewish builder from Brooklyn, recognized the growing demand for inexpensive suburban housing. Levitt had used the techniques of mass production to build housing for

Heading South

Postwar Americans, including Jews, were moving by the thousands to the Sunbelt. Cities like Los Angeles and Miami were magnets for Jews. Many Jewish GIs from the north had done their basic military training in the Sunbelt and had fallen in love with the climate and, sometimes, with a young woman or man from the area. By 1960 there were almost four hundred thousand Jews living in Los Angeles and close to two hundred thousand in Miami. Miami was especially attractive to senior citizens from the Northeast eager to escape the icy winter months. Cheaper air travel and the invention of air conditioning helped speed up the move to the South.

defense workers during the war. Now he quickly built inexpensive homes on Long Island, about twenty miles east of New York City. Soon his technique had spread, and similar suburban communities mushroomed around urban centers throughout North America.

By 1948 there were enough Jews in Levittown, Long Island, to support a synagogue. The popularity of the suburban lifestyle continued to grow, and by 1965 one-third of the American Jewish community was living in suburban communities around the country.

Antisemitism on the Decline

Antisemitism, which peaked just before and during World War II, greatly declined in the late 1940s and into the 1950s. Nazism had made bigotry seem less respectable to most people. Military service also softened prejudices. Americans who had never been exposed to Jews before fought side by side with them. They learned that Jews were loyal fighters and that the similarities between Jews and non-Jews outweighed religious or ethnic differences. Finally, as economic conditions improved, people were less likely to seek scapegoats for their financial problems.

By the 1950s, American Jews were receiving widespread acceptance. Judaism had become acknowledged as America's third great faith, alongside Protestantism and Catholicism. American leaders began to speak routinely of the country's Judeo-Christian values rather than its Christian values. And television stations began wishing viewers not only a Merry Christmas but also a Happy Ḥanukkah.

New York City Mayor Fiorello LaGuardia (center, holding hat) at a pro-tolerance rally circa 1944.

Jews and McCarthyism

Although the increased acceptance helped American Jews feel more secure than ever, many Jews continued to feel vulnerable. They feared that any negative information about the Jewish community could trigger a backlash from the American public.

Some were concerned that such a backlash could result from the rising fear of communism that was sweeping the United States in the late 1940s and early 1950s. Tensions between the United States and the Soviet Union were high, and many Americans worried that Communists might secretly be weakening America from within. The U.S. House of Representatives and Senate held hearings meant to expose Communists in the entertainment industry, the government, and the military. Senator Joseph McCarthy gained notoriety for his aggressive style of accusing witnesses of harboring Communist sympathies, usually without evidence. The attitude displayed and tactics used by McCarthy and his followers would become known as McCarthyism.

Jews were particularly concerned because sizable numbers of them had been members of the Socialist or Communist Party before World War II. Many had broken with communism after Stalin's 1939 alliance with Hitler. Still others had abandoned communism when they learned of Stalin's violent persecution of Jews. But some Jews had remained committed Communists or Socialists. Now Jewish groups had to deal with those members of the community and their impact on the public's view of Jews as a whole.

Many American Jewish organizations responded to the fear and the hysteria of the time by firing employees who were known or even suspected Communists. Some Jewish organizations directed community centers not to invite Communist speakers to their events. In Hollywood, movie studios, including those run by Jews, refused to hire blacklisted talent—those writers, directors, producers, and actors who had, or were suspected of having, ties to the Communist Party.

Many careers and lives were ruined by the time McCarthyism died out in the mid-1950s. But even in its heyday, McCarthyism never developed into an antisemitic movement, and antisemitism in the United States continued to decline.

Remaking Judaism

If a fear of communism was characteristic of postwar America, so, too, was a religious revival. Christian Americans were flocking to churches in greater numbers than during the Depression and World War II. American Jews participated in this revival, joining synagogues and sending their children to religious schools in record numbers, although

Julius and Ethel Rosenberg

In August 1949 the Soviet Union tested its first atomic bomb. Shocked at the speed with which Soviet scientists had developed the bomb, U.S. officials suspected that they must have received secret information from spies in America. The following year, Julius and Ethel Rosenberg were arrested on charges of spying for the Soviet Union.

The Rosenbergs proclaimed their innocence, and left-wing groups insisted that the charges against them were motivated by antisemitism. Yet most Jewish leaders who believed the Rosenbergs might be innocent refused to defend them publicly, even after they were tried and sentenced to death.

The Rosenbergs' guilt has been debated ever since. Today newly discovered documents have convinced most historians that Julius Rosenberg did pass atomic secrets to the Russians. It is believed that Ethel played at most a supportive role in the affair. It is noteworthy that the Rosenbergs were the only convicted spies to be executed during the cold war period, and they remain the only American civilians to be executed for espionage.

their rate of synagogue attendance was nonetheless much lower than the Christians' rate of church attendance.

Increased prosperity and the move to suburbia helped fuel the greatest synagogue building boom in American history. More than a thousand synagogues were built between 1945 and 1965. They included not only sanctuaries for prayer, but also religious-school classrooms, social halls, and sometimes even recreational facilities, such as gyms and swimming pools.

The New Synagogues: Sacred Centers or Social Centers?

Most of the new synagogue centers were established by the Conservative and Reform movements because suburban Jews looked to the synagogue not so much as a house of prayer but as a substitute for the urban ethnic communities they had left behind.

For many members of the new synagogues, the social, recreational, and educational components of the synagogue center were far more central to their daily lives than was the sanctuary. The definition of a "good Jew," for these members, did not require regularly attending prayer services, observing Shabbat, or keeping kosher.

The Conservative movement had continued to grow quickly; it was now growing especially rapidly and soon became the largest movement in American Judaism. While maintaining a great deal of traditional observance, it introduced new approaches and practices. In 1950, for example, its law committee voted to allow Jews to drive to synagogue and to use electricity on Shabbat. Although these innovations angered some traditionalists, they appealed to many second- and third-generation Jews, who wanted a modernized Judaism but wished to maintain their ties to the practices of their youth.

The Reform movement was also growing and evolving. By the late 1950s and early 1960s many Reform rabbis had energized their congregants by emphasizing prophetic Judaism, or the ethical teachings of the Hebrew prophets. In particular they provided leadership on issues of social justice, such as civil rights.

Judaism Continues to Evolve

As Jews became increasingly Americanized, they continued to reshape Judaism. Think about the evolution of the bar mitzvah celebration. It was once a simple synagogue ritual in which a thirteen-year-old boy was called to the Torah for the first time. Then, in the 1960s, bat mitzvah ceremonies became popular in many American communities. And today some adults who did not have a bar or bat mitzvah ceremony as a teenager participate in adult versions of the ritual.

Over time the celebratory parties have become much more lavish, complete with catered food and live entertainment. Today many American synagogues focus on the religious significance of becoming a bar or bat mitzvah by requiring students to participate in mitzvah projects, such as collecting food and clothing for the poor.

Jewish Activists

Thousands of Jews in the 1950s and 1960s, including many college students, participated in the struggle on behalf of civil rights for African Americans. Jews took part in sit-ins, freedom rides, and protest marches. In 1958, The Temple in Atlanta was bombed because its rabbi, Jacob Rothschild, was a passionate supporter of equality for all of Atlanta's citizens. For many Americans the bombing was a wake-up call, a reminder that anyone who dared speak out against social injustice could become a target of hatred.

In the summer of 1964, almost two-thirds of the white volunteers who participated in a black voter-registration drive in Mississippi were Jews. Two of those Jewish civil rights workers, Andrew Goodman and Michael Schwerner, were murdered by Ku Klux Klan members, along with a black colleague, James Earl Chaney.

Not all American Jews were happy about the high-profile involvement of Jews in the civil rights movement, however. Many southern Jews resented the northern Jewish civil rights workers. Indeed, the involvement of northern Jews in desegregation efforts sparked a wave of antisemitism directed against southern Jews. Some Jewish-owned businesses were boycotted and synagogues firebombed.

FAMOUS FIGURES

Abraham Joshua Heschel

Many rabbis were involved in the civil rights struggle. Among them was a leading Jewish thinker, Abraham Joshua Heschel. Born into a distinguished Hasidic family in Warsaw in 1907, Heschel received a traditional yeshiva education and was trained as an Orthodox rabbi. In 1934, he received his doctorate in philosophy in Berlin.

Heschel was deported to Poland by the Nazis in 1938. From Poland he went to England and then to America, where from 1940 to 1945 he taught at the Reform rabbinical seminary, Hebrew Union College, in Cincinnati. He taught at the Conservative movement's seminary, the Jewish Theological Seminary, in New York City from 1945 to his death, in 1972.

In March 1965, Heschel joined Martin Luther King Jr. and other leaders of the civil rights movement in a protest march in Selma, Alabama. "I felt as though my legs were praying," Heschel wrote in describing the event. A refugee from Nazism, he strongly believed that Jewish teachings demand active participation in advancing social justice. "The opposite of good is not evil," Heschel wrote. "The opposite of good is indifference."

Abraham Joshua Heschel and his wife Sylvia, with Pope Paul VI in 1964.

As the 1960s unfolded, American Jews helped lead other movements in the pursuit of justice. They were prominent among those demanding the right to free speech on college campuses, protesting U.S. involvement in Vietnam, and rallying for women's rights. Many were inspired by the prophetic Judaism promoted by liberal rabbis. Sacred teachings such as "Let justice well up as waters and righteousness as a mighty stream" (Amos 5:24) strengthened both their commitment to Judaism and their commitment to the pursuit of justice as Americans. Other American Jews felt alienated from Judaism, associating it with the suburban lifestyle of their parents, which they saw as spiritually hollow and materialistic.

Slugging Out the Conflicts

On most days, there is no conflict between the secular and religious beliefs and obligations of someone who is committed to Jewish life and practice. Such a person can buy a ticket to the movies *and* a kosher snack, go to work during the day *and* light Ḥanukkah candles at night, and sing "The Star Spangled Banner" at the ballpark *and* "Hatikvah" in the synagogue.

But sometimes there *are* conflicts. Two baseball superstars, Hank Greenberg and Sandy Koufax, faced a conflict that required a major decision—to play or not to play on the High Holidays. In 1934, with his Detroit Tigers in a tight pennant race, Hank Greenberg decided to play on Rosh Hashanah but not on Yom Kippur, by which time the Tigers had already clinched their division. In 1965 the Los Angeles Dodgers were in the World Series and wanted Sandy Koufax, their ace pitcher, to start Game 1. But the game fell on Yom Kippur—and Koufax decided not to pitch the game. The Dodgers lost the game but won the series.

The slugger Shawn Green is the latest Jewish star to face this dilemma. When he was playing for the Dodgers, Green sat out a key game in the 2001 play-offs because it was played on Yom Kippur.

The Price of Success

American Jews had made it in America. Antisemitism was on the decline, and increasingly the lifestyles of Jews were becoming similar to those of their non-Jewish neighbors. Jews had become solidly middle class in economic terms and were feeling secure enough to become active in social and political causes. There was no question that postwar America was good for the Jews. But was it good for Judaism?

By the 1950s the Judaism that immigrants had transported across the Atlantic had become thoroughly Americanized. The suburban synagogue building boom, the growth of the Conservative and Reform movements, and the increasing numbers of Jewish youth receiving some kind of Jewish education were hopeful signs for Judaism. But beneath the surface the warning signs were clear. The new synagogues were full only on the High Holidays. Many afternoon religious schools seemed to inspire their students with resentment rather than enthusiasm for Jewish learning and Jewish life. Rituals that were still widely observed in the ethnic city neighborhoods before World War II, like observing Shabbat and keeping kosher, were increasingly being abandoned. Worst of all, American Judaism seemed to lack meaning and value for some members of the younger generation.

Ironically, perhaps it was the success and acceptance of Jews and Judaism in America that had created the new challenges. With greater social acceptance, intermarriage rates were rising. In addition, as American Jews became wealthier and better educated, they were marrying later and having fewer children. These trends were summed up in a 1964 article in *Look* magazine titled "The Vanishing American Jew." How American Jews would respond to these challenges will be told in chapter 27.

Chapter 25

The Diaspora Consolidates
A Shrinking Jewish World

"The Jews are vanishing from Europe!"

This statement was not the jubilant claim of a fanatic antisemite but rather the warning of the respected Jewish historian Bernard Wasserstein, writing in 1996. Before World War II, he observed, Europe had been the home of more than nine million Jews. More than half of them died in the Holocaust. In the following years, European Jewry continued to decline. Some died without having children to carry on Jewish tradition; the rest moved elsewhere or abandoned their Jewish identities. Thus by 2005 there were only about one and a half million Jews in Europe.

What happened in Europe was repeated in much of the rest of the Diaspora. Before World War II, Jews lived in almost every country in the world. Travelers supplied colorful accounts of exotic Jewish communities in such places as China, Ethiopia, and Yemen. Yet since World War II the Jewish world has rapidly shrunk. Today over 80 percent of world Jewry lives in just two countries: the United States and Israel. In fact, by 2005, half of all Jews lived in just five metropolitan areas: Tel Aviv, New York, Los Angeles, Jerusalem, and Haifa.

The Former Soviet Union

The Soviet Union emerged from World War II with the world's second-largest Jewish population—an estimated

TIMELINE

1948 Israeli ambassador Golda Meir visits Soviet Jews in Moscow

1959 Helen Suzman helps form the anti-apartheid Progressive Party in South Africa

World History
1967 *First human heart transplant is performed by Christiaan Barnard in South Africa*

1979 Islamic revolution overthrows the government in Iran; thousands of Jews subsequently flee to escape persecution

1984 Operation Moses begins the airlift of Ethiopian Jews to Israel

1991 Soviet Union collapses; hundreds of thousand of Soviet Jews leave for Israel and the United States

1994 Terrorists bomb the Jewish Community Center in Buenos Aires

two million Jews; the only country with a larger Jewish population was the United States. Before World War II, Joseph Stalin had begun to persecute Soviet Jews, and after the war his policies became even more extreme. He ordered the murder of thousands of Jews and was especially obsessed with executing Jewish intellectuals, writers, and artists.

Romania was under Soviet control from the late 1940s until 1989. As in Russia, Jewish ritual objects were considered contraband. This bar mitzvah boy, Milu Wasserman, is wearing a prayer shawl, or tallit, that his father smuggled out of the Israeli embassy in Bucharest.

Stalin's successor, Nikita Khrushchev, was openly critical of many of Stalin's policies—but not of his antisemitism. Although Khrushchev was less violent, he continued in Stalin's footsteps. He denied Jews the right to practice their religious faith, learn about their heritage, or immigrate to another country. Khrushchev also severely limited Jews' access to top universities and government positions. In the words of the Holocaust survivor and Nobel Prize winner Elie Wiesel, the oppressed Russian Jews had become the Jews of Silence.

Jews around the world responded. The State of Israel established a secret Liaison Bureau in 1952 to help Soviet Jews. Chabad-Lubavitch, a Ḥasidic movement, became involved in secret rescue efforts, as did new grassroots American Jewish organizations, such as the Student Struggle for Soviet Jewry, established in 1964. Civil rights activists joined the cause, and Elie Wiesel wrote *The Jews of Silence* about his travels in Russia.

But by 1967, following Israel's victory in the Six-Day War, growing numbers of Soviet Jews courageously challenged their government. They demanded religious and cultural rights, such as the right to participate in public prayer and to study Hebrew, as well as the right to move to another country. In response, they were fired from their jobs and, in some cases, jailed.

In keeping with the religious teaching that all Jews are responsible for one another, Jews around the world—especially in North America and Israel—responded to the crisis by creating an international movement to free Soviet Jews. Their efforts included both public demonstrations and secret solidarity missions to the Soviet Union. They also lobbied governments to negotiate with Russia on behalf of the Jews.

Responding to this international pressure, the Soviet Union slowly opened its gates. Hundreds, then thousands, and then tens of thousands of Jews left before the fall of the Soviet Union in 1991—and many more have left in the years since. In total, more than one and a half million Jews left the Soviet Union; by 2005, fewer than four hundred thousand Jews remained in the former Soviet Union. Most of the immigrants settled in Israel or the United States.

Golda in Moscow

Just months after Israel declared its independence, Golda Myerson (not yet calling herself Golda Meir) traveled to Moscow as Israel's ambassador to the Soviet Union. It was October 1948, and she planned to attend Rosh Hashanah services in the Great Synagogue in Moscow. But the Jews of the Soviet Union had been warned by the government to stay away. Stalin did not want them to publicly welcome Israel's ambassador or celebrate Israeli independence.

"As we had planned, we went to the synagogue on Rosh Hashanah," Meir later wrote. "Instead of the 2,000-odd Jews who usually came to the synagogue on the holidays, a crowd of close to 50,000 people was waiting for us. . . . They had come—those good, brave Jews—in order to be with us, to demonstrate their sense of kinship and to celebrate the establishment of the State of Israel." After an emotional service, Meir called out to the crowd in Yiddish: "Thank you for having remained Jews!"

Arab Lands

Before World War II, over one million Jews lived in Arab lands, such as Iraq, Syria, Egypt, Yemen, and Morocco. Although Islamic law classified Jews as second-class citizens, many Eidot Hamizraḥ advanced economically and socially through the educational opportunities provided by Western countries and by the French Jewish organization Alliance Israélite Universelle.

Arab nationalists often resented minority groups in the Arab world, Jews in particular. In North African countries like Algeria and Tunisia, the hatred was fueled by the Jews' eagerness to learn French and adopt French culture. Arab nationalists were struggling for their freedom from French rule and saw the Jews as French sympathizers. In response, they targeted local Jews as part of their campaign against Zionism.

East Meets West, Jewish-Style

The schools established by the Alliance Israélite Universelle in communities in North Africa and Iran introduced thousands of Jews to modern ideas and ways of life. Alliance Israélite Universelle instructors insisted that all students learn French and the local language, but they did not teach Judeo-Arabic, the Jewish language that many Jews spoke at home. Instructors also encouraged the Mizrahi Jews to wear Western clothing. Finally, they showed contempt for local Jewish rabbis and for religious practices that they considered superstitious or primitive. Although the schools often distanced their students from traditional Judaism as practiced in the Arab lands, they did prepare them to compete and prosper in the modern world.

Some Arab leaders, such as the Grand Mufti of Jerusalem, had openly sided with Hitler during World War II. Anti-Jewish riots took place in major Arab cities in 1945 and again after the UN vote to partition Palestine in 1947. During the first two decades of Israel's existence, riots continued to take place, especially during the Arab-Israeli wars. In addition, in countries like Iraq, Jews were convicted on false charges of treason and publicly hanged.

France's withdrawal from North Africa by the early 1960s threatened to make the situation for Jews there even worse. The result was a dramatic exodus of Jews from the Arab Middle East, with most finding refuge in Israel and others in France, Canada, and the United States. By 2007 fewer than eight thousand Jews lived in Arab countries.

Iran

Jews have lived in Persia (modern-day Iran) for twenty-six hundred years, since their exile to Babylonia. The biblical story of Purim, told in the Book of Esther, took place there, and the country remained home to thousands of Jews into modern times. Its Jewish population in 1945 was estimated at ninety thousand. From 1941 to 1979, under the favorable rule of Mohammad Reza Shah Pahlavi, who believed in modernization and maintained ties with the West, the Iranian Jews flourished.

The Jewish community of Iran is said to have been one of the wealthiest and most highly educated Jewish communities in the world. The capital, Tehran, boasted Jewish schools, active social and cultural organizations, and some thirty synagogues; Iran and Israel maintained close relations. All of that changed following the Islamic revolution in Iran in 1979. As Iran turned away from the West and its modern influences and came under the control of the Islamic religious establishment, persecution of Jews increased, as did anti-Israel sympathies. Security, freedom, and progress for Jews gave way to insecurity, anxiety, and loss of status.

The leading figure in Iran's Jewish community, Habib Elqānyān, was charged with pro-Zionist activities and was executed in 1979. In 1999 thirteen Jews from Shiraz and Isfahan were arrested on the eve of Passover on charges of spying for Israel (by 2003 they had all been released). By the late 1990s many Jews had left the country, and by 2005 the Jewish population of Iran was estimated at only eleven thousand. Today there are large communities of Iranian Jews in the United States, especially in Southern California.

South Africa

South African Jewry numbered about 100,000 after World War II. Most had moved to South Africa from Lithuania in search of a better life. In a country divided by apartheid, Jews enjoyed the privilege that came with being white. Some Jews courageously joined the battle to fight apartheid and suffered for it. Others believed that radical political change would be harmful to Jews and supported the government. Still others urged gradual moderate change, fearing social revolution.

Apartheid officially ended in 1994, and Nelson Mandela became South Africa's first black president. Under Mandela, many laws designed to benefit the country's oppressed and underprivileged blacks, were introduced. For Jews, though, as for other whites, the new South Africa proved to be a more difficult place to live and work. A great many jobs were reserved for blacks and as often happens when a country undergoes social and political

FAMOUS FIGURES

Helen Suzman

Helen Suzman was born in 1917 in the mining town of Germiston, South Africa. Her parents, Lithuanian Jewish immigrants, had come to South Africa to escape the oppression of Jews in Russia. In 1948, when the pro-apartheid National Party came to power, Suzman joined the moderate United Party and was elected to Parliament in 1953. Six years later, along with eleven other liberal members of Parliament, Suzman helped form the anti-apartheid Progressive Party. Of the twelve founding members, only she was reelected to Parliament in 1961.

For the next thirteen years, Suzman was the sole anti-apartheid member of Parliament. She may have been particularly driven to speak out against apartheid by the indignities and misery of oppression her parents had experienced in Russia. Once, when another member of Parliament criticized her for embarrassing South Africa abroad by raising questions about the government's discriminatory policies, Suzman responded, "It is not my *questions* that embarrass South Africa—it is your *answers*."

As white opposition to apartheid grew, Suzman was joined in Parliament by other white liberals. She retired from Parliament in 1989 but helped oversee South Africa's first democratic election in 1994 and has remained politically active. Suzman visited Nelson Mandela many times in prison and was at his side in 1996 when he signed South Africa's new constitution.

Helen Suzman.

upheaval, crime rates soared. In addition, the new government was highly critical of Israel. As a result, many Jews, particularly younger Jews, joined the other whites who were leaving South Africa. From a peak of around 117,000 Jews, the Jewish population declined to about 75,000 in the early years of the twenty-first century.

Latin America

The Inquisition legally barred Jews from settling in most Latin American colonies until well into the nineteenth century, although the edict was not always applied rigidly. Crypto-Jews had come to the region in the sixteenth century from Spain and Portugal, and initially practiced Judaism secretly. Many of them, especially in Peru and Mexico, later became victims of the Inquisition. Dutch, British, and Danish Caribbean colonies, being non-Catholic, permitted Jews to establish synagogues and communities openly. The majority of the region's Jews, however, arrived more recently.

Four waves of Jews arrived in Latin America: Eastern European Jews during the era of mass immigration, from 1881 to 1914; Sephardic Jews during the dissolution of the Ottoman Empire, beginning in the nineteenth century; European Jews who could not get into the United States after most immigration was cut off in 1924; and German Jews escaping Hitler.

To some extent these groups—particularly the Yiddish-speaking Ashkenazic Jews and the Ladino-speaking Sephardic Jews—remained separate from one another.

Today Argentina has the largest Jewish community in Latin America. Most Jews in Argentina and throughout Latin America live in large cities. They form distinctive communities, often with their own schools and institutions, keeping much more separate from their non-Jewish neighbors than Jews in the United States, although increasing numbers are adapting to the secular Latin-American culture.

Antisemitism has long been characteristic of Latin-American life. After World War II, Argentina became a haven for Nazis, and throughout Latin America Jews have been accused by those on the political right

This poster for the 1939 Hollywood-made Yiddish-language film *Tevye der Milchiger* (*Tevye the Dairyman*) was created for Latin-American audiences.

of being Communists and radicals, even as they have been condemned by Communists for being capitalists.

Tens of thousands of Jews have left Argentina in recent years. This exodus has been due, in part, to the two terrorist bombings in Buenos Aires—of the Israeli embassy in 1992 and of the Asociación Mutual Israelita Argentina (AMIA) community center in 1994—and in large part to the community's severe economic problems.

Other significant Jewish communities are in Brazil, Mexico, Uruguay, Chile, and Venezuela.

The New Face of World Jewry

By 2005, according to the *American Jewish Year Book*, about 97.4 percent of all Jews lived in just fifteen countries.

CENTERS OF WORLD JEWISH POPULATION			
United States	5,280,000	Australia	102,000
Israel	5,237,600	Brazil	96,700
France	494,000	Ukraine	84,000
Canada	372,000	South Africa	72,500
United Kingdom	297,000	Hungary	49,900
Russia	235,000	Mexico	39,800
Argentina	185,000	Belgium	31,200
Germany	115,000		

Millions of Jews have migrated since the end of World War II. For the most part they have abandoned underdeveloped, unstable, and dangerous countries for wealthy, technologically advanced, and politically stable countries that are more tolerant of Jews. About 90 percent of world Jewry now lives in these more economically and socially attractive countries. As a result, no major Jewish community suffers widespread persecution. In addition, because so many Jews live close to one another, they benefit from the strength in numbers. Jewish citizens of larger communities can work together to realize common goals.

The negative side of this shift in population is that most of the world outside these major Jewish communities no longer has firsthand knowledge of Jews and Judaism. Judaism, once a world religion, is now a regional religion.

Chapter 26

Israel in Our Time
An Ongoing Story of Challenge and Triumph

The Big Picture

The modern State of Israel is a place of contrasts, none more stunning than that between old and new. Emek Refaim—where David drove out the Philistines—is now a bustling Jerusalem avenue lined with outdoor cafés, hamburger joints, and trendy clothing stores. Similarly, at the foot of Mount Tabor—where Barak and the biblical prophet Deborah gathered the Israelite army— lies the modern village of Kfar Tavor, the birthplace of the modern Israeli army.

Travel on a city bus and many other contrasts come to light. A Ḥasidic man wearing a distinctive black hat sits next to a bareheaded teen wearing headphones. An Armenian priest gestures to an Arab woman in a long embroidered dress to open the window. A young Israeli soldier from Ethiopia offers an elderly tourist her seat.

Israel's mixture of old and new and its religious and ethnic diversity are just a few of the elements that have created both a dynamic culture and multiple challenges. But one challenge has dominated all others: the need to make peace with its Arab neighbors and with the Palestinians.

New Immigrants

Israel is a country of seven million people. It is composed of 77 percent Jews, nearly 20 percent Arabs, and 4 percent

TIMELINE

1967	Six-Day War is fought
1973	Yom Kippur War is fought
1979	Israel and Egypt sign a peace treaty
1987	Palestinian Intifada begins in Gaza and the West Bank

World History

1989	*World Wide Web is invented*

1994	Israel and Jordan sign a peace treaty
2000	Second Intifada begins
2005	Jewish settlements are removed from Gaza Strip
2006	Hamas wins Palestinian elections

others. Two-thirds of its Jewish population are native-born Israelis, or sabras. Recent waves of immigrants from Ethiopia and the former Soviet Union are changing the face of Israel just as Israel has changed them.

For centuries, Jews lived in Ethiopia cut off from the rest of the Jewish people. They were ill-treated and poverty-stricken; many were malnourished. Most worked in farming but were also well-known for their fine crafts and jewelry.

When Ethiopia suffered a great famine and war in the 1980s, the Jews became especially eager to leave. In 1984, the Israeli government and Jewish organizations from North America worked with the Israeli Airline, El Al, to fly them to Israel. That airlift is known as Operation Moses. For several reasons, including the risk of flying over Arab airspace en route, and the tenuous diplomatic relationships between the countries, the rescue operation was conducted with the utmost secrecy.

The mission to bring the Ethiopian Jews to Israel continued into the 1990s. Today more than fifty-six thousand Ethiopians live in the Jewish State. Thousands of Ethiopian Jews who converted to Christianity in the past and have since returned to Judaism are waiting to be brought to Israel.

At first the Ethiopians were greeted with an outpouring of warmth, but their integration into Israeli life has often not been smooth. Some Ethiopians have complained of Israelis' racist attitudes. But the biggest barrier has been the Ethiopians' lack of education and job skills, which has made it difficult for them to find work.

Beta Israel

Ethiopian Jews call their community Beta Israel (the House of Israel), although other Ethiopians refer to them as Falashas ("Strangers" or "Foreigners"). According to their own traditions, they trace their lineage back to King Solomon and the Queen of Sheba (Sheba was an ancient land on the southern tip of the Arabian Peninsula). But genetic tests indicate that they are descended from native Ethiopians who converted to Judaism or intermarried with Jewish traders from Yemen.

A Jewish prayer
service in Ethiopia.

In recent years the largest number of immigrants has come from the former Soviet Union. Between 1989 and 2000 almost 900,000 Russian Jews arrived in Israel. Some left the former Soviet Union in reaction to the rising antisemitism, but many more came in search of greater economic opportunity.

The Russian immigrants generally have been highly educated and skilled. Russian doctors have brought their expertise to Israeli hospitals, Russian athletes and coaches have strengthened Israel's professional sports and Olympics teams, and Russian engineers have contributed to Israel's electronics and high-tech boom.

Yet Russian immigration has brought its own challenges. For example, many well-educated Russians have not found employment in their professions. But the greatest problems have arisen over religious issues and Jewish identity.

Israel's Law of Return grants automatic citizenship to the families of all immigrants with one Jewish grandparent. But such new citizens often find that they are not considered Jewish in regard to more personal matters—such as marriage and burial rites—which are governed by the stricter Jewish law that requires one's mother to be Jewish. By that standard, about one-third of Russian immigrants are non-Jews. In such cases, unless they convert to Judaism under the supervision of an Orthodox rabbi, they may not be married by an Israeli rabbi, and they are not permitted to be buried in a Jewish cemetery.

A Religious Country or a Secular Country?

About 20 percent of Israel's Jews consider themselves religious, and another 35 percent describe themselves as "traditionalists" but do not strictly observe Jewish law. The remaining

45 percent consider themselves secular. Religious and secular Jews work side by side and share the public space but often disagree on how Israel should balance its Western-style democracy with its Jewish character.

Should all aspects of Israeli life be determined by Jewish religious law? Should Israel be a completely secular country, in which Jewish law and tradition have no special influence? Or should Israel find a balance between these two views? Israeli opinion ranges widely.

Since the founding of the modern State of Israel, the government has adopted certain basic policies regarding Judaism's role in Israeli society. Saturday is observed as the official day of rest; Jewish holidays, such as Passover and Rosh Hashanah, are recognized as official state holidays; and kosher food is served in all army kitchens and in government buildings. In addition, there are religious political parties, which use their influence in the Knesset, Israel's legislature, to strengthen Israel's observance of Jewish law.

Especially problematic to secular Israelis is the religious court's control over issues of personal status—marriage, divorce, funerals, and religious conversion. The religious court requires that all Jewish marriages and conversions conducted in Israel be performed by Orthodox rabbis. Secular resentment is further inflamed by the many young ultra-Orthodox men who use student exemptions to avoid serving in the Israel Defense Forces (IDF).

Whatever differences of opinion there are, most Jewish Israelis agree that the state should be influenced by Jewish traditions and values. In contrast, Israel's Arab community sees the Jewish nature of the state as a barrier to their acceptance as full and equal citizens.

The Azrieli Center, located in Tel Aviv, is a complex of three skyscrapers, two of which are seen here. Development began in the mid-1990s and was completed in 2007. Each tower is a different geometric shape—square, triangular, and round. At 614 feet (with 49 floors), the circular building is the tallest of the three towers.

Many Israelis are attracted to Western pop culture, including dress, music, fast food, and technology.

A Shifting Economy

The communal way of life and back-to-the-soil ideology of the *kibbutzim* made them the pride of Israel's Socialist pioneers. Parents and children lived separately, members ate in communal dining halls, and members' earnings were based on their needs.

This lifestyle has not appealed to the recent generations of Israelis, however, and so there have been changes. Now children live with their parents. Many *kibbutzim* have also stopped serving meals in dining halls. And some base salaries on the status of a job, so that a factory worker will not earn the same wage as a manager.

Israel's national economic policies are changing, too. There is more competition among private companies, and some government-owned companies have been privatized. In addition, the arrival of highly skilled workers from the former Soviet Union combined with the possibility of peace with Israel's Arab neighbors helped create a technology boom in the mid-1990s. Israeli companies have become leaders in software, communications technology, and biotechnology.

Economic growth has brought prosperity to many, but it also has widened the gap between rich and poor. Although for all Israelis there are more goods on which to spend their money, today the neediest receive less government help than did their counterparts in the 1950s and 1960s. By the early twenty-first century, more than 20 percent of Israelis were living below the poverty line.

The Six-Day War

Israel has experienced more than its share of bloodshed and war. In May 1967, Egyptian president Gamal Abdel Nasser blockaded the Strait of Tiran, stopping all ships from entering or leaving Israel's southern port of Eilat. He amassed troops along the border with Israel. Expecting war, Israel struck first, launching a daring air attack against Egypt.

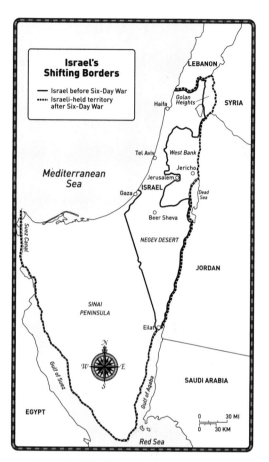

Israel's Shifting Borders

— Israel before Six-Day War
···· Israeli-held territory after Six-Day War

LEBANON

Golan Heights

SYRIA

Haifa

Mediterranean Sea

Tel Aviv

West Bank

Jericho

Jerusalem

ISRAEL

Gaza

Dead Sea

Beer Sheva

NEGEV DESERT

JORDAN

Suez Canal

SINAI PENINSULA

Eilat

Gulf of Suez

Gulf of Aqaba

SAUDI ARABIA

EGYPT

30 MI

30 KM

Red Sea

As a result of the Six-Day War in 1967, the area under Israeli control was expanded to include Gaza, the West Bank, and the Sinai Peninsula.

Israel's first strike on the morning of June 5 destroyed the Egyptian air force. Syria and Jordan entered the war on Egypt's side but were quickly defeated. In what became known as the Six-Day War, Israel captured the Sinai Peninsula and Gaza Strip from Egypt, the West Bank from Jordan, and the Golan Heights from Syria. In addition, it took control of East Jerusalem, including the Old City. Jerusalem was united.

Problems Continue

The new territories tripled Israel's size. They also prevented Egypt and Syria from placing rockets close enough to reach Israel's major cities. But the territories created new problems: first, Jews established settlements in the newly occupied territories, and second, one million Palestinian Arabs were living on land now controlled by Israel. Both problems plague Israel to this day.

Religious Zionists like Rabbi Zvi Yehudah Kook believed that Israel's victory was a sign that the coming of the Messiah was near. His followers helped found Gush Emunim ("Bloc of the Faithful"), which opposed the return of any of the captured land and declared that Jews had a right to the entire biblical land of Israel. Other Israelis warned that governing a people against their will violated Jewish values and would weaken Israel.

The UN and most countries, including the United States, believed that the return of the territories would be part of any future peace agreements between Israel and the Arabs and that the establishment of Jewish settlements would make Israel's withdrawal more difficult.

At first the Israeli government limited Jewish settlement to areas that were critical to national security or had great religious significance. But the Israeli government of the late 1970s encouraged settlements in areas that had previously been off-limits. By 2006, about two hundred thousand Jews—both secular and religious—were living in the West Bank and Golan Heights.

At the same time, high birthrates have greatly increased the Palestinian Arab population in the territories, growing from one million in 1967 to more than three million by the early twenty-first century. Frustrated and angered by Israeli occupation and settlement, Palestinian Arabs sought independence. The West Bank and Gaza became time bombs.

Indeed, in December 1987 a Palestinian uprising began in Gaza and the West Bank. It became known as the Intifada, or "Shaking Off." Starting with demonstrations, it escalated into rock throwing and, eventually, the use of homemade explosives. To much of the world, Palestinians had become the heroic David standing up to the Goliath, Israel.

Palestine Liberation Organization

Palestinian resistance groups outside the West Bank were committed to Israel's destruction. One such group, the Palestine Liberation Organization (PLO), was founded in 1964. Yasir Arafat, who became its chairman in 1969, used acts of terror, targeting innocent civilians to gain sympathy for the Palestinian cause. Although most Palestinians were not terrorists, many began to support the PLO in their belief that Arafat would liberate them.

New Hope

In October 1973 Egypt and Syria surprised Israel with an attack on Yom Kippur. Israeli casualties were high, but the IDF eventually triumphed. A breakthrough in Israel's relations with its neighbors came in November 1977, when Egyptian president Anwar al-Sadat flew to Jerusalem to address the Knesset: "I declare to the whole world that we accept to live with you in a permanent peace based on justice."

Prime Minister Menahem Begin agreed to Israel's withdrawal from the Sinai, and in 1979 Israel and Egypt signed a peace treaty. Two years later Sadat was assassinated by Islamic extremists opposed to his peace efforts; nonetheless the treaty has held. In 1994, Israel and Jordan, which had long maintained secret relations, also signed a formal treaty.

A breakthrough in Israel's conflict with the Palestinians almost came in 1993. Yasir Arafat and the Palestine Liberation Organization (PLO) renounced terrorism and recognized the right of the State of Israel to exist. Prime Minister Yitzḥak Rabin, in turn, recognized the PLO as the representative of the Palestinian people. On September 13, 1993, both sides signed an agreement to end fighting and extend self-rule to the Palestinians in parts of Gaza and the West Bank.

Peace Remains a Dream

Despite high hopes, the conflict continued, and tensions rose in Israel. Rabin was denounced as a traitor at antigovernment rallies even though a majority of Israelis supported his policies. On November 4, 1995, shortly after attending a peace rally, Rabin was assassinated by Yigal Amir, a Jewish extremist who opposed the peace process.

U.S. president Bill Clinton brought both sides together in the summer of 2000 in the hope of stopping the violence and shaping a final agreement, but the negotiations broke down, and the West Bank and Gaza soon broke out in a Second Intifada, more violent and deadly than the first. Suicide bombers brought the violence into the heart of Israel, targeting cafés, nightclubs, and hotels.

To protect its citizens, in 2002 Israel began building a security fence that separates much of the West Bank from Israel. Two years later the violence was quieting down when Arafat died. Many Israelis believed Arafat's death would remove a major obstacle to peace. Israeli prime minister Ariel Sharon, once a leading supporter of settlements in the territories, became convinced that Israel could not hold on to the Gaza Strip and most of the West Bank. In 2005 he evacuated the Jewish settlements in Gaza and pulled out the army.

Security issues are always front-page news in Israel.

FAMOUS FIGURES

Yitzḥak Rabin

Yitzḥak Rabin was born in Palestine in 1922 and served as a senior military commander before becoming prime minister. During his first term (1974–1977) he ordered a daring raid on the airport in Entebbe, Uganda, after a hijacked Air France jetliner landed there. The raid freed all but three of the one hundred and five Jews who were held hostage. In his second term as prime minister (1992–1995), Rabin shifted his goals from winning wars to winning peace. In 1994, Rabin, Shimon Peres (a former Israeli prime minister), and Yasir Arafat were jointly awarded the Nobel Prize for their efforts to bring peace to the Middle East.

After negotiating the peace agreement with Arafat in 1993, Rabin said, "I would have liked to sign a peace agreement with Holland, or Luxembourg, or New Zealand. But there was no need to. . . . One does not make peace with one's friends. One makes peace with one's enemies."

Standing with their Nobel Peace Prize, from left to right: Yasir Arafat, Shimon Peres, and Yitzḥak Rabin.

But efforts to advance the peace process were hurt by the victory of Hamas, the Islamic Resistance Movement, in the 2006 Palestinian elections. Hamas gained the support of many Palestinians through its promise to end the corruption that existed under the PLO and by providing medical care, education, and other social services. But Hamas also carried out many terror attacks in Israel and was committed to Israel's destruction.

Efforts to negotiate a peace between Israel and Syria have thus far also failed, and Israel's northern border with Lebanon has been a source of constant problems. Lebanon, a weak country, has been unable to prevent militant groups in its southern region from launching attacks on Israel. In June 1982, Israel invaded Lebanon to drive out the PLO, which had taken hold of the southern region. Israel's campaign was successful, but at a high cost in terms of Lebanese and Israeli lives.

The 1982 War and Israel's occupation of a security zone in southern Lebanon from 1985 until May 2000 were among the key factors that led to the creation of Hezbollah ("Party of God"), an Islamist political party and militant group. Hezbollah played on the resentment that some Lebanese felt toward Israel, and like Hamas in Gaza, it won support by meeting critical social needs, running hospitals and schools, for example. Meanwhile, Hezbollah fighters were trained and armed by Iran and carried out attacks on Israeli soldiers and civilians. In 2006, in southern Lebanon and northern Israel, Israel and Hezbollah fought a war with no clear results other than considerable destruction and loss of life.

Are hopes for a peaceful future realistic? The Arab-Israeli conflict boils down to two people's claims on one land. A solution will require compromise on dreams that are dear and beliefs that are deep. 🦁

Chapter 27

American Jewry Today
Making the Choice to Survive and Thrive

On June 3, 1972, one year after the publication of "The Jew Who Wasn't There: Halakha and the Jewish Woman," a controversial article by the theologian Rachel Adler, Sally Priesand became the first woman to be publicly ordained as a rabbi. Though many Reform congregations in 1972 were not ready to accept women as rabbis, Priesand was hired by the Stephen Wise Free Synagogue in New York City.

Momentum for change continued to build. In February 1973 more than five hundred women from the United States and Canada gathered to attend the first National Conference of Jewish Women in New York City. The event provided a public forum for issues that until that point had concerned only a handful of visionaries; by the end of the conference, a movement had been born.

Adler and Priesand and the women who followed in their paths became role models for thousands of girls and a powerful force in the revitalization of American Jewry. Indeed, in many ways that force has symbolized the energy and diversity within today's North American Jewish community.

Jewish Pride

During the late 1960s and early 1970s, Americans began to take an interest in exploring their ethnic and racial heritage.

TIMELINE

1960 English-language edition of *Night* by Elie Weisel is published

1969 "Freedom Seder" is held in Washington, D.C.

1972 Sally Priesand becomes the first woman to be publicly ordained as a rabbi

1991 Shoshana Cardin becomes the first female chair of the Conference of Presidents of Major American Jewish Organizations

1993 U.S. Holocaust Memorial Museum opens in Washington, D.C.

2000 Joseph Lieberman, an observant Jew, is the Democratic vice-presidential nominee

World History
2001 *Terrorist attacks on the World Trade Center and Pentagon on September 11 kill nearly 3,000 people*

Participants in the Israel Independence Day Parade in New York City expressing their support of Israel.

As a result of the civil rights and black power movements, there was an increasing acceptance and celebration of the ethnic differences in American society. American Jews expressed their pride by openly wearing *magen David* pendants (often called Jewish stars) and skullcaps.

The publication of the English-language edition of Elie Wiesel's book *Night,* in 1960, helped make Holocaust remembrance a top priority among American Jews. When in May of that same year, Israeli agents in Buenos Aires arrested Adolf Eichmann, supervisor of the plan to systematically annihilate European Jewry, Holocaust awareness rose even higher. Eichmann was brought to trial in Israel. As American Jews followed the trial, they began to openly discuss their memories of and thoughts about the Holocaust.

In the following decades, observance of Holocaust Remembrance Day, Yom Hashoah, became widespread. The Holocaust became the subject of study in secular and religious classrooms. By the late 1980s there were twelve Holocaust memorials and nineteen museums dedicated to Holocaust remembrance in the United States. The U.S. Holocaust Memorial Museum, a project of the federal government, opened in Washington, D.C., in 1993. That same year, Steven Spielberg's film about the Holocaust, *Schindler's List,* won top honors at the Academy Awards.

American Jews' Connection to Israel

Just seven years after the arrest of Eichmann, American Jewry was again confronted with the possible destruction of millions of Jews. In the weeks leading up to the June 1967 Six-Day War, they listened to broadcasts of Egyptian president Gamal Abdel Nasser's anti-Israel propaganda and his plans to destroy the young Jewish State. Israel's extraordinary victory gave American Jews reason to swell with ethnic pride.

American Jews' deep concern for Israel's survival was reflected in the hundreds of millions of dollars they contributed on its behalf. But financial support was not the only way in which American Jews expressed their identification with the Jewish state. In the years after 1967, American Jewish tourism to Israel increased. Zionism and Israeli history were taught almost universally in Jewish schools. And the organized American Jewish community became tireless supporters of Israel. Reflecting the growing importance of Israel to American Jews, the American Israel Public Affairs Committee (AIPAC) grew into a powerful lobbying organization, dedicated to influencing U.S. foreign policy in support of Israel.

In recent years, however, there has been concern about the relationship between American and Israeli Jews. One challenge is the wedge between some American and Israeli Jews that has been created by their differing views on how to address the Arab-Israeli conflict. Other sources of friction include the Israeli government's refusal to give legal status to non-Orthodox movements—for example, its refusal to permit non-Orthodox rabbis to perform Jewish wedding ceremonies and conversions.

Recent polls have registered a decline in American Jewish identification with Israel, especially among young people. American Jewish leaders hope that ties between the two communities can be strengthened through visits of American Jews to Israel as tourists and as participants in volunteer projects and study programs.

Jewish Activism

Since the late 1960s, when some Jewish civil rights activists began to explore ways in which Judaism could help them live more meaningful lives, the teachings of prophetic Judaism and *tikun olam*—acts of social justice—have grown in popularity among American

Today many liberal synagogues sponsor social action projects and their religious schools require students to participate in *tikun olam* projects.

Jews. Jewish sacred texts have inspired many to pursue justice and help the poor in a variety of ways, such as through participation in voter registration and literacy programs, the Peace Corps, and synagogue High Holiday food drives.

Jewish Feminism

By the early 1970s the American Jewish community had begun to recognize ways in which Judaism treated women and men differently. At this time, women were achieving greater equality in the workplace and in the larger culture. So it seemed increasingly inappropriate and out-of-date that men and women were treated differently in synagogue. Women were not permitted to be ordained as rabbis. In most synagogues, women were not permitted to receive an *aliyah* (the honor of reciting the blessings over the reading of the Torah) or to be counted in a minyan, the quorum of ten Jewish adults required for a prayer service.

But times changed. Two years after Sally Priesand was ordained by the Hebrew Union College, Sandy Sasso was ordained by the Reconstructionist Rabbinical College, and in 1985 the Jewish Theological Seminary ordained its first woman rabbi, Amy Eilberg. By the late twentieth century, except in the Orthodox movements, Jewish women were permitted to participate equally in most aspects of synagogue life. A woman could be called to the Torah for an *aliyah*, counted in a minyan, and serve as a synagogue board member or congregation president.

Social Justice and Passover

Members of Jews for Urban Justice, an organization that worked to alleviate poverty and end other forms of social injustice, found a modern way to express the strong ties between social justice and Judaism. On the third day of Passover in 1969—the first anniversary of the assassination of civil rights leader Martin Luther King Jr.—they held a "freedom seder" in the basement of an African-American church. A diverse crowd of Jews and non-Jews sat at tables set with a traditional seder plate. They read from a haggadah that combined traditional prayers with readings on the themes of freedom and the struggle for social justice in America.

FAMOUS FIGURES

Shoshana S. Cardin

Shoshana Cardin was born in Tel Aviv in 1926 and moved to Baltimore with her family when she was three years old. Her life has been guided by the value of community service. As a child, Cardin gave political speeches, raised money for the Jewish National Fund, and served as president of her Zionist youth group. As an adult she became a feminist, civic leader, and social activist.

Beginning in 1984, Cardin achieved a number of firsts: She became the first woman to serve as president of the Council of Jewish Federations; the first woman to chair the National Conference on Soviet Jewry; and the first woman to chair the Conference of Presidents of Major American Jewish Organizations. In 2003, she became chair of the Shoshana S. Cardin Jewish Community High School in Baltimore. She has also chaired secular organizations, including the Maryland Commission for Women and the Maryland Volunteer Network.

Cardin's many accomplishments also include helping to provide services for women with financial credit needs and battered women. Through her negotiations with such world leaders as George H. W. Bush and Soviet president Mikhail S. Gorbachev, she helped to win aid for Israel and for Soviet Jews who wished to immigrate to Israel.

Shoshana Cardin visiting a Jewish community in the mountains of Azerbaijan.

Lilith is a Jewish American feminist magazine. Published quarterly since 1976, it is named after Lilith, who, according to Jewish tradition, was the first woman, created before Eve. Stories of Lilith often portray her as independent, strong, and vocal.

By the 1970s and 1980s some Orthodox women had begun to organize prayer groups in their synagogues, in which they read from the Torah. A few began to put on prayer shawls (*tallitot*). And today many more Orthodox women have an advanced education in Jewish studies. While most Orthodox rabbis continue to believe that Jewish law prevents women from being ordained, the role and religious authority of women in Orthodox communities continue to expand.

Orthodox Judaism

In the mid-twentieth century, the American Orthodox community seemed to be shrinking. But as American society has become more tolerant of diversity, Orthodox Jews have found greater acceptance. The result has been an increase in religious observance, with more Jews keeping kosher and attending synagogue, for example, and a significant growth in Orthodox day school education. In addition, most adults who grew up in an Orthodox homes are choosing to remain within the movement. Another factor contributing to the movement's growth is Orthodox couples' tendency to have large families.

The Ḥasidic community and the ultra-Orthodox yeshiva world are also flourishing. Both realms benefited from a wave of European refugees immediately before and after World War II. Most Ḥasidic Jews choose to isolate themselves from the secular world by living in separate communities and creating their own business, social, and religious organizations.

Liberal Judaism

The Reform movement has grown in recent years. About 35 percent of American Jews identify themselves as Reform, making it the largest Jewish movement in the United States today. Two trends within the movement help account for this growth: increasing observance of Jewish tradition in ways that help families personalize and deepen their Jewish identities, and outreach to those outside the mainstream, including interfaith families. A growing number of Reform Jews have begun to send their children to Reform and community-sponsored day schools, and summer camps and youth groups continue to attract large numbers of children from committed Reform families.

Approximately 26 percent of American Jews who are members of a synagogue identify themselves as Conservative, making Conservative Judaism the second largest movement in the United States. Yet Conservative Judaism faces a serious challenge: One out of every

Equality for Lesbians and Gay Men

In the 1980s a new front opened in the continuing tug-of-war between tradition and modernity, this one involving the equality of lesbians and gay men. Synagogues whose members were largely lesbian and gay were founded in major urban centers during the 1970s and 1980s. But as gay men and lesbians pushed for greater acceptance in American society, they also wanted to be included in mainstream Jewish life. In 1984 the Reconstructionist Rabbinical College voted to admit openly lesbian and gay students, and by the 1990s mainstream synagogues were welcoming lesbians and gay men. In the past few years, some liberal rabbis have begun to officiate at same-sex commitment ceremonies and marriages, and the Reform movement has established a center for the study of sexuality and gender.

The issue of gay and lesbian equality within Judaism continues to be debated. Opponents argue that Jewish law allows for no compromise on this issue.

two adults who was raised a Conservative Jew no longer identifies with the movement. Conservative Judaism must find a way to attract more members, especially young people. Still, the Conservative Ramah camping movement and the network of Solomon Schechter day schools continue to produce highly committed youngsters who are well educated in Judaism. They are the people who are most likely to determine the movement's future.

Reconstructionist Judaism is the mainstream movement with the smallest number of members. It remains an attractive choice for those seeking a worship experience that emphasizes intellectual exploration and a democratic approach to synagogue organization. According to the Reconstructionist philosophy of Jewish decision making, halachah can strongly influence but not fully determine decisions. This approach has helped encourage ritual experimentation and the reaching out to interfaith families.

Looking to the Future

The American Jewish community has continually met the challenge of changing conditions and opportunities by adapting in diverse and creative ways. In our time, Judaism has been enriched by the Jewish feminist movement, social activism, and the creative innovations of communal and personal religious rituals. Today many couples include personalized rituals in their Jewish wedding ceremonies, and some families weave their life experiences into the retelling of the Exodus story at the Passover seder. In addition, many American Jews strongly support Israel and are influential in matters of American and world politics, and synagogue adult and family education programs are evermore diverse and popular.

As we experiment and adapt, we develop new practices and rituals that can strengthen us.

The Ḥavurah and Jewish Renewal Movements

In the early 1960s some Reconstructionist Jews began to come together in small informal gatherings, or *havurot,* to pray and engage in religious study and discussions. By the late 1960s and early 1970s Jewish social activists had developed an interest in Jewish religious observance and helped start their own *havurot* in Washington, D.C., Boston, New York, Los Angeles, and other communities. The *havurot* held weekly Shabbat services and sponsored cultural activities.

Combining the idealism, individualism, and informality of 1960s culture with traditional Judaism, *havurot* attracted young Jews who rejected what they saw as the materialistic and impersonal aspects of the suburban world in which they were raised. Most *havurot* prayer services were led by group members rather than rabbis or cantors, and there was great openness to personalizing the prayer experience.

In recent years the increased interest in spirituality has fueled the growth of the Jewish Renewal movement. Its guiding force, Rabbi Zalman Schachter-Shalomi, has encouraged followers to enrich and deepen their spiritual lives through song, dance, prayer, and meditation. Some Jews believe that Jewish Renewal may become a fifth movement within Judaism, but its greatest impact may be on the Reconstructionist, Reform, and Conservative movements. Many synagogues, for example, have integrated the songs and creativity that are characteristic of Jewish Renewal into their prayer services.

As of 2001, the three largest centers of Jewish population in North America were—by far—the New York metropolitan area (2,051,000), Greater Los Angeles (668,000), and southern Florida (498,000).

Yet there are challenges with which Jews continue to struggle. Increased rates of intermarriage and total assimilation, a decreased birthrate among Jews, and a decreased rate of conversion to Judaism cause some people to wonder whether Judaism will continue to thrive. Indeed, the American Jewish population is becoming an ever-smaller percentage of the total population.

The commitment to Jewish peoplehood—the traditional idea that all Jews, wherever they live, are related to and responsible for one another—has declined as assimilation and intermarriage have risen. A survey in 1998 found that only 52 percent of American Jews agreed with the statement "I look at the entire Jewish community as my extended family," and only 47 percent agreed that "I have a special responsibility to take care of Jews in need around the world."

The modern Jewish community of North America brings enormous resources to help meet these challenges. Its members are diversely talented, holding positions of accomplishment in business, government, education, the arts, and sciences—in fact, throughout society. It has achieved much and surely will achieve more.

But despite the multitude of resources, questions remain. For example, which innovations in religious practice will be incorporated into Jewish tradition? What levels and styles of participation in Jewish communal life will become most common? How will the ties among the communities of the Diaspora be strengthened and challenged, and what relationship will Diaspora Jews have with the Jews of Israel?

The answers are not for this book to tell, for they are not yet known. The Jewish people will determine them by the lives they live and the choices they make. Indeed, the answers will unfold—along with new questions—day by day, community by community, individual by individual, to be woven by time into the rich tapestry of Jewish history.

Index